D0554748

Frontispiece: Although the black immigrant movement to the United States in the first half of the 20th century had its roots in the British West Indies, it also drew immigrants from elsewhere in the Caribbean. Most of this latter group came from Cuba; others came from the Danish West Indies, which was acquired by the United States in 1917; still more came from the Dutch and French West Indies.

Preceding pages: Migrants from Florida make their way to Cranberry, New Jersey, to pick potatoes. The photograph was taken near Shawboro, North Carolina, in July 1940.

One of the world's largest nonprofit scientific and educational organizations, the National Geographic Society was founded in 1888 "for the increase and diffusion of geographic knowledge." Fulfilling this mission, the Society educates and inspires millions every day through its magazines, books, television programs, videos, maps and atlases, research grants, the National Geographic Bee, teacher workshops, and innovative classroom materials. The Society is supported through membership dues, charitable gifts, and income from the sale of its educational products. This support is vital to National Geographic's mission to increase global understanding and promote conservation of our planet through exploration, research, and education.

For more information, please call 1-800-NGS LINE (647-5463) or write to the following address:
National Geographic Society
1145 17th Street N.W.
Washington, D.C. 20036-4688 U.S.A.
Visit the Society's Web site at www.nationalgeographic.com.

Library of Congress Cataloging-in-Publication Data

Dodson, Howard.
    In motion : the African-American migration experience / by Howard Dodson and
  Sylviane A. Diouf ; Schomburg Center for Research in Black Culture.
       p. cm.
    Includes biographical references and index.
    ISBN 0-7922-7385-0
    1. African Americans--Migrations--History. 2. Migration, Internal--United
  States--History. 3. United States--Emigration and immigration--History I. Diouf,
  Sylviane A. (Sylviane Anna), 1952- II. Schomburg Center for Research in Black Culture.
  III. Title.

  E185.D625 2005
  304.8'089'96073--dc22

                                                                    2004057903

IN MOTION

The African-American Migration Experience

COMPILED AND EDITED BY
HOWARD DODSON AND SYLVIANE A. DIOUF

THE SCHOMBURG CENTER FOR RESEARCH IN BLACK CULTURE

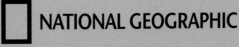

NATIONAL GEOGRAPHIC

WASHINGTON, D.C.

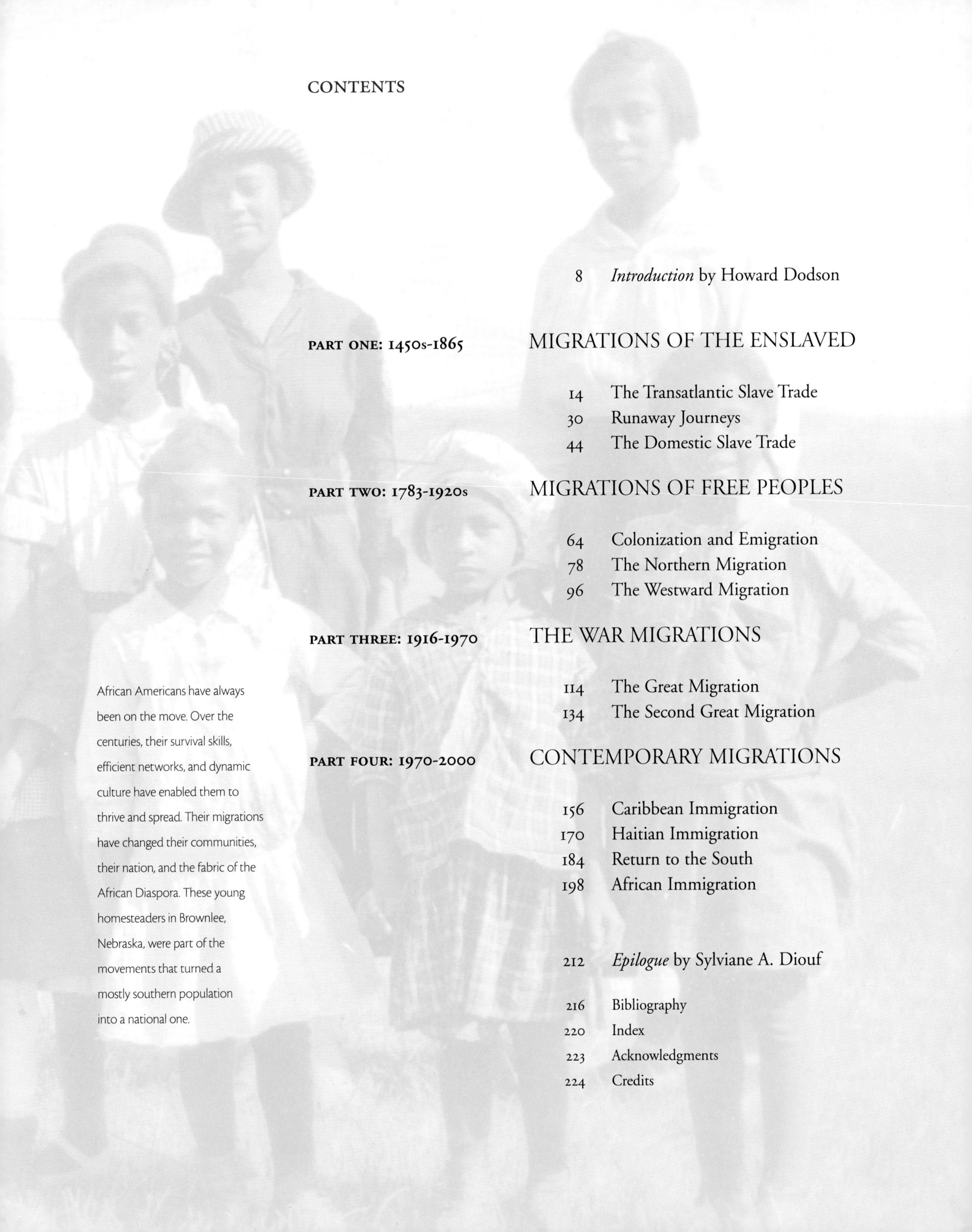

CONTENTS

African Americans have always been on the move. Over the centuries, their survival skills, efficient networks, and dynamic culture have enabled them to thrive and spread. Their migrations have changed their communities, their nation, and the fabric of the African Diaspora. These young homesteaders in Brownlee, Nebraska, were part of the movements that turned a mostly southern population into a national one.

8   *Introduction* by Howard Dodson

PART ONE: 1450s–1865

MIGRATIONS OF THE ENSLAVED

14   The Transatlantic Slave Trade
30   Runaway Journeys
44   The Domestic Slave Trade

PART TWO: 1783–1920s

MIGRATIONS OF FREE PEOPLES

64   Colonization and Emigration
78   The Northern Migration
96   The Westward Migration

PART THREE: 1916–1970

THE WAR MIGRATIONS

114   The Great Migration
134   The Second Great Migration

PART FOUR: 1970–2000

CONTEMPORARY MIGRATIONS

156   Caribbean Immigration
170   Haitian Immigration
184   Return to the South
198   African Immigration

212   *Epilogue* by Sylviane A. Diouf

216   Bibliography
220   Index
223   Acknowledgments
224   Credits

by Howard Dodson

New societies, new peoples, new communities usually originate in acts of migration. Individuals or groups decide to move from one place to another. They choose a new destination, sever their ties with their traditional community or society, and set out in search of new opportunities, new challenges, new lives, new worlds. Most societies in human history have a migration narrative in their stories of origin. All communities in American society trace their origins in the United States to one or more migration experiences. America, after all, is "a nation of immigrants."

Until recently, people of African descent have not been counted as part of America's migratory tradition. The slave trade, after all, was a forced rather than voluntary migration of African peoples to the United States. In the minds of many Americans, the Great Migration of the second and third decades of the 20th century (1916-1930) was inspired, at least in part, by the boll weevil and the lynching epidemic that engulfed the American South after Reconstruction ended. It, too, was mistakenly perceived as a forced, involuntary migration. What is more, studies of African societies of the 19th and 20th centuries concluded that African societies (like African-descended peoples themselves) were by nature static, tradition-bound cultures incapable of innovation, creativity, and development. *In Motion: The African American Migration Experience* challenges these myths and false assumptions about the nature of African-descended peoples in the United States and documents their unique histories of migration to, within, and out of the United States over the last five centuries.

African Americans, perhaps more than any other population in the Americas, have been shaped by migrations. Their culture and history are the products of black peoples' various movements, coerced and voluntary, that started in the Western Hemisphere five hundred years ago. Theirs is the story of men and women forcibly removed from Africa; of enslaved peoples moved from the southeastern coast of the United States to the Deep South; of fugitives walking to freedom across the country and beyond; of colonists leaving the United States to settle on foreign shores; of southerners migrating west and north; of African Americans of the north and west returning to the south; and of waves of immigrants arriving from the Caribbean, South America, and Africa.

The transatlantic slave trade is usually considered the primary determinant of the African presence in the United States. While most people of African descent in the United States trace their origin to the slave trade, it is centuries of additional, largely voluntary migrations that have given shape to the African-American presence in the nation as a whole. These migrations to, within, and out of the United States have been central to the definition of the African-American experience.

Between 1492 and 1776, an estimated 6.5 million people migrated to the Americas. More than five out of six were Africans. The major colonial labor force, they laid the economic and cultural foundations of North, Central, and South America. Though only 500,000 Africans settled in the original 13 colonies of the United States, by 1860 they numbered more than 4 million, and as a result of the domestic slave trade and the self-initiative of "fugitives" who stole themselves and ran away from systems of slavery and injustice, the Africans' presence had extended into Alabama, Mississippi, Missouri, and Texas by the outbreak of the Civil War. Their migrations continued after slavery. Between 1916 and 1970, 6.5 million African Americans left the South for northern and western cities. With this internal Great Migration, African Americans transformed themselves from a southern, rural population into a national, largely urban one.

The men and women of the Great Migration not only transformed the cities they settled in, but their neighborhoods became primary destinations for black people arriving from the Caribbean, Africa, and South America. These immigrants often retained their national and ethnic identities, and brought new resources into the African-American community. With each wave of migration, changes in the demographic, cultural, religious, economic, and political life of the recipient communities occurred.

At the same time, from the earliest days, thousands of African Americans have left the United States when it appeared that they could not find the security, freedom, and equality they aspired to. Their quest for liberty and better opportunities took them to Canada, Mexico, the Caribbean, and Africa.

Today's 35 million African Americans are heirs to all the migrations that have formed and transformed African Americans, their communities, the United States, and the African Diaspora. They are the offspring of diverse African ethnicities who also include, in their genetic makeup, Europeans, Native Americans, and Asians. They represent the most diverse population in the United States, a population that has embraced its varied heritages created by millions of men and women constantly on the move, looking for better opportunities, starting over, paving the way, and making sacrifices for future generations.

This book, *In Motion: The African-American Migration Experience,* derives from and is a companion volume to the extraordinary website of the same name, organized and curated by the Schomburg Center for Research in Black Culture. The website documents and interprets the 13 migrations of African peoples to, within, and out of the United States that defined in many ways the dynamic quality of the African-American experience. Comprised of some 8,000 images and over 16,000 pages of texts—narrative histories of each migration, scholarly essays on each, related articles, book chapters, manuscript sources, and lesson plans—In Motion, the website, is an extraordinary resource for anyone looking for in-depth knowledge of migration as a central theme in African-American history and culture. *In Motion,* the book, offers readers a compact introduction to the subject.

Individuals move from one place to another. Families move. Communities and groups move. These movements are the stuff of which migrations are made. But individuals or even a group moving from one place to another does not a migration make. Thousands upon thousands of people relocating from one or more regions, countries, or communities within a specified time period transform the communities of origin, the migrants themselves, and the communities in which they settle and attempt to start life anew. Mass movements of people to new destinations make migrations.

The mass migrations of people of African descent documented in this book have had an extraordinary impact on African Americans and America's political, economic, social, and cultural development. They have changed the political geography of the nation as a whole, as well as the communities of origin and destination. They have been bearers of traditional cultures as well as creators of new cultures. They have led local, state, and federal jurisdictions to pass new laws that have changed the constitutional and legal structures of society. They have spotted America's urban landscapes with urban ghettos and given lily-white suburbs a tinge of chocolate. They have created new laboratories of African diasporan, social, and cultural transformation—creating each day still newer, New World Africans. Finally, these African American, African, and African diasporan migrations have Africanized America. *In Motion* is not simply an exploration of the African-American experience. It is, in fundamental ways, a profound interpretation and affirmation of the African presence as part of the total American reality.

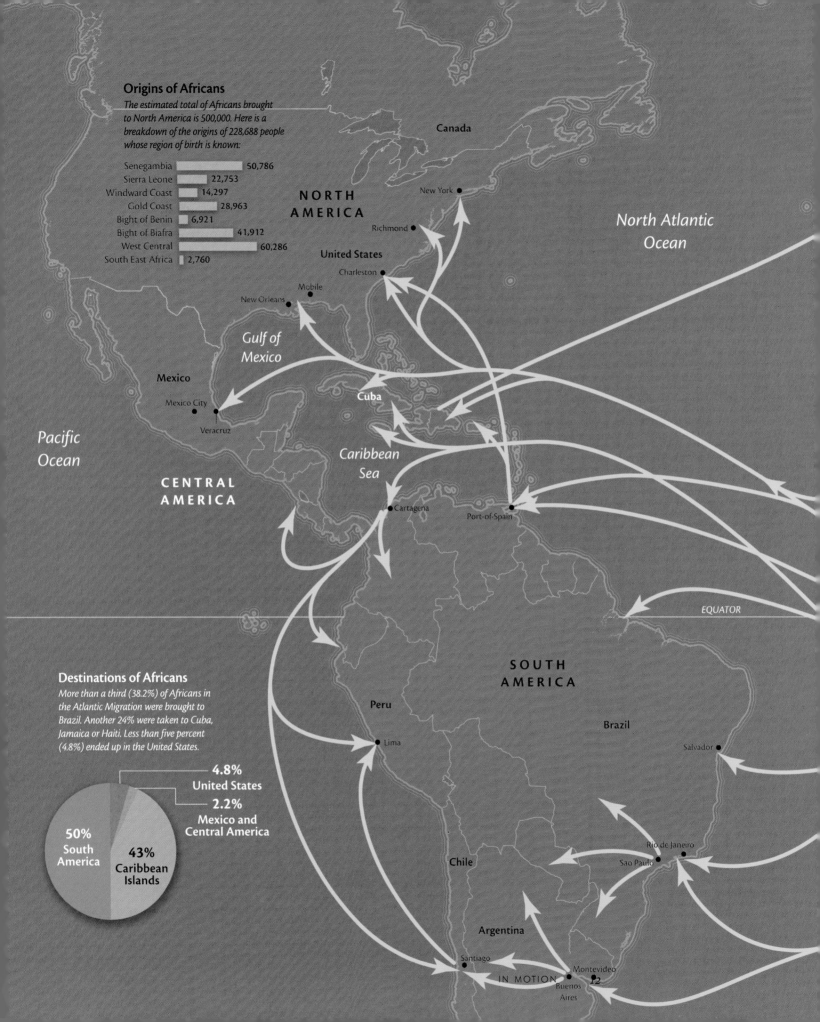

Origins of Africans

The estimated total of Africans brought to North America is 500,000. Here is a breakdown of the origins of 228,688 people whose region of birth is known:

Senegambia	50,786
Sierra Leone	22,753
Windward Coast	14,297
Gold Coast	28,963
Bight of Benin	6,921
Bight of Biafra	41,912
West Central	60,286
South East Africa	2,760

Canada

NORTH AMERICA

North Atlantic Ocean

New York

Richmond

United States

Charleston

Mobile

New Orleans

Gulf of Mexico

Mexico

Mexico City

Veracruz

Pacific Ocean

Cuba

CENTRAL AMERICA

Caribbean Sea

Cartagena

Port-of-Spain

EQUATOR

SOUTH AMERICA

Peru

Lima

Brazil

Salvador

Destinations of Africans

More than a third (38.2%) of Africans in the Atlantic Migration were brought to Brazil. Another 24% were taken to Cuba, Jamaica or Haiti. Less than five percent (4.8%) ended up in the United States.

4.8%
United States

2.2%
Mexico and Central America

50%
South America

43%
Caribbean Islands

Rio de Janeiro

Sao Paulo

Chile

Argentina

Santiago

IN MOTION

Montevideo

Buenos Aires

12

Migrations of the Enslaved

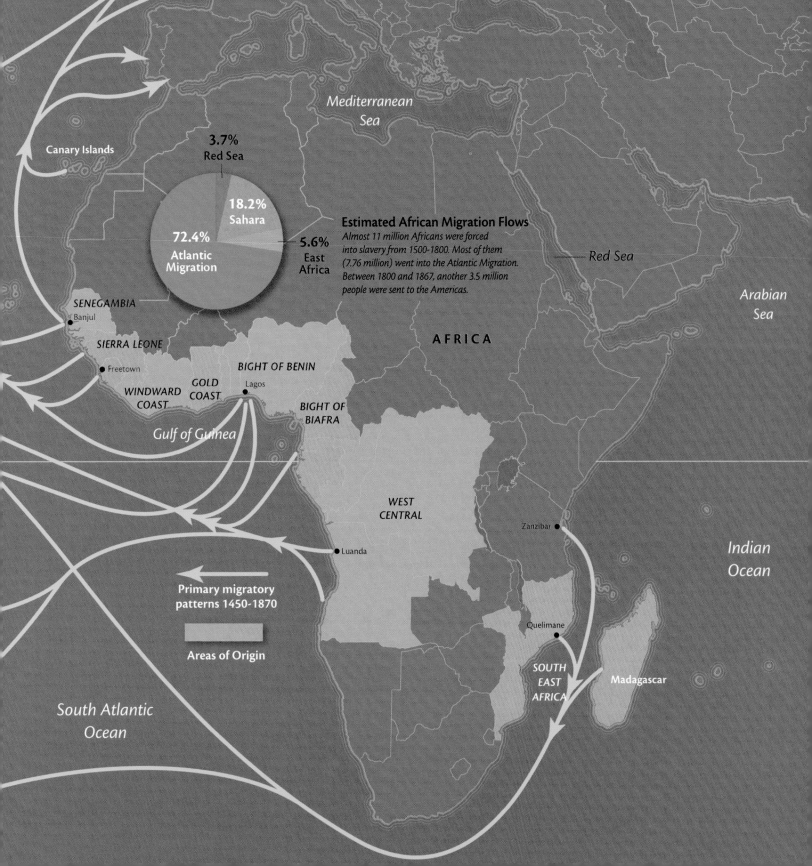

EUROPE

Mediterranean
Sea

Canary Islands

3.7%
Red Sea

18.2%
Sahara

72.4%
**Atlantic
Migration**

5.6%
**East
Africa**

Red Sea

Arabian
Sea

Estimated African Migration Flows
*Almost 11 million Africans were forced
into slavery from 1500-1800. Most of them
(7.76 million) went into the Atlantic Migration.
Between 1800 and 1867, another 3.5 million
people were sent to the Americas.*

AFRICA

SENEGAMBIA
• Banjul

SIERRA LEONE
• Freetown

GOLD
COAST

BIGHT OF BENIN
• Lagos

WINDWARD
COAST

BIGHT OF
BIAFRA

Gulf of Guinea

WEST
CENTRAL

Zanzibar •

Indian
Ocean

• Luanda

→ **Primary migratory
patterns 1450-1870**

Areas of Origin

Quelimane •

SOUTH
EAST
AFRICA

Madagascar

South Atlantic
Ocean

The Transatlantic Slave Trade

1450s TO 1865

Over the course of more than three and a half centuries, the forcible transportation in bondage of at least 12 million men, women, and children from their African homelands to the Americas changed forever the face and character of the modern world. In the Americas the importation and subsequent enslavement of the Africans would be the major factor in the resettlement of the continents following the disastrous decline in their indigenous population. The transatlantic slave trade laid the foundation for modern capitalism, generating immense wealth for business enterprises in America and Europe. On the other hand, the African continent experienced the loss of a significant part of its able-bodied population, which played a part in the social and political weakening of its societies that left them open, in the 19th century, to colonial domination and exploitation.

Between 1501 and the 1860s, at least 12 million African men, women, and children were transported in the transatlantic slave trade. Among them were farmers, fishermen, cattle herders, craftspeople, notables, scholars, slaves, musicians, as well as political and religious leaders. The woman shown here is a Bambara from Mali.

THE DEVELOPMENT OF THE TRADE | In the mid-15th century, Portuguese ships sailed down the West African coast in a maneuver designed to bypass the Muslim North Africans, who had a virtual monopoly on the sub-Saharan gold, spices, and other commodities that Europe wanted. These voyages resulted in maritime discoveries and advances in shipbuilding that later would make it easier for European vessels to navigate the Atlantic. Over time, the Portuguese vessels added another commodity to their cargo: African men, women, and children.

For the first hundred years, captives in small numbers were transported to Europe. By the close of the 15th century, 10 percent of the population of Lisbon was of African origin. Other captives were taken to islands off the African shore, including Madeira, Cape Verde, and especially São Tomé, where the Portuguese established sugar plantations using enslaved labor on a scale that foreshadowed the development of plantation slavery in the Americas. Enslaved Africans could also be found in North Africa, the Middle East, Persia, India, the Indian Ocean islands, and in Europe as far as Russia.

English and Dutch ships soon joined Portugal's vessels trading along the African coast. They preyed on the Portuguese ships, while raiding and pillaging the African mainland as well. During this initial period, European interest was particularly concentrated on Senegambia. The region had a long, glorious history. It was the site of the ancient Kingdom of Ghana and the medieval empires of Mali and Songhay. Its interior regions of Bure and Bambuk were rich in gold. It reached the Mediterranean and hence Europe from Songhay. The slave trade was closely linked to the Europeans' insatiable hunger for gold, and the arrival of the Portuguese on the "Gold Coast" (Ghana) in the 1470s tapped these inland sources.

Later, they developed commercial and political relations with the kingdoms of Benin (in present-day Nigeria) and Kongo. The Kongo state became Christianized and, in the process, was undermined by the spread of the slave trade. Benin, however, restricted Portuguese influence and somewhat limited the trade in human beings.

Starting in 1492, Africans were part of every expedition into the regions that became the American Spanish colonies. By the beginning of the 16th century, they were brought as slaves to grow sugar and mine gold on Hispaniola, and were forced to drain the shallow lakes of the Mexican plateau, thereby finalizing the subjugation of the Aztec nation. In a bitter twist, the Africans were often forced to perform tasks that would help advance the genocide that would resolve the vexing "Indian question."

By the middle of the 17th century, the slave trade entered its second and most intense phase. The creation of ever larger sugar plantations and the introduction of other crops such as indigo, rice, tobacco, coffee, cocoa, and cotton would lead to the displacement of an estimated seven million Africans between 1650 and 1807. The demand for labor resulted in numerous innovations, encouraged opportunists and entrepreneurs, and accrued deceptions and barbarities, upon which the slave trade rested. Some slave traders—often well-respected men in their communities—made fortunes for themselves and their descendants. The corresponding impact on Africa was intensified as larger parts of west and central Africa came into the slavers' orbit.

The third and final period of the international slave trade began with the ban on the importation of captives imposed by Britain and the United States in 1807 that lasted until the 1860s. Brazil, Cuba, and Puerto Rico were the principal destinations for Africans, since they could no longer legally be brought into North America, the British or French colonies in the Caribbean, or the independent countries of Spanish America. Despite this restricted market, the numbers of deported Africans did not decline until the late 1840s. Many were smuggled into the United States. At the same time, tens of thousands of Africans rescued from the slave ships were forcibly settled in Sierra Leone, Liberia, and several islands of the Caribbean.

CAPTURE AND ENSLAVEMENT | War, slave raiding, kidnapping, and politico-religious struggle accounted for the vast majority of Africans transported to the Americas. Several wars resulted in massive enslavement, including the export of prisoners across the Atlantic as well as the use of captives as slaves within Africa itself.

A Vast Empire

Opposite, left: This 17th-century image of Benin city depicts the capital of a vast empire. By the mid-16th century, it stretched from the region of northern Lagos to the Niger River delta. Presided over by the *oba*, or king, the city was both a major trading center and the religious and political capital of the Edo people.

Opposite, right: Rebellious captives were held in this crawl space under the stairs leading to the trader's apartment on Gorée Island, Senegal. Throughout the 18th century, numerous revolts linked to the slave trade broke out in Senegambia. Fort St Joseph, on the Senegal River, was attacked, and all commerce was interrupted for six years. Several conspiracies and actual revolts erupted on Gorée Island, resulting in the death of the governor and several soldiers. In addition, the crews of several slave ships were killed on the River Gambia.

The Akan wars of the late 17th century and the first half of the 18th century were a struggle for power among states in the Gold Coast hinterland. Akwamu, Akyem, Denkyira, Fante, and Asante groups battled for control of the region. By the mid-18th century, Asante emerged as the dominant force. By 1650, Oyo had become a consolidated imperial power in the interior of the Bight of Benin by defeating the Bariba and Nupe in the north and other Yoruba states to the south. The wars between various Gbe groups resulted in the rise of Dahomey and its victory over Allada in 1724. The winners occupied the port of Whydah three years later but were then forced to pay tribute to the more powerful Oyo. These wars accounted for the deportation of over a million Africans along the Bight of Benin coast. The 60-year period of the Kongo civil wars, ending in 1740, was responsible for the capture and enslavement of many. Among them were the followers of the Catholic martyr Beatrice of Kongo, who tried to end the wars through pacifist protest.

The spread of militant Islam across West Africa began in Senegambia during the late 17th century. It led to two major political transformations: the emergence in the late 18th century of the Muslim states of Futa Jallon in the Guinea highlands and Futa Toro on the Senegal River. The jihad movement continued into the 19th century, especially with the outbreak of war in 1804 in the Hausa states under the leadership of Sheikh Usman dan Fodio. These wars in turn exacerbated political tensions in Oyo, which resulted in a Muslim uprising and the collapse of the Oyo state between 1817 and 1833. New strongholds were created at Ibadan, Abeokuta, and Ijebu, and the conflict intensified over attempts to replace or resurrect the Oyo state.

Continental Atrocities

Left: Europeans gave names, such as the Gold Coast, or the Slave Coast to some parts of the West African coast according to the "goods"—including people—they could find there, as shown on this map of Africa from the 1600s.

Inset, left: The slave raids resulted in social and economic devastation. As children and young adults were taken away, infants and the elderly were left behind or killed. Entire communities had to relocate in difficult, hard-to-reach terrain, leading to stagnation or even regression.

Above: Tukulor, Wolof, Fulani, Serer, Manding, and Sarakole were among the ethnic groups of Senegambians transported to the United States, in particular to the Virginia-Maryland region and Louisiana.

After 1700, the importation of firearms heightened the intensity of many of the wars. European forces intervened in some of the localized fighting and in warfare all along the Atlantic coast. They sought to obtain captives directly in battle or as political rewards for having backed the winning side. Working from their permanent colonies at Luanda, Benguela, and other coastal points, the Portuguese conducted joint military ventures into the hinterlands with their African allies.

Africans also became enslaved through non-military means. Judicial and religious sanctions and punishments removed alleged criminals, people accused of witchcraft, and social misfits through enslavement and banishment. Rebellious family members might be expelled from their homes through enslavement. Human pawns, especially children, held as collateral for debt were almost always protected from enslavement by relatives and customary practices. However, debts and the collateral for those debts were sometimes subjected to illegal demands, and pawned individuals, especially children, were sometimes "sold" or otherwise removed from the watchful eyes of the relatives and communities that had tried to safeguard their rights.

Africans were also kidnapped, though kidnapping was a crime in most communities, and sold into slavery. Captives were sometimes ransomed, but this practice often encouraged the taking of prisoners for monetary rewards.

As the slave trade destroyed families and communities, people tried to protect their loved ones. Various governments and communal institutions developed means and policies that limited the trade's impact. Muslims were particularly concerned with protecting the freedom of their co-religionists. Qur'anic law stated that those of the Faith born free must remain free. But this precept was often violated.

Throughout Africa, people of all beliefs tried to safeguard their own. Some offered themselves as slaves in exchange for the release of their loved ones. Others tried to have their kin redeemed even after they had been shipped away. Resistance took the form of attacks on slave depots and ships, as well as revolts in the forts, in barracoons, and on slave ships.

But at a higher level, political fragmentation made it virtually impossible to develop methods of government that could effectively resist the impact of the slave trade. Personal gain and the interests of the small commercial elites who dominated trade routes, ports, and secret societies also worked against the freeing of captives, offenders, and displaced children, who could easily end up in the slave trade.

TRADERS AND TRADE | Western European countries established distinct national trades. The European port cities most involved in this growth industry were Bristol, Liverpool, and London in England; Amsterdam in Holland; Lisbon, the Portuguese capital; and Nantes, located on the western French coast.

On the African side most captives were traded from only a few ports: Luanda (Angola), Whydah (Bight of Benin), Bonny (Bight of Biafra), and the adjacent "castles" at Koromantin and Winneba on the Gold Coast, which accounted for at least a third of the Africans transported to the Americas. Other major ports included Old Calabar (Bight of Biafra), Benguela (Southern Angola), Cabinda (north of the Congo River), and Lagos in the Bight of Benin. These nine ports accounted for at least half of all the Africans deported to the Americas.

The European countries attempted, though not successfully, to regulate the trade by chartering various national companies established under royal decree or parliamentary order. But these efforts to create monopolies, such as England's Royal African Company (RAC), were soon undermined by private merchant companies and pirates who opened up new markets in the Bight of Biafra and the northern Angola coast, and challenged the RAC on the Gold Coast and in the Gambia.

Each of the nations and their slave ports experimented with innovative marketing and trading techniques. Sometimes this competition required the maintenance of trading depots and forts—the slave castles, or factories—as was the case in the Gold Coast and the Bight of Benin, as well as in lesser ports along the Upper Guinea coast, Senegambia, and Angola.

The trade was propelled by credit flowing outward from Europe and used by merchants to purchase men, women, and children in West Africa. They advanced goods on credit in lieu of payment in captives. The wares sent to Africa in exchange for captives included those that could be used as money—cowry shells, strips of cloth, iron bars, copper bracelets (manillas), silver coins, and gold. These goods also had value as commodities: cloth could be turned into clothing, iron into hoes and other tools. Consumer goods included textiles, alcohol, and jewelry.

Military goods, principally firearms, were also exchanged for captives. They were instrumental in the 18th-century Gold Coast wars that enslaved multitudes and led to the Asante people's political ascendancy in the region. With the exception of the Gold Coast wars, guns played little role at first in local conflicts, due in part to the difficulty of keeping powder dry in tropical regions. For example, the rise of Oyo, which became the dominant slaving power in the interior of the Bight of Benin, was mostly effected by the use of cavalry.

The trade was a high-risk enterprise. The commodity was people; they could escape, be murdered, commit suicide, or fall victim to epidemics or natural disasters. Local traders could disappear with their payment and never produce the captives stipulated in the contract. Since the slave trade went across political and cultural frontiers, there was little recourse to courts and governments in the event of commercial dishonesty. No international court or judicial system existed to handle the

Active Resistance

Above: More than 390 insurrections on board ships have been documented, mostly for the British, French, and Dutch trades. Resistance added costs to the trade, and research shows that if Africans had not resisted transportation and enslavement, about 9 percent more, or an estimated one million people, could have been deported.

Right, top: For the first 50 years of the Atlantic slave trade, children under 15 represented about 10 percent of the captives. Starting in 1800 and continuing until the end of the trade, children under 15 represented about 40 percent of the deportees.

Right, bottom: This engraving shows captives, wearing shackles, held on the French slave ship *Vigilante.*.

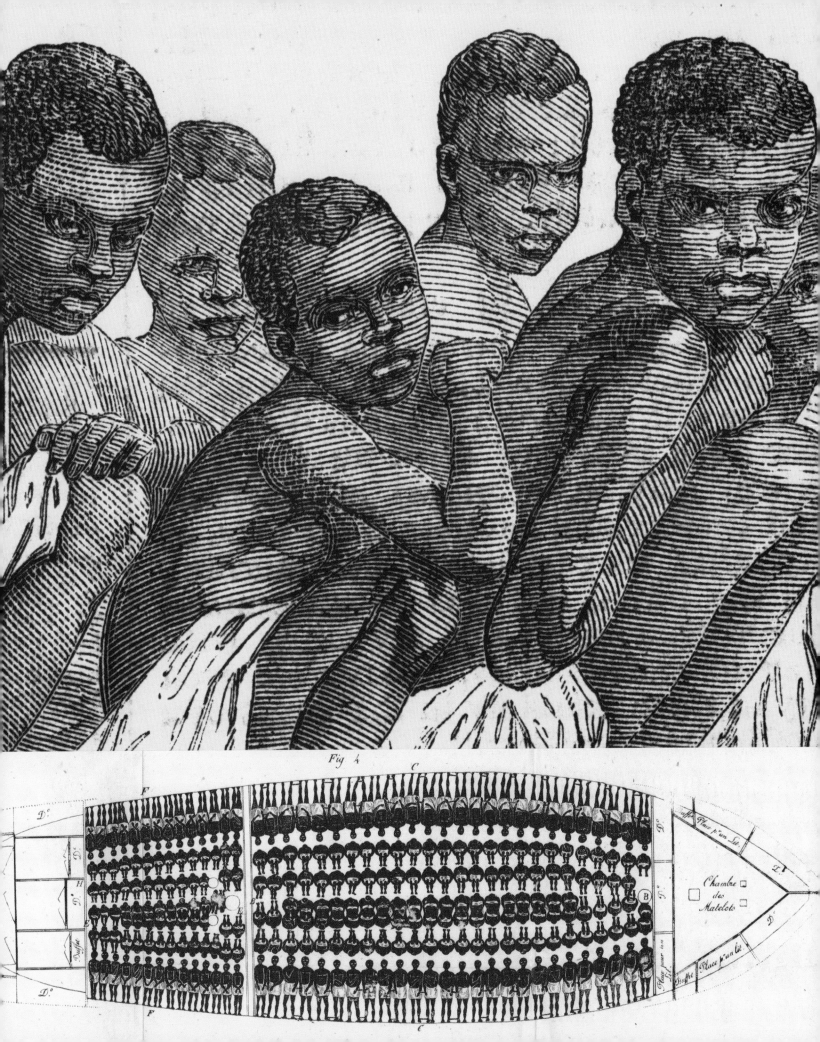

Fig. 4

Chambre des Matelots

Place p.' un Lit.

extraordinary violations of human rights that defined every aspect of the slave trade.

The slave trade was driven by both demand and greed. The customers in the Americas who could afford it desperately needed labor and did not care how it was obtained. Traders could benefit immensely from theft, plunder, kidnapping, ransoming, and the sale of human beings as commodities. These slavers took advantage of African political troubles, religious differences, legal technicalities, economic crises, and outright callousness to exploit helpless individuals.

THE MIDDLE PASSAGE | On the first leg of their three-part journey, often called the Triangular Trade, European ships brought manufactured goods to Africa; on the second, they transported African men, women, and children to the Americas; and on the third leg, they exported to Europe the sugar, rum, cotton, and tobacco produced by slave labor. There was also a direct trade between Brazil and Angola that did not include the European leg. Traders referred to the Africa-Americas part of the voyage as the "Middle Passage," and the term has survived to denote the Africans' ordeal.

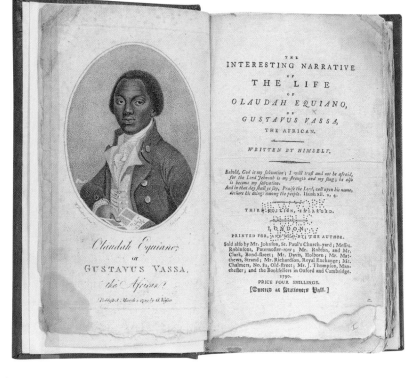

Well over 30,000 voyages from Africa to the Americas have been documented. But numbers and statistics alone cannot convey the horror of the experience. However, the records provide detailed information on some aspects of this tragedy.

The dreadful Middle Passage could last from one to three months and epitomized the role of violence in the trade. Based on regulations, ships could transport only about 350 people, but some carried more than 800 men, women, and children. Branded, stripped naked for the duration of the voyage, lying down amidst filth, enduring almost unbearable heat, compelled by the lash to dance on deck to straighten their limbs, all captives went through a frightening, incredibly brutal, and dehumanizing experience. Men were shackled under deck, and all Africans were subjected to abuse and punishment. Some people tried to starve themselves to death, but the crew forced them to take food by whipping them, torturing them with hot coal, or forcing their mouths open by using special instruments or by breaking their teeth. The personal identity of the captives was denied. Women and boys were often used for the pleasure of the crew. Ottobah Cugoano, who endured the Middle Passage in the 18th century, recalled "it was common for the dirty filthy sailors to take the African women and lie upon their bodies."

Mortality brought about by malnutrition, dysentery, smallpox, and other diseases was very high. Depending on the times, upwards of 20 percent died from various epidemics or committed suicide. Venture Smith, describing his ordeal, wrote: "After an ordinary passage, except great mortality by the small pox, which broke out on board, we arrived at the island of Barbadoes: but when we reached it, there were found out of the two hundred and sixty that sailed from Africa, not more than two hundred alive." It was not unusual for captains and crew to toss the sick overboard; some even disposed of an entire cargo for insurance purposes.

On board slave ships, in the midst of their oppression, the Africans, who were often as much strangers to each other as to their European captors, forged the first links with their new American identities. Relationships established during the Middle Passage frequently resulted in revolts and other forms of resistance that bound them in new social and political alliances. Ottobah Cugoano described the attempted revolt organized on the ship that took him from the Gold Coast to Grenada: "When we found ourselves at last taken away, death was more preferable than life; and a plan was concerted amongst us, that we might burn and blow up the ship, and to perish all together in the flames....It was the women and boys which were to burn the ship, with the approbation and groans of the rest; though that was prevented, the discovery was likewise a cruel bloody scene."

The special relations created on the ship lasted a lifetime and were regarded by the deported Africans, torn from their loved ones, as strongly as kinship. They had special names for those who had shared their ordeal. They were called *bâtiments* in Creole-speaking areas (from the French for ship), *sippi* in Suriname (from ship), and shipmate in Jamaica. Far from wiping out all traces of their cultural, social, and personal past, the Middle Passage experience provided Africans with opportunities to draw on their collective heritage to make themselves a new people.

AFRICANS IN AMERICA | Of the estimated ten million men, women, and children who survived the Middle Passage, approximately 450,000 Africans disembarked on North America's shores. They thus represented only a fraction of those transported during the 350-year history of the international slave trade. Brazil and the Caribbean each received about nine times as many captives.

The labor of enslaved Africans proved crucial in the development of South Carolina, Georgia, Virginia, and Maryland, and contributed indirectly through commerce to the fortunes of New York, Massachusetts, and Pennsylvania. Though the enforced destination of Africans was primarily to plantations and farms for work in cash-crop agriculture, they were also used in mining and servicing the commercial economy. Slaves were placed in towns and port cities as domestic servants, and many urban residents performed essential commercial duties working as porters, teamsters, and craftsmen.

In 18th-century America, Africans were concentrated in the agricultural lowlands of South Carolina and Georgia, especially in the Sea Islands, where they grew

TO BE SOLD on board the Ship *Bance-Island*, on tuesday the 6th of *May* next, at *Ashley-Ferry*; a choice cargo of about 250 fine healthy

NEGROES,

just arrived from the Windward & Rice Coast. —The utmost care has already been taken, and shall be continued, to keep them free from the least danger of being infected with the SMALL-POX, no boat having been on board, and all other communication with people from *Charles-Town* prevented.

Austin, Laurens, & Appleby.

N. B. Full one Half of the above Negroes have had the SMALL-POX in their own Country.

Early Trade

Above: A newspaper advertisement from the 1780s announces the sale, near Charleston, South Carolina, of Africans from Sierra Leone who were familiar with rice cultivation. Contrary to the myth that planters purposely mixed workers of different ethnic origins to promote division, they were more interested in buying gangs of people of the same provenance who were already familiar with the crops under cultivation.

Right: The first Africans to enter the English colonies of North America arrived in 1619 in Virginia. Dutch sailors had captured them from a Spanish ship, and exchanged them for food with the settlers at Jamestown.

rice, cotton, indigo, and other crops. In Louisiana they labored on sugarcane plantations. They were employed on tobacco farms in the tidewater region of Virginia and Maryland. The tidewater, together with the Georgia and South Carolina lowlands, accounted for at least two-thirds of the Africans brought into North America prior to the end of legal importation in 1807.

ETHNICITIES IN THE UNITED STATES | The largest number of Africans in the lowlands (34 percent) came from Bantu-speaking regions of west-central Africa. Twenty percent were transported from Senegambia, while the Gold Coast and Sierra Leone each accounted for about 15 percent. Others came from the Bight of Biafra and the Windward Coast. The enslaved population of Virginia/Maryland was composed mostly of Africans from the Bight of Biafra, some 39 percent. Senegambia accounted for 21 percent of the Africans in this region. Another 17 percent were of Bantu origin, and 10 percent were originally from the Gold Coast.

Therefore, nearly 90 percent of the Africans in these two major regions came from only four zones in Africa. Most came from the west-central area of Angola and Congo where languages (Kikongo, Kimbundu) and culture (often referred to as Bantu) were closely related. Many more ended up in the tidewater than in the lowlands, but they comprised nearly a third of all migrants in both sectors.

The Senegambians were much more prominent in North America than in South America and the Caribbean. Senegambia was strongly influenced by Islam, to a greater degree than any other coastal region where enslaved Africans originated. More Muslims were enslaved in North America than anywhere else in the New World except for Brazil. Their presence was especially pronounced in Louisiana, to which many Manding people—almost all males—had been transported. This state also had a large presence of non-Muslim Bambara from Mali.

The Upper South had a considerable population of migrants from the Bight of Biafra, as did lowland South Carolina and Georgia. In all probability, a large number of the many Africans whose origins are not known actually came from this area. These Igbo and Ibibio people would develop a distinct subculture. Women made up a relatively high number among those groups. They gave birth to a new generation, ensuring some transmission of their cultural values and beliefs. Men and women from Sierra Leone and the adjacent Windward Coast were heavily concentrated in the low country, and most were involved in cultivating rice. Noticeably absent from North America's African population were substantial numbers of people from the Slave Coast (Togo, Benin, and western Nigeria).

THE SUPPRESSION OF THE SLAVE TRADE | Article I, Section 9, Clause 1 of the U.S. Constitution (1787) stipulated: "The Migration or Importation of such Persons as any of the States now existing shall think proper to admit, shall not be prohibited by the

Wounded Dignity

Many more people of Bantu origin ended up in the Maryland/Virginia area than in the Georgia/Carolina region, but they comprised nearly a third of all migrants in both sectors, and had an important influence on the religion and culture of the enslaved population in North America. In 1850 Harvard biologist Louis Agassiz commissioned portraits of enslaved Africans in South Carolina, to illustrate his theory that human groups did not have a common origin. To show that the Africans were a different (and inferior) species, he had seven men and women born in Africa or of African-born parents photographed, front, back, and in profile. In some pictures they are entirely naked. Their expressions tell a terrible story of wounded dignity.

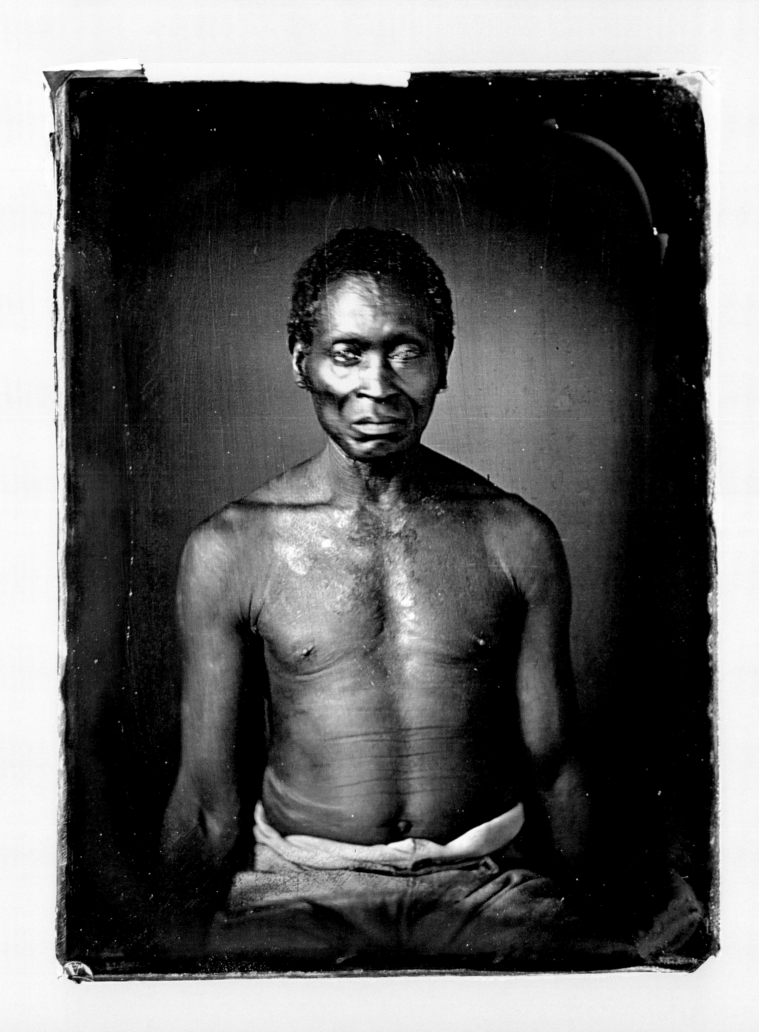

Congress prior to the Year one thousand eight hundred and eight, but a Tax or duty may be imposed on such Importation, not exceeding ten dollars for each Person."

In consequence, the United States abolished its slave trade from Africa, effective January 1, 1808. But slave trading, now illegal, continued unabated until 1860. The U.S. Slave Trade Act, enacted by a vote of 63 in favor and 49 against in February 1807, was a half victory for the slavers because it specified that the Africans illegally brought to slaveholding states would still be sold and enslaved. Penalties consisted merely of fines. With the authorities turning a blind eye and refusing to enforce their own law, the illegal slave trade flourished for several decades, particularly in Texas (Spanish until 1821), Florida (Spanish until 1818), Louisiana, and South Carolina.

Africans were sold with little secrecy. As recounted by a slave smuggler, it was an easy task: "I soon learned how readily, and at what profits, the Florida negroes were sold into the neighboring American States. The kaffle [coffle]...[was to] cross the boundary into Georgia, where some of our wild Africans were mixed with various squads of native blacks, and driven inland, till sold off, singly or by couples, on the road." The introduction of African captives took such proportions that President Madison wrote to Congress, saying "it appears that American citizens are instrumental in carrying on a traffic in enslaved Africans, equally in violation of the laws of humanity, and in defiance of those of their own country."

Congress passed a tougher law in 1820 making international slave trading an act of piracy punishable by death. Even though the traffic went on, only one American was ever executed for this crime. In addition, American slavers, particularly from New York and Rhode Island, shipped Africans to Cuba, Puerto Rico, and Brazil, where the slave trade was still legal. More than 3.3 million Africans were transported between 1801 and 1867, the vast majority to Brazil and Cuba. Half came from west-central Africa, and more than 40 percent were originally from the Bights of Benin and Biafra, and Southeast Africa (Mozambique and Madagascar).

In the 1850s a movement developed in the South to reopen the international slave trade. It was defeated, but the illegal importation of Africans increased between 1850 and 1860, even though the African Squadron, established by the U.S. government in 1843, patrolled the harbors of the African coast. Countless ships eluded them, but the U.S. Navy managed to capture more than a hundred slavers before 1861, including a boat prepared to take on 1,800 people in Angola.

Although their respective countries had officially outlawed the Atlantic slave trade, American and British slavers and traders continued to be openly involved in it, and their activities brought money and work to shipbuilders, crews, insurance companies, and manufacturers of various trade goods, guns, and shackles. Slave ships brought Africans until the Civil War. The *Clotilda* landed more than a hundred men, women, and children from Dahomey (Benin) and Nigeria in the summer of 1860 at Mobile, Alabama.

LEGACIES IN AMERICA | The slave trade and slavery left a legacy of violence. Brutality, often of near-bestial proportions, was the principal condition shaping the character of the enforced migration, whether along a trade route, on board ship, or on an American plantation. The degree of power concentrated in the hands of North American slave owners, interested only in maximizing their profits, allowed excessive levels of physical punishment and the perpetuation of sexual abuse and exploitation that have marked in many ways the development of the African-American community.

There was a marked sexual component to the assaults; rape was common. Kinship was disregarded, particularly the paternity of children. Their status reflected the slave status of their mothers, no matter who their father might have been. Slave owners treated their unpaid, overworked labor forces as mere chattel.

Avoiding and resisting violence were determining characteristics of the responses of the Africans to their forced migration experience. Individuals attempted to evade physical abuse through strategies of accommodation, escape, and on several occasions, violent rebellion. The preservation and adaptation of African cultural forms to respond to the new needs of the enslaved population was also an act of resistance to the imposition of European norms.

Unlike earlier slave systems, in the Americas racial distinctions were used to keep the enslaved population in bondage. Contrary to what happened in Latin America, where racial stratification was more complex, in North America, any person of identifiable African descent, no matter the degree of "white" ancestry, was classified as colored, Negro, or black. A racial caste system was established, and as a result racialized attitudes and racism became an inherent and lasting part of North American culture.

Though enslaved individuals came from widely different backgrounds, and the number of ethnic groups and markers of identity were extensive, certain ethnicities, cultural forms, and languages—usually in pidgin and creolized forms—as well as religions proved sustainable and were maintained, sometimes exaggerated, and manipulated during the process of adjusting to slave life in the Americas.

The overarching result of African migration during the slavery era was an "American" culture, neither "European" nor "African," created in a political and economic context of inequality and oppression. The African contribution to this new culture was a towering legacy, hugely impacting on language, religion, music, dance, art, and cuisine. Most important, an enduring sense of African-American community developed in the face of white racism.

Abache and Cudjoe Kazoola Lewis, 1912

Cudjoe Lewis and Abache were among the last group of Africans forcibly transported to the United States. Originally from present-day Benin and Nigeria, 110 men, women, and children disembarked in Mobile, Alabama, from the *Clotilda* in 1860. After Emancipation, they asked in vain to be repatriated.. Very attached to their traditions, they eventually founded their own town, Africatown. The last survivor, Cudjoe Lewis, died in 1935. The descendants of the *Clotilda* Africans still live in Africatown.

Runaway Journeys

1630s TO 1865

From the beginnings of slavery until the Civil War, African Americans attempted to make or succeeded in making their way to freedom. It was during the 19th century, however, that the migration of fugitives within the United States and to Canada and Mexico became widespread. It is estimated that at least 50,000 men, women, and children ran away each year, and among them a few thousand made it to freedom.

A few fugitives became prominent abolitionists who wrote autobiographies, thus contributing to a unique American literary genre, the Slave Narrative. At enormous risk, countless others helped their families and friends and even strangers secure their own freedom.

MANY REASONS TO LEAVE | The great majority of the runaways absconded for a few days or weeks only to be captured or to return on their own. Some ran away to reunite with family members who had been sold away or to sustain familial or romantic liaisons. But for others the goal was to secure permanent freedom and leave behind the horrors of a system that brutalized and exploited them. Many planned their escapes for weeks, even months, waiting for the right moment. Their quest for freedom often meant leaving loved ones behind in slavery, and the pain and anguish of such separations remained strong. Fear and anxiety about being caught and returned to bondage were a constant reminder that at no time did runaways have any right to freedom. Local and federal laws, indeed the Constitution itself, protected the rights of slaveholders to retrieve their "property."

Successful fugitives were extremely self-confident and self-reliant individuals—resourceful, willful, focused, and purposeful. Their owners often described them as "artful," "cunning," "wily," "bold," and "intelligent." They took enormous risks and faced extraordinary hardships. They knew they would meet harsh punishments if caught. Many had seen firsthand the brutality experienced by those who had failed. Severe whippings of three hundred lashes—followed by rubs of salt, vinegar and hot pepper—were among the most severe punishments and left many permanently injured.

Even fugitives who had been caught previously and were still wearing the instruments that were supposed to prevent them from absconding again were among the runaways. These contraptions were designed and used to torture fugitives and break their spirits, so as to make them more submissive to white rule. However, the cruel and unusual punishments many times persuaded them to abscond.

Some, like Jade, who stole money to pay for his passage North, never recovered. A man who witnessed his punishment stated, "They took him and whupped him for near fifteen minutes. We could hear him holler 'way up at the big house. Jade, he never got over that whupping. He died three days later."

Notwithstanding the dangers and threats, men, women, and children—alone, in small family units, or in groups—dared to embark on a road to freedom that could take up to a year to travel.

THE PEAKS OF MIGRATION | During the colonial period, the number of runaways remained small, and those who succeeded usually posed as free blacks in towns and cities. But during and after the American Revolution, the flow of fugitives increased as the war disrupted the plantation system in the South and ushered in the gradual abolition of slavery in the North. During the war, thousands fled to the British lines. For instance, in 1775 Lord Dunmore, royal governor of Virginia, offered slaves their freedom if they bore arms for the British. Between five hundred and six hundred men immediately responded to Dunmore's "proclamation." Too often, however, the British promise of freedom was an empty one. At the end of the war, they sent a number of Black Loyalists to the West Indies in chains.

The disruption caused by the war between the United States and Great Britain in 1812–1815 also sparked a migration of fugitives. To break the will of the South, British commanders occupied New Orleans with black troops. Adm. Alexander Cochrane even recruited runaways to fight against the Americans in Louisiana. In South Carolina and Georgia, black Sea Islanders left their plantations when British troops appeared. Roswell King, overseer on Pierce Butler's plantation on St. Simons Island, witnessed such an exodus among his boss's five hundred slaves. "I can never git over the Baseness of your ungrateful Negroes," he wrote Butler, telling him of 138 people who had escaped.

After the closing of the African slave trade in 1808 and the great expansion of the domestic slave trade from the Upper South to the lower Mississippi River valley, the migration increasingly turned to the northern states and Canada.

PROFILE OF THE FUGITIVES | A profile of fugitives both within the South and in the North and Canada reveals that the great majority were young men in their teens and twenties. They ran away in greater numbers because they had not yet married or, if they had, had not yet begun a family. Once away from the plantation or farm, they could better defend themselves and were willing to resist capture.

Women were less likely to be fugitives because they had often begun to raise families by their late teens and early twenties. With youngsters to care for, it was difficult to contemplate either leaving them behind or taking them along in an escape attempt. Nevertheless, many women embarked on the migration to freedom.

Going Home

John Thompson, born in Virginia, was sold "down the river" to Alabama. Wanting to reunite with his family, he escaped in 1857. He traveled at night on top of train cars (*top*), hiding in the woods during the day. He finally reached Virginia, where he was caught and sold again. He managed to escape once more with the help of the Underground Railroad and settled in New York. Learning that his former owner was in town to arrest him, John sailed to London. *Bottom:* An illustration depicts the culminating episode in the flight of Henry Brown, who escaped from Richmond, Virginia, in a box. In the office of the Pennsylvania Anti-Slavery Society, Brown emerges from a crate as several figures, including Frederick Douglass (holding a claw hammer at left) look on. The box itself became an abolitionist metaphor for the inhumanity and spiritual suffocation of slavery.

Among the most notable was North Carolina native Linda Brent—later known as Harriet Jacobs—who escaped in 1835 and hid in an attic for nearly seven years before running to the North. She later became a reformer, abolitionist, and educa-

tor, and wrote her autobiography, *Incidents in the Life of a Slave Girl, Written by Herself,* in 1861. When she escaped, a wanted poster was displayed for miles around. Sometimes entire families made it to freedom, like Harriet Shepard and her five children, who, along with five other men and women, fled in an owner's carriage. In a few instances, extended families of ten or more made it across the Ohio River.

Besides tremendous courage, fugitives displayed ingenuity and organizational skills. They had to discreetly gather food for the trip and, if possible, changes of clothes. Most runaway advertisements described the clothing they were wearing when they left, and as a consequence, many runaways modified their appearance, and even disguised their gender. Those light-skinned enough to pass for white had to behave and talk like white people. All had to provide believable explanations when asked questions, and became masters at deceit and secrecy.

Henry "Box" Brown of Virginia made one of the most unusual escapes from slavery. After his owner sold his wife and children to a North Carolina planter, Brown resolved to flee from bondage. With the help of a friend, he folded his five-foot-eight-inch, two-hundred-pound body into a specially constructed wooden box, two feet eight inches deep and two feet wide. His friend took the trunk-like box to the Adams Express Company in Richmond and sent it off to a Philadelphia abolitionist. Twenty-seven hours and 350 miles later, Brown arrived at his destination.

Most fugitives chose one of the five major destinations that evolved during the period from the American Revolution to the Civil War: towns and cities in the South, remote areas near the plantations, the West, the North, and Canada. A few fled to Mexico, Central America, or the Caribbean.

ESCAPE TO CITIES AND TOWNS | Perhaps a majority of successful runaways escaped to towns and cities. Even in colonial days these urban areas offered them opportunities for autonomy and anonymity. By the early 1800s, most Southern cities had hundreds and sometimes thousands of hired slaves, making it possible for escapees to blend in. Resourceful fugitives could find ways to conceal their identities, create new ones, perhaps find shelter with relatives, and possibly lose themselves in growing free black populations. Many who succeeded in hiding their true identities were literate,

On to Liberty

Left: Throughout the history of North American slavery, men, women, and children fled the brutality and oppression they were subjected to. They embarked on long and risky journeys to regain their right to freedom, as seen in this 1867 painting by Theodor Kaufmann.

Above: During the 19th century, the migration of fugitives from the Deep and Upper South to the North accelerated. Many, like Polly Jackson, traveled to Ohio. According to legend, she fought off slave catchers with a kettle full of hot water and a butcher knife. It was difficult for women to defend themselves against male pursuers.

$50.00 Reward!!

Ran away from the Yard Corner of Jackson & Broad Streets, Augusta Ga. — on the evening of Tuesday 7th April 1863 a Woman "Dolly", whose likeness is here seen. —

She is thirty years of age, light Complexion — hesitates somewhat when spoken to, and is not a very healthy woman — but rather good looking, with a fine set of teeth. Never changed her Owner, and has been a house Servant always. —— It is thought she has been enticed off by some White Man, being herself a Stranger to this City, and belonging to a Charleston Family. ——

For further particulars apply to Antoine Poullain Esqr. Augusta Ga. —— !!

Augusta Police Station

Louis Manigault Owner of Dolly

possessed marketable skills, and could pass as free. They knew what whites wanted to hear and could produce a plausible explanation of their backgrounds. Males found work as laborers, carpenters, masons, bricklayers, mechanics, shoemakers, and tradesmen; women were employed as cooks, maids, and laundresses.

Although escapees still faced the constant danger of being stopped and questioned, control was less intensive than in the countryside, where black strangers were scrutinized and often arrested. As Baltimore, Washington, D.C., Richmond, Louisville, Nashville, Mobile, New Orleans, and St. Louis grew, it became increasingly difficult for authorities to keep track of the expanding black populations, and residential patterns impeded their ability to check the identities of black men and women who lived in alleys behind town houses, in rundown houses along the rivers, and in residential areas and suburbs where they worked as house servants.

Although detailed statistics do not exist, local police records suggest that there was a continual flow of fugitives into urban areas. In these cities where fugitives might have relatives and friends, there were also free blacks willing to assist and religious institutions that would take them in. In the Upper South cities, many legally free blacks, who had recently emerged from bondage, sympathized with the fugitives' plight and provided aid and comfort. A free mulatto in Camden, Delaware, Samuel D. Burris, was described as "notorious" for providing protection to fugitives. Despite a previous conviction, an observer reported, "Burris still persists in the nefarious practice of enticing Servants and Slaves away from their Masters."

MAROON COMMUNITIES | The second migratory path led into the most remote, isolated backcountry, dense forests, bayous, swamps, or Indian territories. There, the runaways formed maroon communities—organized enclaves of fugitives—that developed in the earliest days and continued through abolition. As early as 1690, farmers in Harlem, New York, were complaining about the inhabitants of a maroon colony who were attacking the settlers.

The first known free black community in North America was a settlement of fugitive Africans called Gracia Real de Santa Teresa de Mose. Located near St. Augustine in Spanish Florida, it operated from 1739 to 1763. Some fugitives established camps in Elliott's Cut, between the Ashepoo and Pon Pon Rivers in South Carolina; and in the Indian nations of Alabama and Mississippi. In the 18th century, others had taken refuge in Spanish Florida with the Seminole Indians. Black and native Seminoles joined forces against the U.S. Army during two wars in 1812 and 1835.

During the 1790s, runaways in Virginia and the Carolinas hid in woods and swamps during the day, and emerged at night to commit "various depredations" on farms and plantations. By the 19th century, several thousand lived in the Great Dismal Swamp on the border between Virginia and North Carolina. Slaveholders often ran advertisements mentioning that the fugitives were heading there: "Bonaparte ran away last Christmas without cause or provocation. He is about six feet high and rather slim yet very strong, twenty-eight years old, not of very dark complexion, full eyes, large mouth, fine set of teeth, speaks fluently. I have received information that he is lurking about the Dismal Swamp." (*Southern Argus,* April 16, 1852.)

Maroons have been described as "some of the most hate-filled and angry slaves." Before fleeing, they had often committed acts of violence against their owners, overseers, or other whites. Many vowed never to return to bondage. Joe, who murdered a slave owner in South Carolina, fled deep into the woods. He recruited others to join him and became the leader of a band of fugitives. He was then given the nickname Forest, as he had made the deep woods his refuge. A group of slave owners petitioned the State Senate in 1824, saying in part:

"[Joe] was so cunning and artful as to elude pursuit and so daring and bold...as to put every thing at defiance....Embolden [sic] by his successes and his seeming good fortune he plunged deeper and deeper into Crime until neither fear nor danger could deter him first from threatening and then from executing a train of mischief we believe without parallel in this Country."

Forest remained at large and was caught only when a former companion betrayed him and revealed his location. The maroon leader was shot in the forest where he had successfully lived free for more than two years.

The maroons, or "outlyers" as contemporaries called them, maintained their cohesion for years, sometimes for more than a generation. They made forays into populated farming sections for food, clothing, livestock, and trading items. Sometimes they bartered with free blacks, plantation slaves, and nonslaveholding whites, and in a few instances white outlaws joined them. It is estimated that at least 50 maroon communities were active in the South between 1672 and 1864.

GOING SOUTH AND WEST | For some fugitives, the path to freedom went south and west. Men and women in Texas, Arkansas, and Louisiana could escape north into Indian Territory, west toward the frontier, or south to Mexico. Of the three destinations, Mexico proved the most attractive. "Sometimes, someone would come 'long and try to get us to run up North and be free," declared San Antonio former slave Felix Haywood. "We used to laugh at that. There was no reason to run up North. All we had to do was to walk...south, and we'd be free as soon as we crossed the Rio Grande."

Haywood's views were confirmed by the San Antonio *Ledger,* a pro-slavery newspaper that noted in 1852 that Mexico had "long been regarded by the Texas slave as his El Dorado for accumulation, his utopia for political rights, and his Paradise for happiness." By the eve of the Civil War, nearly ten thousand runaways lived south of the Rio Grande.

Missouri slaves sought freedom in another western sanctuary, Kansas. Between 1861 and 1865, 12,000 fugitives crossed the Kansas-Missouri border to freedom. Some fled to Kansas Territory, seeking Lawrence, a major stop on the western

Seminoles

Long before Florida became a state in 1845, runaway slaves joined up with the Seminole Indians. Blacks often dressed like the Seminole but maintained Christian practices. Although they were technically considered the property of the Seminole, they paid only small fees to their "owners." They were also influential during the wars, serving as soldiers and as interpreters and advisers to the Indians. After their defeat in the Second Seminole War (1835-42), the federal government relocated the Seminole Indians to the American West along with about 240 black Seminoles. Others were returned to their former owners, or escaped deep into the swamps. This picture depicts Renty and Mary Grayson, who lived in Brackettville, Texas, a town many black Seminoles migrated to after leaving Florida and, later, Indian Territory.

Underground Railroad. Opportunities for flight increased dramatically after the Civil War began. When Kansas Senator James H. Lane led Union forces into southwest Missouri in August 1861, runaways began to enter his military camp. Without authorization from Washington, Lane signed up the men as soldiers and sent the women and children to safety in Kansas. His impetuous act created the first African-American troops in the Union Army during the Civil War and encouraged other Missouri refugees from Arkansas and Indian Territory to make their way to Kansas and freedom.

UP NORTH | During the 19th century, the northern exodus of runaways increased as slavery was abolished in Pennsylvania, New Jersey, New York, the New England states, Ohio, Indiana, Illinois, and Michigan. Those who succeeded in making it to freedom usually came from the Upper South states of Maryland, Virginia, Delaware, Kentucky, and Missouri.

The routes they took after crossing into free territory varied. One corridor led to Philadelphia, through eastern Pennsylvania, and on to New York and Boston. Some came into western Pennsylvania and moved north before entering western New York. Others crossed the Ohio River at Louisville or Cincinnati and journeyed overland to Cleveland, getting assistance along the way in Oberlin, Xenia, and other towns. More than a few found refuge in all-black communities in Ohio's Brown and Mercer counties. Fugitives also went to Quaker areas like Richmond, Indiana, and to larger cities such as Indianapolis and Chicago.

In rarer instances, the fugitives made it to the North from the Deep South states. They sometimes trekked more than a thousand miles, over hills, rivers, and mountains. They would sleep during the day, hiding out in dense woods, curled up in barns, outbuildings, or slave cabins. They traveled primarily at night to avoid the patrols. The North Star was their navigational guide.

In 1837 Charles Ball escaped from a South Carolina farm and headed north: "From dark until ten or eleven o'clock at night, the patrol are watchful, and always traversing the country in quest of negroes, but towards midnight, these gentlemen grow cold, or sleepy, or weary, and generally betake themselves to some house, where they can procure a comfortable fire."

Sometimes, escapees from the Deep South stowed away on Mississippi steamboats and Atlantic coast vessels. Others posed as free blacks and boarded trains. William and Ellen Craft combined many of these techniques and ingeniously escaped from Georgia to Boston in 1848. Ellen, the daughter of her owner and very

light-skinned, posed as her husband's deaf and ailing master—her arm in a sling to cover her inability to write and her head wrapped in a bandage to camouflage her lack of a beard. Despite a near discovery in Baltimore, they reached their destination. Later, when two slave catchers appeared in Boston, they fled to Nova Scotia and eventually emigrated to England where they lived for 17 years. Ellen stated at the time, "I would much rather starve in England, a free woman, than be a slave for the best man that ever breathed upon the American Continent."

The fugitives quickly found out that the North was not the "Promised Land"; rather, they met there with discrimination and poverty, and found their dreams and hopes shattered. In southern Ohio, Indiana, and Illinois, white residents held strong sympathies for the slaveholding South. They did little to assist runaways and had few qualms about turning them over to owners or slave catchers who came to claim them. African Americans' social networks in the North were often family- and community-oriented. Many fugitives settled in black neighborhoods in Cincinnati, Pittsburgh, Philadelphia, Newark, and Boston.

In the 19th century, runaways could find help from the loosely organized anti-slavery advocates who became known as "conductors" on the Underground Railroad. The most outstanding of the black conductors was Harriet Tubman. She escaped slavery herself and led her family and hundreds of others to freedom during the course of 19 trips into the South. The network was especially active in the western territories after the War of 1812. By 1830 it had spread through 14 northern states. The network derived its name from the comment of a Kentucky slaveholder who had vainly pursued a fugitive into Ohio. He remarked that the man "must have gone off an underground railroad."

Quite a few fugitives in the North became active in the abolition movement. The most famous runaway, Frederick Douglass—one of the country's greatest orators—is regarded by many as the century's leading abolitionist spokesman. Douglass's writings and speeches gave an authentic voice to the abolitionist crusade.

Josiah Hanson, Anthony Burns, Samuel Ringgold Ward, William Wells Brown, Henry "Box" Brown, and others wrote about their experiences in slavery and became highly sought-after speakers on the anti-slavery lecture circuit. Their moving stories about their lives in bondage had a profound effect in converting northerners to the abolitionist cause. As historian Larry Gara wrote, "The eyewitness accounts of these former slaves had more impact in the anti-slavery cause than hundreds of theoretical speeches and pamphlets."

CANADA, THE PROMISED LAND | The stage was set for the black migration into Canada in 1772, when England declared that any slave reaching Canadian soil was automatically free. Following the War of 1812, sizable numbers of fugitives started to settle in Canada. People began to call it the "Promised Land," a term that came into wider usage after slavery was banned in 1834 throughout the British colonies. Over the next 30 years, between one and two thousand African Americans entered Canada each year.

The passage of the Fugitive Slave Act of 1850—which gave a slave owner or his appointed agent the authority to retrieve a fugitive even in the North with the assistance of local authorities—caused many escapees living in the northern states to cross into Canada. According to the British and Foreign Anti-Slavery Society, within a year of the bill's passage, some five thousand black people had emigrated. Among them were free men and women whose very liberty was threatened by kidnappers, who increasingly abducted and sold them South; and others who felt they were not completely free. Most escapees settled in what are now the Ontario Province cities of Toronto, Chatham, London, and Windsor; in rural areas along Lakes Erie and Ontario; and in the all-black communities of Dawn, Wilberforce, Dresden, and Buxton. By the eve of the Civil War, perhaps 30,000 fugitives lived in Canada.

THE CIVIL WAR | The dynamics of flight changed dramatically during the Civil War. Beginning in June 1861, enslaved people near Fortress Monroe, Virginia, began to trickle into Union lines and offer their services to the federal authorities. Gen. Benjamin Butler called them "contraband." In the following months, the trickle turned into a torrent as thousands escaped and made their way to Army lines. Some Union generals refused to accept these runaways, returning them to their owners, but Congress prohibited this early in 1862. By the time Lincoln

Harriet Tubman

In 1851 Harriet Tubman took members of her family, including her 70-year-old parents, to St. Catharines, in what is today Ontario, on perilous journeys out of bondage. Until 1857, when she moved to Auburn, New York, the Canadian town was her base of operations. This picture was taken around 1887 in Auburn. Left to right: Harriet Tubman, Gertie Davis (Tubman's adopted daughter), Nelson Davis (Tubman's husband), Lee Cheney; "Pop" Alexander, Walter Green, and Sarah Parker ("Blind Auntie" Parker).

signed the Emancipation Proclamation on January 1, 1863, tens of thousands of men, women, and children had made it out of slavery.

THE CONSEQUENCES OF THE MIGRATION | The number of runaways who made it to safety can only be estimated. In 1850 and 1860, United States census takers asked each slave owner in the South how many of his or her slaves had run away during the previous year and remained at large. They reported 1,011 in 1850 and 803 in 1860. But many owners did not wish to admit that their slaves had become

successful fugitives, and so the census reports were almost surely far below the actual numbers. The records of northern anti-slavery societies as well as newspaper notices of runaways in the southern states suggest that probably several thousand fugitives made it to freedom each year during the antebellum era. While this figure is low compared with the total number of slaves—3.2 million in 1850 and 4 million in 1860—over time it amounted to a significant migration. The migration of the maroons to remote areas caused great fear among slave owners and represented a continuing problem in maintaining control over their human property. Indeed, existence of these outlying groups served as a counterpoint to the pro-slavery ideology that promoted the institution as benign and paternalistic.

The western movement of fugitives led white Kansans to recognize the permanence of African-American settlement in their state in 1862. Lawrence abolitionist Richard Cordley acknowledged their presence when he declared, "The Negroes are not coming. They are here. They will stay here. They are to be our neighbors, whatever we may think about it, whatever we may do about it." Supported by the mostly white Kansas Emancipation League, the refugees founded Freedman's Church in Lawrence on September 28, 1862, creating the first of the many African-American community institutions that existed throughout Kansas by the end of the Civil War.

In the North and Canada, runaways became symbols of the evils of slavery. Their increasing presence—as important and often charismatic figures in the abolition movement—played a major role in energizing the struggle against slavery. The fugitives would come to symbolize the inherent contradiction in the national creed: America as a land of liberty and equality, and America as a land of slavery and oppression.

THE PARTING "Buy us too".

The Domestic Slave Trade

1760s TO 1865

The domestic slave trade within the United States did not begin, as is often assumed, with the abolition of the international slave trade in 1807. It originated half a century earlier in the 1760s, and overlapped with the trade from Africa. It was extensive even between 1787 and 1807, a period in which more Africans were forced to these shores than in any two decades in North American history. The domestic trade continued into the 1860s and displaced some 1.2 million men, women, and children, the vast majority of whom were born in America.

At the cost of immense human suffering, this forced migration unlocked a great reservoir of slave labor and made possible the rapid expansion of the "Peculiar Institution." The domestic slave trade brought misery, separating families and increasing the climate of insecurity in the community. It also distributed the African-American population throughout the South in a migration that greatly surpassed in volume the transatlantic slave trade to North America.

A card shows a man being separated from his wife and child. The domestic slave trade caused immense suffering to the African-American population. It separated families and took chained people on long journeys across the country to a life of misery on the cotton and sugar plantations of the Deep South.

EXPORTERS AND IMPORTERS | The first key factor in creating the domestic slave trade was an insatiable demand for labor from expanding plantation regions in the South. The second essential element was the availability of a ready supply of enslaved people—a supply made possible because North American slave numbers, unlike those in the rest of the Americas, grew by natural increase (that is, numbers of births exceeded numbers of deaths). By the 1730s the enslaved populations of Maryland, Delaware, and Virginia were rapidly growing. A decade or so later, even those of colonies south of Virginia began to experience continuous and rapid natural increase. In the latter colonies, though, the expansion of the plantation regime was so great that the importation of enslaved men, women, and children was seen as essential.

In the 1760s Pennsylvania, New York, New Jersey, and Massachusetts were exporting some of their bondspeople to the southern colonies. This trend is verified, for example, by evidence in the South Carolina *Gazette,* where advertisements referred to numerous men and women who had been brought from these northern colonies. In the 1770s slave traders, also called speculators, regularly advertised in the Boston *Gazette* for "healthy slaves....Male or Female who have been some years in the Country, of twenty Years of Age or under." As slavery declined in the mid-Atlantic and northern states, owners began to sell their slaves to traders who moved them farther south. The scale of the trade from the North is suggested by alarm in South Carolina that northern blacks might undermine the discipline of local slaves. In 1792, for example, citizens of Beaufort, South Carolina, petitioned the state legislature complaining about the "notorious" practice of Northerners, who "have for a number of years past been in the habit of shipping to these Southern states, slaves who are scandalously infamous and incorrigible."

The export trade from Delaware, Maryland, and Virginia was very well established by the 1780s. At the Constitutional Convention of 1787, Charles C. Pinckney explained that Virginia "will gain by stopping importation [from Africa]. Her slaves will rise in value and she has more than she wants." South Carolina and Georgia whites called out for slaves, and newspaper advertisements of 1787 show that Virginia was ready to supply them. The trader Austin Moses advertised in Richmond, Virginia, for "one hundred Negroes from 20 to 30 years old for which a good price will be given. They are to be sent out of state, therefore we shall not be particular respecting character of any of them—hearty and well made is all that is necessary." Moses was one of many who regularly sent enslaved Virginians to the expanding plantation regions farther south and west.

The interregional movement of the enslaved population was made up of two elements. The substantial majority—from 60 to 70 percent (or 1.2 million people)—migrated by the long-distance domestic slave trade, while the rest were part of planter migrations. In the latter case, planters looking for new opportunities moved all or most of their slaves together to work new western land.

By the 1790s Maryland, Delaware, and Virginia had become the main exporting areas, the bulk of their "shipments" going to Georgia, Tennessee, Kentucky, the Carolinas, and the sugar-planting regions of Louisiana. But by the 1820s the Carolinas and Kentucky were exporting more people than they were importing. Thirty years later Tennessee, Missouri, Georgia and Alabama had joined the ranks of net exporters. From 1760 until the Civil War, the number of men, women, and children traded to the South and West increased substantially during each decade, with the exception of the 1840s when numbers slackened.

Some historians have argued that selling south occurred because land in the exporting states was exhausted. According to this argument, "soil exhaustion" meant that agriculture was in decline in the exporting states, and those states could not support a growing enslaved population. This traditional argument seems to misrepresent the true situation, however. In fact, farming still flourished in the exporting

states, but slave selling offered the chance of further profit. For example, in South Carolina during the 1850s, 65,000 African Americans were transported out of state, but still the state's cotton production rose by 50,000 bales and its enslaved population increased by 17,000.

The trade was motivated purely by profit, and slaves went to markets that offered the highest profits. Some of the enslaved were sold at major urban marketplaces such as New Orleans and Natchez, but most were dispatched directly to scattered rural communities. In 1846 speculator T. W. Burton wrote from Lowndes County, Alabama, "There is a vast quantity of negroes in the Market here," and traders were offering slaves in every village in the county. The area, he said, was "full of negroes." Moving on to Mississippi, Burton found that "there is negroes [offered by traders] all through the state." Most traders covered several counties in seeking out buyers. A fellow speculator reported that Dr. Thomas C. Weatherly, a typical trader, "lives in his tents. He told me he sold ten negroes last week at fair prices. [As a means of meeting customers] he is following the counties round attending the courts."

MODES OF TRANSPORTATION | The great majority of forced migrants trekked southward chained together in coffles. Sella Martin described such a convoy in which he and his mother had made "that dreaded and despairing journey [from North Carolina] to Georgia":

A long row of men chained two-and-two together, called a coffle and numbering about thirty persons, was the first to march forth from the pen, then came the quiet slaves—that is, those who were tame and degraded—then came the unmarried women, or those without children; after these came the children who were able to walk; and following them came mothers with their infants and young children in their arms.

Charles Ball was marched from Maryland to South Carolina in a 50-slave coffle:

The women were tied together with a rope, about the size of a bed cord, which was tied like a halter round the neck of each; but the men...were very differently caparisoned. A strong iron collar was closely fitted by means of a padlock round each of our necks. A chain of iron about a hundred feet long was passed through the hasp of each padlock, except at the two ends, where the hasps of the padlocks passed through a link of the chain. In addition to this we were handcuffed in pairs.

Torn from Home
John, born in Maryland, was uprooted when his owner settled in Alabama. He was part of a minority of slaves who were not transported to the Deep South by speculators, but moved with their owners' households.

Major traders moved south with "droves" of up to 300 people. These terrible journeys usually took seven to eight weeks and covered up to 600 miles. En route, the captives would sleep in tents or other rough accommodations. On reaching their destinations, the traders would often remove the chains, as they prepared their "product'" for market, while wielding guns and whips to keep the people under control.

Though coffles were the primary means of transport, as railroad routes became more extensive they also were used. In 1856 Lyman Abbot, a Northern visitor to the South, found that "every train south has slaves on board...twenty or more, and [has] a "nigger car," which is generally also the smokers' car, and sometimes the baggage car." Sometimes buyers, as they made their purchases in ones or twos, sent people down the line to be collected by their trading partners.

Traders also moved gangs of people along waterways: the Mississippi River from St. Louis to Natchez and New Orleans; the Alabama River from Montgomery to Mobile, and then on by sea to New Orleans. The coastal shipping route was of importance in supplying part of New Orleans' slave importations, but the coastal traffic probably made up only 5 percent of the total interstate trade, and even in New Orleans about half came by land and river. Those arriving by sea originated mostly from Chesapeake ports (Washington, Baltimore, and the Virginia cities of Alexandria, Richmond, and Petersburg) and from Charleston, South Carolina. Specially equipped ships made month-long journeys carrying up to 150 people from these ports to New Orleans and Natchez. Joshua Levitt, an anti-slavery clergyman, gave this description in 1834:

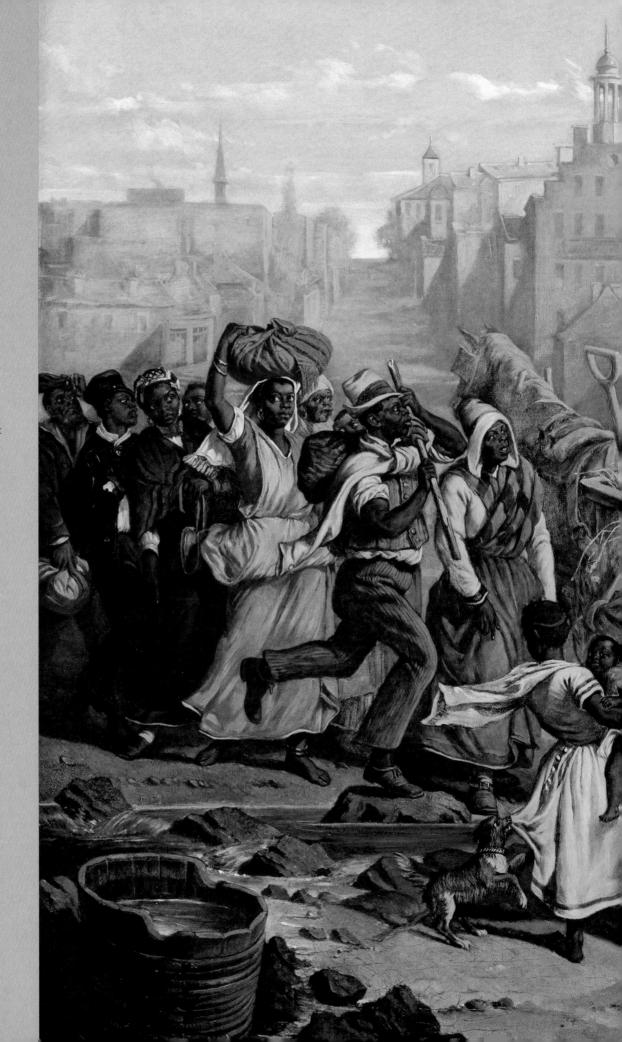

After the Sale

Bought by different traders and slaveholders, families were broken up and could be sent to various cities and states. The destruction of families that the domestic slave trade entailed was one of the most traumatic events in the life of the African-American community.

For Sale,

A LIKELY, HEALTHY, YOUNG
NEGRO WENCH,

BETWEEN fifteen and sixteen Years old:
She has been used to the Farming Busi-
ness. Sold for want of Employ.—Enquire at
No. 81, William-street.

The Innocents

Above: Between 1770 and 1820, as the northern states were dismantling slavery, numerous people were sold south, including free men and women who had been kidnapped by slave traders.

Left, top: Children under ten years of age comprised about 18 percent of the trade. Many were sold with their mothers, but a significant number (especially of those age eight or nine) were sold on their own, as attested by bills of sale and advertisements. In the exporting states, one in three children under 14 were separated by sale from one or both parents.

Left, bottom: The young woman advertised as a farm worker may have been bought and employed by a local slaveholder, or she may have been sold to a slave trader who would have taken her south. By the end of the 18th century, some northern states, such as New York, were already selling African Americans to the southern states.

The hold was appropriated to the slaves, and is divided into two compartments. The after-hold will carry about eighty women, and the other about one hundred men. On one side [of the hold] were two platforms running the whole length; one raised a few inches, and the other half way up the deck. They were about five or six feet deep. On these the slaves lie, as close as they can be stowed.

THE VICTIMS OF THE TRADE | During the century of the domestic trade, roughly equal numbers of males and females were sold away. The exception was the Louisiana sugar plantations, whose population made up some 6 percent of the nation's enslaved. Importation to New Orleans, where many sugar planters bought their slaves, was about 58 percent male, and traders sent very few young children to that market. The exhausting labor in the cane fields took an exceptionally heavy toll on the laborers' health, and the demands of the sugar planters meant that the southern Louisiana market tended to import particularly strong workers. The shortage of women in their childbearing years due to the gender imbalance in purchasing practice made the region unique in North America for having a marked excess of slave deaths over births.

Speculators preferred to purchase what they termed "young and likely Negroes" —mainly teenagers and young adults. They wanted men with the immediate ability to perform hard labor and the potential for a long work career. The merchants also looked for young women with many years of childbearing ahead of them. Only about 5 percent of the males and 6 percent of the females sold were over 30. Documentary evidence shows that with the exception of Louisiana, males between 10 and 29 years old comprised 72 percent of the trade but only 43 percent of the United States' total enslaved population. Children under ten made up about 18 percent of the trade and most, especially the under-eights, were sold together with their mothers.

To be "sold down the river" was one of the most dreaded prospects of the enslaved population. Some destinations, particularly the Louisiana sugar plantations, had especially grim reputations. But it was the destruction of family that made the domestic slave trade so terrifying. Francis Fedric, who was born in Virginia and sold away in Kentucky, recalled the scene:

> Men and women down on their knees begging to be purchased to go with their wives or husbands,…children crying and imploring not to have their parents sent away from them; but all their beseeching and tears were of no avail. They were ruthlessly separated, most of them for ever.

The experience of separation was traumatic. Traders bought selectively, without regard to family, picking individuals on whom they thought they could make the most profit. Bills of sale show that they almost never bought husbands and wives together, and such records indicate that the trade would have disrupted one in five marriages of all slaves in the selling states. Since the long-distance trade did not, however, break up the majority of marriages, the enslaved community could maintain a strong sense of family. The importance that the black population placed on families is shown by the fact that owners—as a means of coercion—constantly used the threat of sale and family destruction.

As well as spouses being separated by the trade, one-third of the children under 14 were separated from one or both of their parents. John Brown from Virginia was about ten when he endured the misery of being sent to Georgia, far from his mother:

> Finney agreed to purchase me by the pound....A rope was brought, both ends of which were tied together, so that it formed a large noose or loop. This was hitched over the hook of the stilyard, and I was seated in the loop. After I had been weighed, there was a deduction made for the rope. I do not recollect what I weighed, but the price I was sold for amounted to three hundred and ten dollars. Within five minutes after, Finney paid the money, and I was marched off. I looked round and saw my poor mother stretching out her hands after me. She ran up, and overtook us, but Finney, who was behind me, and between me and my mother, would not let her approach, though she begged and prayed to be allowed to kiss me for the last time, and bid me good bye.

The pattern of long-distance separation that characterized the trade was hugely significant, not only in the suffering that it inflicted on the individuals, the families, and the communities, but also for its impact on master-slave relationships. The emotional toll of this forced migration can be seen in the southern papers that routinely carried advertisements seeking the apprehension of runaways. Vast numbers of these advertisements pointed out that the fugitive was likely trying to get back to the place from which he or she had been sold—and where family still lived.

After the passage of the Fugitive Slave Act in 1850, the abduction of free people for sale in the domestic slave trade increased. As slave catchers were allowed to claim fugitives in the North and take them back to the South, free people who could not prove their status became victims of unscrupulous men who declared they were, in reality, runaways. Many free people were kidnapped in northern cities and sold in the interregional slave trade that took them to the Deep South.

To the forced migrants and the communities they left behind, the slave trade sent the stark message that the threat of sale and family separation would be with them as long as they lived. For a great many, then, the enduring result of the system was an ever heightened distrust of their owners and an awareness that most whites did not think of them as people capable of real feelings.

The Price of Blood

Opposite, left: In this painting, a slaveholder sells his mulatto son to a speculator. Far from being benevolent and paternalistic, slaveholders and slave traders alike were not averse to selling their own children when the monetary incentives were high enough. The slave trade was motivated by greed, and neither the sellers nor the buyers had moral qualms about it.

Opposite, right: Nathan Bedford Forrest (1821–1877), who came from a poor rural family and remained quasi illiterate all his life, operated in Memphis, Tennessee, where he made a fortune as a slave trader. Forrest was a celebrated Confederate general during the Civil War, and the first grand wizard of the Ku Klux Klan.

Bottom: Speculators were not outcasts from society, but reputable men who advertised their services in newspapers and city directories, and who were backed by banks. Many were elected to public office, and traders were often seen as leaders of their communities.

THE SLAVE TRADERS | The trade has always posed problems for those seeking to portray slavery as a benign and paternal institution in which slave owners saw their main mission as "civilizing Negroes." Long after slavery ended, conservative white Southerners still pretended that the slave traders had been social outcasts and that their business had been of minimal importance to southern life. In his 1904 history of the trade, the southern historian Winfield H. Collins wrote that their ill repute was such that "they were accounted the abhorrence of everyone....Their descendants, when known, had a blot upon them and the property acquired in the traffic as well." Nothing could be further from the truth. In reality, traders were very often prominent citizens and respected leaders of their communities. Slave trading was not a poor man's occupation. A coffle of 40 slaves might cost the trader well over $30,000 in cash, a huge sum in the 19th century that is equivalent to about $600,000 in today's dollars. Major traders nearly always came from wealthy planter families. The traffic in human beings made them even richer.

Some examples from South Carolina during the 1850s show the kind of social positions that traders held. The very high-profile traders Alexander McDonald, J. S. Riggs, Thomas Ryan, Ziba Oakes, and A. J. Salinas served as aldermen in Charleston. Col. C. Weatherly of Marlboro District combined extensive slave trading with his role as a member of the state's House of Representatives, later serving in the State Senate. Maj. George Seaborn was another trader/planter and a gentleman of very high standing. In 1850 a financial agency reported that he was a "planter aged 50, v[ery] fine char[acter] and w[orth] in land and negroes some $20,[000]." He was also joint editor and publisher of the *Farmers' and Planters' Magazine*.

In the early decades of the trade, its speculators did attract some criticism in the South. Some feared that enslaved persons from the northern and middle colonies would bring with them undesirable ideas of freedom. Prosperous planters in older sections of states—sections where the slave system was long established and where planters no longer felt the need for new importations—resented traders who brought slaves into the newer, still-growing regions in their states. They were greatly concerned that any increase in the black population would undermine the prices of both crops and slaves. Despite these apprehensions, they were quite happy to sell to traders as long as they transported their purchases out of state. Many planters also resented the profit gouging and crooked practices with which some traders were identified.

The traders' high social status was deliberately concealed in the slaveholders' propaganda efforts. The truth about "Negro speculation" would have made it impossible to defend the "morality" of slavery. As James Stirling, a Scottish visitor, observed in the 1850s: "The slave traffic was a sore subject with the defenders of slavery.... They fain would load all the iniquities of the system on the trader's unlucky back." Thus, the trader was invariably portrayed as an outcast and a scoundrel in pro-slavery novels and polemics, in marked contrast to the picture they painted of a righteous, humanitarian plantation owner who only sold slaves as a last resort to clear his debts. J. T. Randolph's 1852 novel *The Cabin and the Parlor* claimed:

> The slaves...were all purchased to remain in the district. Even among those planters who showed little concern for the ruined Courtneys, there was a sentiment of honor on this point.... A trader who made his appearance was hustled away rather rudely by one or two present, so that after making a few ineffectual bids, he thought it prudent to retire.

Southern whites and their Northern sympathizers would pass down this self-serving view of slavery over many generations. It still resonates today. Guides routinely tell tourists visiting the grandly restored plantations throughout the South: "On this plantation they never sold any of their slaves," and "they never broke up families." This flies in the face of evidence that virtually all slave owners would have dealt with traders.

After the Civil War, chains of evidence that might otherwise have led historians to the trade were often deliberately broken. White Southerners, keen to invent and

Slave Pens

Above: Located at 283 Duke Street, in Alexandria, Virginia, the dealership of Price, Birch & Co. was an important center of trade. The offices occupied three stories while the slave pens flanked the central building.

Inset, right: The jails where men, women, and children awaited departure to distant states often turned into places of torture where the rebellious were whipped and paddled.

Right: The interior of a slave pen in Alexandria, Virginia, shows the cells where people were held prior to being sold.

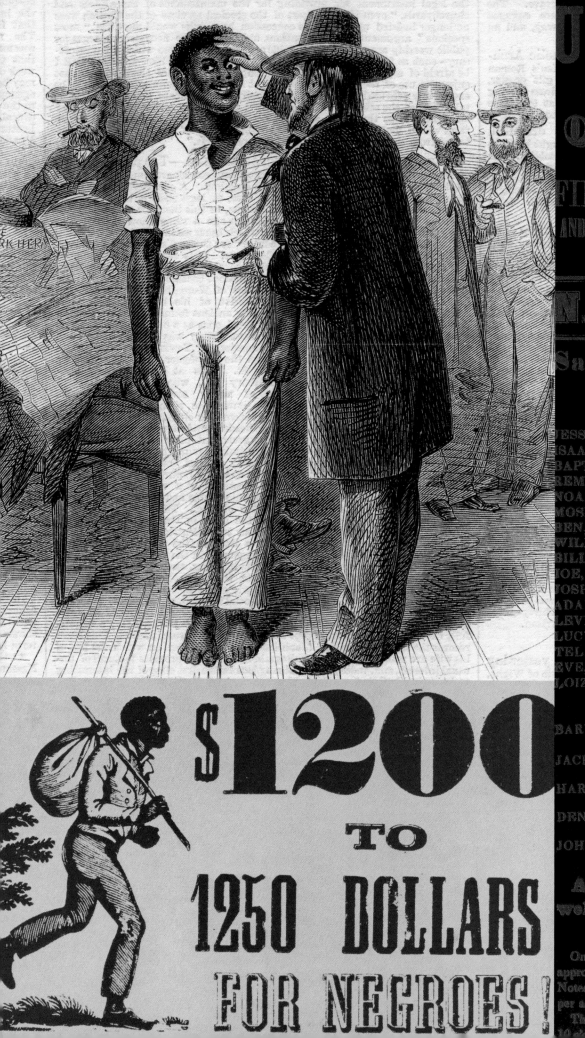

promote a history of the benevolent Southland, tended to write the trader out of history. In obituaries, biographical directories, and county histories, profiles of prominent citizens who had been slave traders tended to omit that aspect of their lives. When the notorious trader and prominent South Carolina politician Col. Weatherly was discussed in an 1897 history of his county, his political career was referenced, but his slave trading went unmentioned. The death of the highly successful slave trader Charles Logan in 1903 was well covered in South Carolina's newspaper, the *State*. He was remembered as one whose wealth had been accumulated through "speculative deals of various sorts," and as a benefactor of the Catholic Church, a hospital, a school, and to officials charged with preventing cruelty to animals. Without the faintest trace of irony, the *State* concluded, "Next to the care of children, kindness to animals is the mark of a good heart." No mention was made of his slave-trading career.

Apart from the deliberate hiding of slave traders, the nature of surviving documentary records complicates the task of reconstructing the trade. Slave traders' advertisements in antebellum newspapers provide hugely valuable clues. It is clear, however, that this source of evidence reveals only a fraction of the trade. This is shown by the fact that a very important trader like Ziba Oakes of Charleston, South Carolina, almost never used newspaper advertisements. For itinerant rural traders, newspapers often did not circulate quickly enough to be of great value either in achieving sales or in making purchases, and most found it better to approach their customers directly rather than through advertisements.

Official state records sometimes provide significant data. This is especially so for the coastal branch of the trade. Anti-smuggling legislation connected with the closure of the African slave trade in 1807 required coastwise shipments of slaves to be officially recorded; this means that for the coastal branch of the trade we have a store of ships' manifests which, although incomplete, is still massive. The vast bulk of the trade, however, was not coastal but instead operated in the countryside and in villages and small towns scattered across the South. Since in this land-based trade there was rarely any legal requirement to record trading activity, considerable effort is needed to reconstruct this highly dispersed traffic.

Some help in identifying traders is provided by occupational descriptions in the federal censuses of 1850 and 1860, but these descriptions are complicated by the fact that traders were often men of considerable wealth, with interests including planting and perhaps a general store. On a great many occasions, therefore, individuals known to have been active slave traders appear simply as "merchant" or "planter" rather than "Negro trader." Furthermore, the census often abbreviated "Negro trader" or "Negro speculator" to "trader" or "speculator." A combination of census data, advertisements, traders' letters, business documents, and court records reveals, however, a traffic of massive proportions.

Humans on the Block

Opposite, top: Former slaves revealed that they had to put on a joyful face and ask slaveholders to buy them if they wanted to avoid being beaten by the dealers, who did not want to miss a sale. Those who were brought back to the dealer after a failed trial with their new owners were threatened with sale to the worst possible owner and might be brutally paddled or whipped.

Opposite, bottom: Ziba Oakes was a broker working out of Charleston, South Carolina. He acquired slaves from agents, and also did his own buying. The people he bought were held in a large depot, and sold to long-distance traders. Oakes had clients all over the South.

Opposite, right: Missouri, which was part of the Louisiana Purchase, had an important French-speaking population. This poster for a sale of 24 enslaved men, women, and children was printed in both English and French to reach a wider public. It describes their ages and skills, and other traits of interest to the buyer.

THE NATIONAL DEBATE | Until the Civil War settled the issue once and for all, conflict raged between the northern abolitionists and the southern traditionalists, with Southerners fiercely defending their right to own human beings. Abolitionists contended that the domestic trade was vital to slavery's survival and exemplified the worst aspects of a totally corrupt system. Slaves, they argued, were inefficient workers because they lacked any positive incentives to work well. Plantation monoculture led to soil exhaustion and therefore slave-based agriculture was hopelessly unprofitable in the Upper South. The abolitionists believed that the slave system was kept alive in the Upper South only through the supplementary incomes gained from selling slaves to professional Negro speculators and from deliberately breeding and rearing people for sale. Alvan Stewart proclaimed that the domestic trade was so important that ending it would break open "the great door to the slave Bastille." Without the long-distance market "the slaves of Maryland and Virginia would eat up their masters, and the masters must emancipate in self-defense to save themselves from destruction." As for the Deep South, Stewart prophesied:

> In Alabama, Louisiana and Mississippi] there is such havoc annually by death among the slaves of the great planters...that in less than seven years, if no slave could be imported into those southern regions, one half of the plantations would lie uncultivated for want of slaves.

The abolitionists viewed white Southerners as inhumanly callous and so deeply corrupted morally that in return for the slave traders' cash they were happy to break up families and send individuals on long-distance, forced migrations. Those who benefited from the domestic slave trade developed rationalizations to justify their activities. Pro-slavery propagandists maintained that owners only reluctantly—when under financial duress—resorted to selling their slaves and breaking up families. There is ample evidence available to refute this proposition. Traders' bills of sale suggest that no more than 5 percent of their slaves were acquired at debt, probate, or other court-mandated sales. Rarely were slave owners staving off imminent financial crisis when they sold to the traders. They were, in fact, further increasing their profits.

Records also give the lie to another major claim propounded by slave-trade apologists—that the people they sold were most often recaptured runaways or "criminals" being punished for their transgressions. These groups comprised only a very small portion of the trade. Runaways were predominantly male, while the trade was made up of roughly equal numbers of men and women. The bodies of fugitives and "criminals" would have borne the scars of the lash, and traders would have regarded them as extremely risky buys.

Many owners lived under the delusion that they treated their bondspersons well and were loved and respected by them. They clung to this belief by embracing

Expanding Population

Above: Contrary to the experience in the Caribbean and Latin America, where sugar cultivation extracted such extreme labor from the workers that deaths greatly outnumbered births, in the United States the African-American population experienced natural increase. The fact that there was a ready "supply" of enslaved people in the Old South was a contributing factor in the expansion of the domestic slave trade.
Right: This slave block, photographed in 1915, was located in the St. Louis Hotel in New Orleans. Slave trading continued until the end of the Civil War. Men, women, and children were transported and sold at slave pens or directly to planters in rural areas up to the very last days of the conflict.

an absurd rationalization: Black people, they claimed, were emotionally shallow and, unlike whites, did not have strong attachments to their families. The history of the slave trade lays bare the mythmaking that made up the "plantation legend."

In the end, the abolitionist position on the slave trade was essentially correct about its size and about the character of its participants. At the same time, they greatly overestimated the problem of the planters' debts. By buying into the myth that most sales were made to ease the owners' financial problems, they underestimated the slaveholders' voluntary participation in the trade. The abolitionists also exaggerated the extent of systematic slave breeding. Slaveholders took great interest in the growth of their "stock" of people. But there does not seem to be any significant evidence to support an abolitionist claim that the selling states developed a system of specialized "breeding farms."

THE END OF THE DOMESTIC SLAVE TRADE | The displacement of enslaved men, women, and children continued, despite much disruption, until near the very end of the Civil War, although exportation from Maryland, Missouri, Kentucky, and Delaware—all of which remained in the Union—was significantly reduced. Prices, expressed in constant dollars, rather than the highly inflated Confederate currency, declined dramatically. When New Orleans fell in 1862, a major urban market was lost to the trade. But the "Negro speculators" were nothing if not resourceful. Henry Badgett had been moving people from North Carolina to Georgia since the 1840s and was still reporting good profits in 1863. In Savannah one leading trader, described by contemporaries as "a bitter old rebel," did not evacuate his stock of slaves until General Sherman's army approached the city in December 1864.

In Virginia, the Omohundro brothers, Silas and R. F., supplied people to traders operating out of Richmond until at least 1863, as did the auctioneer Hector Davis. In late 1863, E. H. Stokes was still buying people in Virginia and selling them in Georgia. But the dubious distinction of dancing the terrible institution's last waltz probably belongs to veteran trader Robert Lumpkin. In April 1865 Charles Carleton Coffin, traveling with the advancing Union Army days before the fall of Richmond, found Lumpkin "shipping out fifty men, women and children.... This sad and weeping fifty, in handcuffs and chains were [he declared] the last slave coffle that ever shall tread the soil of America."

Ironically, the greatest significance of the trade was, in the long term, positive. This inhuman traffic did not succeed in crushing its victims. The enslaved were not just victims but people who resisted. They clung to a sense of family and developed life-saving and heritage-preserving coping devices against a hostile white world. They learned to value themselves and their families in a society that looked upon them with loathing. And they learned to build a community that would grow into an extraordinarily dynamic and creative force in the nation through which they were moved in chains.

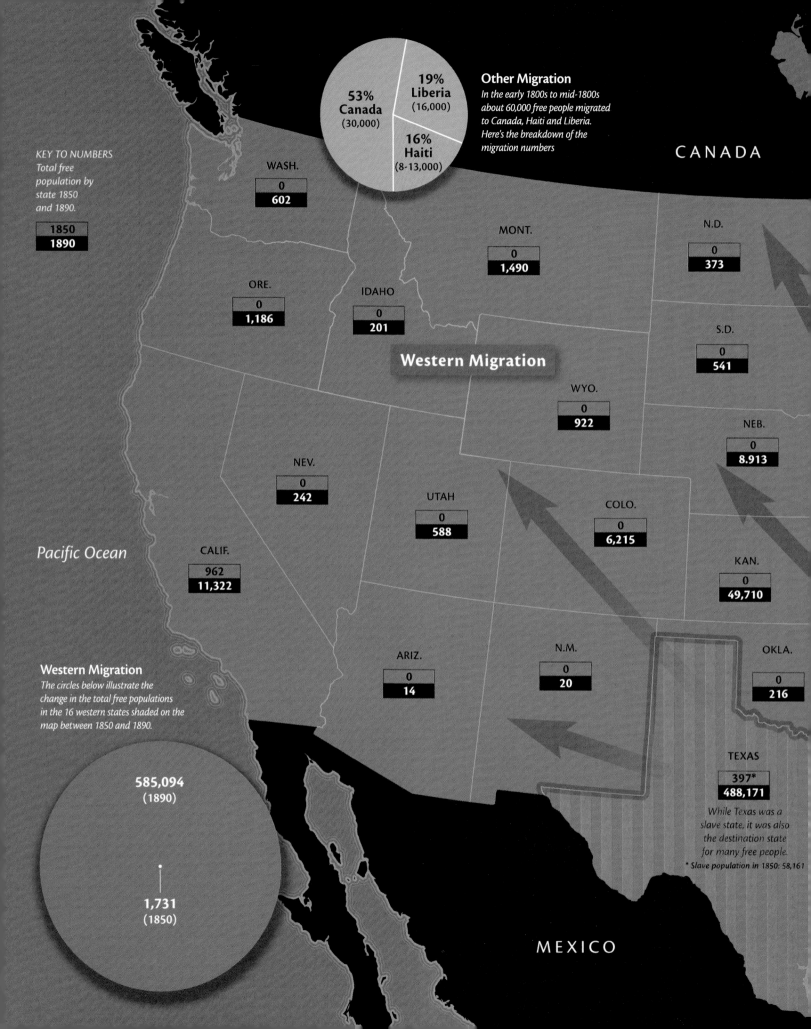

Other Migration

In the early 1800s to mid-1800s about 60,000 free people migrated to Canada, Haiti and Liberia. Here's the breakdown of the migration numbers

53% Canada (30,000)

19% Liberia (16,000)

16% Haiti (8-13,000)

CANADA

KEY TO NUMBERS
Total free
population by
state 1850
and 1890.

| 1850 |
| 1890 |

WASH.
| 0 |
| 602 |

MONT.
| 0 |
| 1,490 |

N.D.
| 0 |
| 373 |

ORE.
| 0 |
| 1,186 |

IDAHO
| 0 |
| 201 |

S.D.
| 0 |
| 541 |

Western Migration

WYO.
| 0 |
| 922 |

NEB.
| 0 |
| 8.913 |

NEV.
| 0 |
| 242 |

UTAH
| 0 |
| 588 |

COLO.
| 0 |
| 6,215 |

KAN.
| 0 |
| 49,710 |

Pacific Ocean

CALIF.
| 962 |
| 11,322 |

ARIZ.
| 0 |
| 14 |

N.M.
| 0 |
| 20 |

OKLA.
| 0 |
| 216 |

Western Migration

The circles below illustrate the change in the total free populations in the 16 western states shaded on the map between 1850 and 1890.

TEXAS
| 397* |
| 488,171 |

While Texas was a
slave state, it was also
the destination state
for many free people.
* Slave population in 1850: 58,161

585,094
(1890)

1,731
(1850)

MEXICO

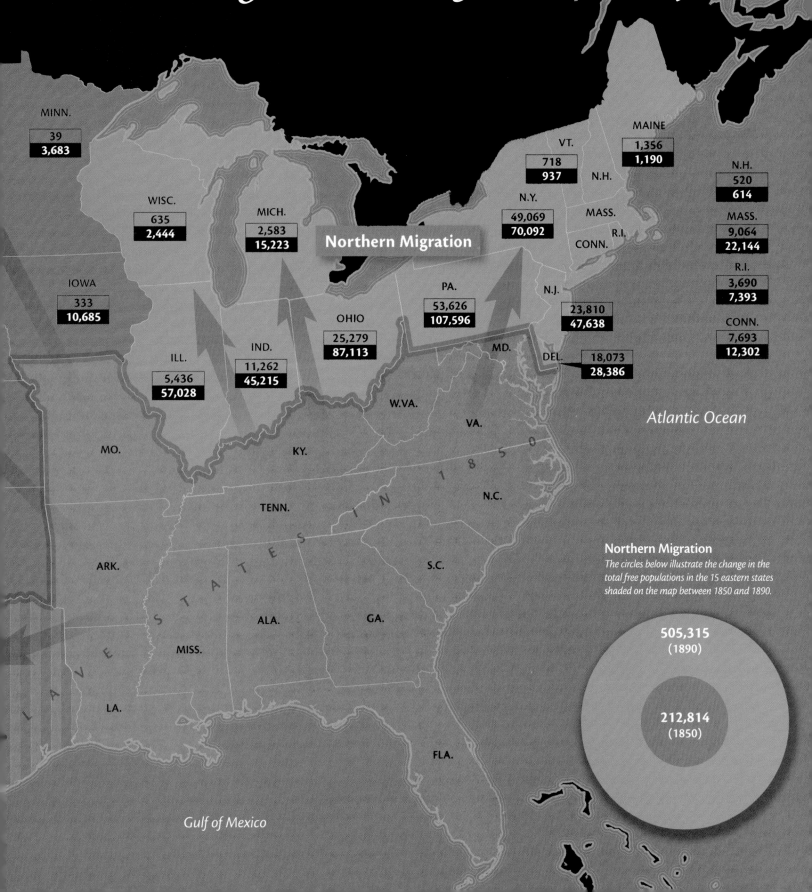

Migrations of Free Peoples

MINN.
39
3,683

WISC.
635
2,444

MICH.
2,583
15,223

VT.
718
937

MAINE
1,356
1,190

N.H.

N.Y.
49,069
70,092

MASS.

CONN.

R.I.

N.H.
520
614

MASS.
9,064
22,144

R.I.
3,690
7,393

CONN.
7,693
12,302

Northern Migration

IOWA
333
10,685

PA.
53,626
107,596

N.J.
23,810
47,638

OHIO
25,279
87,113

ILL.
5,436
57,028

IND.
11,262
45,215

MD.

DEL.
18,073
28,386

W.VA.

VA.

Atlantic Ocean

MO.

KY.

S L A V E   S T A T E S   I N   1850

N.C.

TENN.

ARK.

S.C.

Northern Migration

The circles below illustrate the change in the total free populations in the 15 eastern states shaded on the map between 1850 and 1890.

ALA.

GA.

MISS.

505,315
(1890)

212,814
(1850)

LA.

FLA.

Gulf of Mexico

Colonization and Emigration

1783 TO 1920s

The migration of African Americans to other lands in search of freedom during the late 18th and 19th centuries was an expression of their belief that they would never achieve a position of true equality in the United States. The only solution to this problem, they felt, was to establish separate, self-governing societies or nations. Though migrants found their way to Canada, Haiti, the West Indies, and Mexico, Africa was, most often, the refuge of choice. Emigration and colonization were controversial within the African-American community, and some of the consequences of these migrations were negative for the receiving populations.

THE REASONS FOR EMIGRATION AND COLONIZATION | African Americans' interest in colonization was engendered by the dramatic increase in restrictions placed on them during the late 18th and 19th centuries. The slave system in the South was progressively intensified. The region's agriculturally derived economic prosperity depended on slavery: one-third of its population consisted of blacks in bondage. Throughout the South, laws were passed that prohibited their manumission.

Meanwhile, rising racism made conditions for Northern blacks more oppressive. The growth of the free black population—500,000 by 1860—was yet another factor in the effort to keep the nation's African Americans on an ever tightening leash. They faced voting restrictions and were, for all intents and purposes, excluded from the justice system. By the 1830s, state and federal regulations, popular pressure, and social custom had dispatched them to the very bottom rungs of the social, economic, and political ladders.

In the immediate aftermath of the Civil War, the constitutional amendments giving blacks citizenship and voting rights led many African Americans to hope they would finally be integrated into American society, but by the end of Reconstruction in 1877, white Northerners' interest in the problems of freed people had cooled. The return of the Democratic Party to power in the South was accompanied by mounting Ku Klux Klan violence and intimidation.

A small minority of black abolitionists supported the colonization movement and moved to Liberia. Mrs. Urias R. McGill was living there with her husband when this photograph was taken in 1855. Going to Africa involved chartering ships and was a more difficult endeavor than migrating to Canada or Mexico. It could only be achieved through the assistance of well-funded organizations such as the American Colonization Society.

In the South, African Americans were relegated back to the farm and, with little or no money to buy land, they had no choice but to work as tenant farmers or share-croppers on white-owned property or as agricultural laborers earning meager wages.

Within a people who had continuously struggled against bias and oppression, there were always some who believed that ameliorating their condition was ultimately impossible. They favored emigration, and some advocated the establishment of colonies in Africa.

THE COLONIZATION OF SIERRA LEONE | The first known colonization effort took place in Sierra Leone, home to the Temne, Mandingo, Fulani, Bullom, and Kru ethnic groups. The original settlers, 450 destitute black men and women from England, called the Black Poor, arrived in 1787. In 1792, they were joined by 1,200 Black Loyalists from Canada—former U.S. slaves who had fought alongside the British Army during the Revolutionary War—who were dissatisfied with conditions in Nova Scotia, where they had been sent. Jamaican Maroons, runaways who had been deceitfully deported to Canada after they had signed a peace treaty with the British, followed them in 1800.

In its early years, the settlement was governed by the Sierra Leone Company, an organization founded by British humanitarians with the goal of developing agricultural and other products for trade with England. Its population rapidly increased after 1807 with Africans recaptured from slave ships after the British and American abolition of the international slave trade. These "recaptives" or Liberated Africans came from throughout western, central, and southeastern Africa. About 58,000 were eventually settled in Sierra Leone.

African-American involvement in Sierra Leone began in 1811 when Paul Cuffee, a prosperous black and American-Indian Quaker, shipowner, and lifelong campaigner for black people's rights, set sail from Massachusetts for Freetown with a crew of nine black seamen. The journey came in response to an invitation from England's Royal African Society to visit the colony.

While there, Cuffee decided to develop trade between blacks in England, Sierra Leone, and the United States. He also began to consider the possibility of relocating skilled African Americans to the colony, and founded the Friendly Society of Sierra Leone to put his ideas into practice. In 1815 he took 38 emigrants to the colony.

THE COLONIZATION OF LIBERIA | Though Sierra Leone would continue to receive African-American immigrants over the years, their primary destination soon became Liberia, the country of the Vai, Kru, Kissi, Grebo, Bassa, Kpelle, Mandingo, and other populations. The controversial American Colonization Society (ACS) helped them in this endeavor. It was founded in 1816 with the expressed aim to colonize free blacks in Africa or wherever else it saw fit. An organization with mostly white

Going Away

Above: In 1815 Capt. Paul Cuffee took 38 emigrants to Sierra Leone in what was the first migration of African Americans to Africa. *Right:* In the late 1870s, several thousand African Americans left the South and immigrated to Arkansas. However, racial tension and economic hardship led some to consider leaving the United States altogether as a solution to their plight. In April 1880, 150 Arkansans were housed at Mount Olivet Baptist Church in New York City while they waited for transportation to Liberia. The regular ship, scheduled to leave on May 1, had been entirely booked by the American Colonization Society, and the Arkansans had to wait for another boat.

members and supporters, many of whom were slaveholders, the ACS did not gain widespread support among African Americans, who saw it as a means by which whites hoped to deport free blacks. Nonetheless, some people, dissatisfied with their lives in the United States, sought help from the society. Its first vessel, the *Elizabeth,* set sail in 1820 with some 80 migrants on board. They were unable to acquire land in Liberia and took refuge in Sierra Leone.

A year later, the ACS was successful in obtaining acreage, and a ship carrying 33 African Americans landed at Cape Mesuardo—later to become Monrovia, after U.S. President James Monroe. Over the course of the 19th century, the ACS transported an estimated 16,000 migrants to Liberia. The migration peaked between 1848 and 1854; during this period the ACS chartered 41 ships, carrying over 4,000 colonists to new lives in a new land. Most were free blacks who had either lived in the North all their lives or had been born in the South and later moved across the Mason-Dixon Line. They came from almost all the southern states and from as far west as Colorado. Many of the southern migrants were born free, but a large number had been freed on the expressed condition that they leave the United States.

Gen. Robert E. Lee freed most of his slaves before the Civil War. He offered to pay the expenses of those, like William and Rosabella Burke and their children, who wanted to go to Liberia. Burke went to the seminary in Monrovia and became a Presbyterian minister in 1857. A year later, he wrote a friend back home:

Persons coming to Africa should expect to go through many hardships, such as are common to the first settlement in any new country. I expected it and was not disappointed or discouraged at any thing that I met with; and so far from being dissatisfied with the country, I bless the Lord that ever my lot was cast in this part of the earth.

In a letter to Mary Custis Lee, Rosabella Burke noted, "I love Africa and would not exchange it for America."

The colonists were predominantly male, and often traveled in family groups. Many were under 20 years old. During the 1820-1828 period, women made up 43 percent of those going to Liberia. Freeborn migrants were mostly artisans, involved in agriculture in some way, or skilled and unskilled laborers; a few were professionals.

Departure of the Horsa

Left: The International Migration Society was formed in 1894 by four white Alabamians who hoped to make a profit by establishing "a steamship line between the United States and Africa direct . . . to do a general migration business." In 1895 a train took about two hundred farmers and skilled workers from Memphis to Savannah, where they boarded a ship to Liberia. About one thousand African Americans left for Liberia between 1890 and 1910.

Inset, left: The Seal of Liberia

Above: American Presbyterians pose in front of their banner for the "stranger mission" in Liberia.

As the 19th century progressed, an increasing number came from the middle and professional class. The migration was not always without problems—many prospective settlers died en route. They succumbed to fevers, tuberculosis, pleurisy, and other lung diseases. The primary reason for black Americans to seek freedom through emigration was their perception that there was no other alternative to a hopeless situation. But they also came to Africa because it was the land of their ancestors. Another reason was that the ACS paid their passage. Most could scarcely have afforded it and would have remained in the United States had the society not paid their way.

In the early years the ACS ran Liberia's government, but the settlers soon demanded control of their own affairs. In 1837 the Commonwealth was formed, and virtually all power devolved to the emigrants. The society retained only the right to choose the governor. A decade later Liberia became an independent nation, and in 1848, Joseph Jenkins Roberts—a Monrovia merchant who had emigrated from Virginia 20 years earlier—was elected president.

Even as they left the United States behind, the colonists made concerted efforts to create a sort of "little America" in their new surroundings. They spoke English, and their manners, clothing, and even the construction of their homes reflected their previous place of residence. They were not always welcome in Liberia. Heavily influenced by Christian values, many exhibited a missionary zeal toward the indigenous Africans. They wished to "civilize" and Christianize people whom they often perceived as "heathen savages."

Immigration to Africa continued on a small scale into the 20th century. Between 1890 and 1910, some one thousand African Americans immigrated to Liberia. In 1913, 60 Oklahomans settled in Ghana under the leadership of Chief Alfred Sam. Though small in number, these efforts were not insignificant, as in most cases they represented self-initiated migrations, heavily influenced by nationalist ideas. Although individuals continued to migrate to the continent, there were few organized movements. Events in Africa itself may have been the reason. The 1884 partition of the continent resulted in full-scale domination by Europe. African nations, with the exception of Liberia and Ethiopia, came under European rule. In this climate, it was difficult for African Americans to consider emigration schemes.

MIGRATION TO HAITI | Because of its association with the ACS, many African Americans opposed Liberian emigration. Other sites were proposed—Central America, the Caribbean islands, the Niger Valley, Canada, and Haiti. For a short while, Haiti proved the most popular of these alternatives.

The first black republic and the second country to gain independence, under the leadership of François Dominique Toussaint L'Ouverture, Haiti had served as a place of asylum for runaways and free men and women over the years. This fact, plus its proximity to the United States and its history of self-liberation and Christianity, made the island attractive to black proponents of emigration. White advocates saw Haiti as another site to which undesirable free blacks could be deported.

In 1824 the New York Colonization Society received a commitment from Haitian president Jean-Pierre Boyer to pay the passage of U.S. emigrants. Boyer also promised to support them for their first four months and to grant them land. The same year, African-American leaders, including wealthy Philadelphia business-man James Forten and Bishop Richard Allen, formed the Haytian Emigration Society of Coloured People. They arranged for the transportation of several hundred people, not only to Haiti but also to Santo Domingo, the Spanish-speaking western part of the island of Hispaniola that had been conquered by Haiti in 1822.

New efforts to settle African Americans in Haiti were launched in the mid-19th century. Emperor Faustin Soulouque and James Theodore Holly entered into discussions in 1855 on the settling of African Americans in the island state. After Soulouque was deposed, the new president, Nicolas Fabre Geffrard, appointed his own representative, James Redpath, a white American reporter, as general agent. His mission was to attract immigrants to the island. One of Redpath's agents was Holly, who emerged as the leading advocate of Haitian emigration. He believed that African Americans could profoundly influence the development of the Haitian Republic:

> Our brethren of Hayti, who stand in the vanguard of the race, have already made a name, and a fame for us, that is as imperishable as the world's history....It becomes then an important question for the negro race in America...to contribute to the continued advancement of this negro nationality of the New World until its glory and renown shall overspread the whole earth, and redeem and regenerate by its influence in the future, the benighted Fatherland of the race in Africa.

In the early 1860s, partly as a result of Holly's relentless proselytizing, black American interest in colonization increased. Haiti's president, Fabre Geffrard, hoping to ease the island's labor shortage, promoted policies that encouraged immigration but were not as generous as those offered in the 1820s.

In March 1861 Holly sailed to Haiti with 111 migrants from Connecticut and Canada. During the course of the year, several other journeys brought 800 more to the island nation. Most were unprepared for life in a different environment. Many complained about the climate and the language barrier, and expressed contempt for Vodou and Catholicism. Haitians were often suspicious of the immigrants, whom they described as lazy and uncooperative. Most immigrants, who came from

James Holly

In the mid-19th century, James Theodore Holly (1829–1911)—a fourth-generation Northern free man—was one of the strongest proponents of immigration to Haiti. In his calls for emigration, Holly cited the need for missionary work and the possibilities for self-determination. As an agent of the Haitian Bureau of Emigration, he led a group of emigrants from New Haven, Connecticut, and Canada to Haiti in 1861. His wife, his mother, and two of his children died shortly after their arrival. Although many settlers left the country, Holly remained on the island until his death. He became the first Episcopal bishop of Haiti in 1874.

American cities, did not want to work on farms and sold the land they had received for free in order to settle in the urban centers, where they could not find work. In addition, the government's subsidy policy depleted the country's already minimal treasury by funding emigrants who often left after their four months were over. The majority of the Americans returned home, but others kept on arriving.

President Abraham Lincoln had for some years advocated the removal of freed slaves as a partial solution to the nation's race problem. In 1863 he supported the transportation of 453 men and women to L'Ile-à-Vache, an island off the Haitian coast. The experiment failed due to inadequate planning and poor leadership. In less than a year, the survivors were returned to the United States.

Many Americans, black and white, were opposed to Haitian immigration. Their attacks were not as strong as those against Liberia, mainly because it was a movement initiated, for the most part, by African Americans. In fact, the 1854 National Emigration Convention actually endorsed Haitian immigration. But the opponents of Haiti were numerous. Frederick Douglass, who was opposed to emigration but had finally encouraged the Haitian movement, later abandoned the cause.

Widespread migration to Haiti never materialized. Estimates of the number of African Americans who made the trip range from 8,000 to 13,000, but most returned to the United States. Unlike the situation in Liberia, the island's fairly large but mostly transient African-American community left no lasting evidence of its presence.

RIGHT REV. JAMES T. HOLLY, D.D.
First Bishop of the National Haitien Church.
Consecrated in Grace Church, New York City, November 8th 1874.

MIGRATIONS TO OTHER LANDS | Other Caribbean islands were also proposed as possible destinations, and small numbers of African Americans did immigrate to various colonies. In the aftermath of the 1812 war between the United States and Great Britain, several hundred African-American soldiers who had sided with England were sent to Trinidad. They received 16 acres of land and quickly became assimilated into Trinidadian society. Between 1839 and 1847, another 1,301 Americans migrated to the island.

Canada's first critical mass of black immigrants comprised 5,000 free and enslaved Loyalists. Most had fought alongside the British during the American War for Independence, while a third had been brought by their British owners. After the War of 1812 between the United States and Britain, about 2,000 African Americans crossed the border. Long a safe haven for American fugitives, Canada became a land of immigration for free blacks after the Fugitive Slave Act of 1850 put them at risk of being fraudulently sold into slavery. Canadian migration was advocated by James Holly, Henry Bibb—a fugitive who founded the newspaper

NEW-YORK, 21 *April* 1783.

THIS is to certify to whomſoever it may concern, that the Bearer hereof *Cato Ramſay* a Negro, reſorted to the Britiſh Lines, in conſequence of the Proclamations of Sir William Howe, and Sir Henry Clinton, late Commanders in Chief in America; and that the ſaid Negro has hereby his Excellency Sir Guy Carleton's Permiſſion to go to Nova-Scotia, or wherever elſe *He* may think proper. —

By Order of Brigadier General Birch,

To Canada and Freedom

Though there were African Americans who fought on the American side in the American Revolution, many more joined the British, who had promised them freedom. Only 3,000 black men and women who had joined the British were recognized as free after the war, given certificates of freedom (above), and evacuated to Canada. *Left:* After the Civil War, about two-thirds of the newly arrived African Americans left Canada to go back to the United States, generally to be reunited with their families. But immigration to Canada that had started in the 18th century continued, especially after the end of Reconstruction. One of the most celebrated immigrants was John Ware, the "Negro Cowboy," who arrived with his family, pictured here, in 1882.

The Voice of the Fugitive—and Mary Ann Shadd, editor of the *Provincial Freeman.* By the mid-19th century, the country had about 40 black settlements, but it is estimated that 30,000 black Canadians left during and after the Civil War to fight with the Union Army and be reunited with their families.

Immigration to Canada was revived in the 20th century when more than a thousand African Americans settled in the provinces of Saskatchewan and Alberta between 1905 and 1912. Some arrived from Kansas and Texas, but most came from Oklahoma. The latter left behind a state where racial violence and segregation were on the rise, and where their right to vote had been largely taken away in 1910. Many had moved there from the Deep South to escape racism and discrimination, and once again, they were ready to pack up and leave in search of freedom. Henry Sneed, an African American from Texas who had migrated to Oklahoma, organized the first group of 194 Canadian settlers. They left with nine railroad carloads of farm implements and livestock. But the movement north stopped in 1912 because of growing opposition from Canada's government and citizens, as well as anti-emigration black advocates.

THE DEBATE OVER EMIGRATION AND COLONIZATION | The Rev. Henry Highland Garnet and Martin R. Delany, both prominent abolitionists, did much to advance the colonization/emigration movement. In 1858 Garnet formed the African Civilization Society with the aim of encouraging the concept of Black Nationalism. Though initially opposed to emigration, he came to the conclusion that African Americans had little chance of attaining true independence in their country. Blacks returning to Africa, he argued, could benefit continental Africans by bringing "civilization" and Christianity while gaining freedom for themselves. Garnet countered the argument that emigrationists were abandoning their enslaved comrades by stating that although he was totally opposed to that institution, "No man should deprive me of my love for Africa, the land of my ancestors." He also advocated migration to the Caribbean islands and spent several years as a missionary in Jamaica. In November 1882 Garnet, by then an old man, immigrated to Liberia, where he died soon after.

Martin Robison Delany was, perhaps, an even more forceful proponent of Black Nationalism than Garnet. He was a journalist, firebrand abolitionist, and one of Frederick Douglass's closest friends. Douglass said of him, "I thank God for making me a man, simply, but Delany always thanks Him for making him a black man." After a short and unpleasant stay at Harvard Medical School, Delany published *The Condition, Elevation, Emigration and Destiny of the Colored People of the United States* (1852), supporting black emigration.

Vigorously opposed to the American Colonization Society because it was created by white men, he was an unbending advocate of black autonomy and self-reliance. In 1859 he went to Africa to explore emigration possibilities and negotiated for an American settlement in Abeokuta (Nigeria), but nothing came of his effort. In 1877 Delany established the Liberian Joint Stock Steamship Line. The company's only voyage came a year later, when the ship *Azor*, carrying 206 migrants, sailed from Charleston to Liberia.

Edward Wilmot Blyden, born in St. Thomas in what was then the Danish Virgin Islands, immigrated to Liberia in 1851. He eventually became president of Liberia College. Blyden was convinced that the only way his people could gain the world's respect was by building progressive new "empires" in Africa. However, his work on behalf of the ACS put him at odds with some emigrationists as well as those African Americans who believed their people should pursue a policy of assimilation.

By the 1890s, Henry McNeal Turner had become the most outspoken African-American advocate of emigration. Turner's "Back to Africa" message was well received by many poor southern farmers. They often endured great hardships in their efforts to find passage to Liberia. In 1876 Turner came under heavy criticism when he became vice president of the ACS. He traveled to Africa four times during the 1890s.

Despite these various efforts, emigration and colonization had always met with strong opposition from the black community. The Negro Convention movement, black America's most important arena for political expression and protest during the 19th century, was a direct response to the formation of the American Colonization Society and Liberian colonization. In 1818, 3,000 free African Americans answered a call from James Forten and the Bishop of the African Methodist Episcopal Church, Richard Allen, to convene in Philadelphia. The assembly denounced the ACS's colonization scheme as an "outrage having no other object in view than the slaveholding interests of the country."

Individual African Americans also noted their views on the subject. In 1834 Peter Williams, an Episcopal priest in New York City, objected to the idea that African Americans were best suited to colonization in Africa. "We are NATIVES of this country," he asserted, and "ask only to be treated as well as FOREIGNERS... we ask only to share equal privileges with those who come from distant lands, to enjoy the fruits of our labor. Let these modest requests be granted, and we need not to go to Africa nor anywhere else to be improved and happy."

Back to Africa

Above: This parade of uniformed women marched down Seventh Avenue in Harlem during the 1924 Convention of Negroes organized by the Universal Negro Improvement Association. The first convention, held in 1920, lasted for 31 days, with many thousands in attendance. It issued a manifesto of rights and developed plans for a settlement in Liberia.

Right: Marcus Garvey (1887–1940) rallied African Americans with his Back-to-Africa initiative. Garvey argued that race assimilation was impossible in the context of the United States, mainly because white Americans would not allow it.

MARCUS GARVEY'S BACK-TO-AFRICA MOVEMENT | In the early 20th century, Marcus Garvey and his movement, the Universal Negro Improvement Association (UNIA), founded in his native Jamaica in 1914, boosted emigration sentiment. Three years later Garvey immigrated to New York and set up headquarters in Harlem. Though scorned by the black middle and professional classes, his Back-to-Africa mantra and charismatic leadership rallied many African Americans. The UNIA became the largest mass movement in African-American history, and attracted followers throughout the Caribbean, Africa, South America, and Great Britain.

Garvey's version of Black Nationalism argued that black Americans' quest for social equality was a delusion. They were fated to be a permanent minority who could never assimilate because white Americans would never let them. African Americans, therefore, could not improve their condition or gain autonomy in the United States. Only in Africa was self-emancipation possible. Garvey drew his following largely from the lower end of the economic scale. Southerners who had come North during the Great Migration that accompanied World War I, servicemen returning from the European battlefields, and his fellow West Indians seemed particularly attuned to his philosophy.

The UNIA's first convention, held in 1920 in New York, lasted for 31 days with many thousands in attendance. It issued a manifesto, the Declaration of Rights for the Negro People of the World, and developed plans for a settlement in Liberia. The UNIA sold millions of shares in the Black Star Line, its own shipping company, to its members. Three steamships were purchased, and black officers and crew were contracted to sail the emigrants across the Atlantic. The Black Star fleet did carry passengers on several journeys from New York to Central America and the Caribbean, but it never reached Liberia. As the line faced bankruptcy resulting from shady dealings by some UNIA officials, the federal government launched an unrelenting investigation of the man millions revered as the "Black Messiah." He was convicted in 1925 of defrauding investors, sentenced to five years in prison, and, after serving half of his term, deported to Jamaica. In 1940, Marcus Garvey died in London.

Although his efforts at sending African Americans back to Africa ultimately failed, Garvey's influence remained strong and inspired some to migrate, on their own, to the land of their ancestors.

CONSEQUENCES | The most enduring consequence of colonization for African Americans was the sense of freedom and liberty the experience provided. In their letters home, they frequently stressed the deep satisfaction they derived from living free in a nondiscriminatory environment. For people who had suffered enslavement, doomed to live and die in bondage, emigration represented an opportunity to start new and independent lives. But some migrants returned home, disappointed that Africa was not the promised land they had hoped for.

For many Africans, the arrival of black Americans was, at best, a mixed blessing. The newcomers often exploited and mistreated them, and did not accept them as citizens or as equals. People were dispossessed of thousands of square miles of territory. In 1843 United States cruisers helped put down a revolt of native Liberians against the exploitative trade measures imposed by the Americo-Liberians, as they called themselves. An all-out war erupted in 1875 between the colonists and the Grebo, and violent conflicts persisted until the turn of the 20th century.

The colonists saw themselves as bringing Christianity and Western "civilization" to the local population. Their ethnic and cultural chauvinism often served to devalue the rights, aspirations, and cultures of the native people. The identities the migrants created for themselves were often in conflict with the African context and way of life. Nevertheless, some settlers tried to strike a balance between their Eurocentric worldview and the perspectives of their African neighbors. One of the more positive effects of the migration was the establishment of a journalistic tradition in West Africa. A lasting free-press tradition was established that, over the years, influenced Africans to demand change in their societies.

The importance of colonization and emigration lies not so much in its numbers, but in the fact that the issue raised the nationalist consciousness of America's black population. Perhaps its most enduring legacy was the Pan-African movement, which blossomed in the late 19th and early 20th centuries. A concept pioneered by Martin R. Delany, Edward Wilmot Blyden, and others, it led to the recognition that until Africa was free of oppression, black people around the world could not become free.

The Northern Migration

Studies of African-American migration most often focus on the 20th century, when millions of black people left the South, moving northward to industrial cities of the East and West. Yet an earlier migration was also important. Although not as dramatic in sheer numbers, and less well studied, it too had a profound impact on the course of American history. This was the migration that took place during the decades before and just after the American Civil War. In the antebellum period, much of this movement was forced and occurred in the South, as people from the Upper South were sold into the domestic slave trade. But there was also a voluntary migration of runaways, and of free African Americans leaving the South for a perceived better, less restricted life in the northern states.

In the North they clustered in small communities in the larger cities. They established stable families, built their own institutions, and, although most were denied full citizenship, nevertheless became a vigorous force in regional and national politics. Free African Americans represented only about 10 percent of the total black population at the time of the Civil War, but their role in the issues that led to Southern secession was in great disproportion to their numbers.

FREE BLACKS IN THE SOUTH | For free African Americans, the South was never a comfortable place. In a slave society their presence was always suspect, and slaveholders went to great lengths to limit their numbers. In the 1830s, for example, Virginia was one of a number of southern states whose laws required that a freed slave must leave the state within a year of emancipation. States like North Carolina prohibited free blacks from entering their territory. In several states, including Maryland, free blacks convicted on the most minor charges were sold into slavery. In 1858 one free black man in South Carolina was convicted for stealing a pot valued at less than a dollar; he escaped after he was delivered to a slave dealer for sale. In the 1850s Charleston's free blacks were forced to wear badges in order to work, and their entrance into the mechanical trades was severely limited. In Washington,

Added to racism, the gender conventions of the 19th century limited the employment opportunities available to African-American women. They also set aside certain work as the purview of women. Sybil Harber worked as a midwife, one of the few skilled professions open to African-American women. Some women were also teachers in black schools. In 1880, 8 percent of the female Southern migrants in Boston worked in skilled and professional jobs, but their percentage declined with time; by 1900 those jobs were mostly held by black women born in Massachusetts.

D.C., free African Americans were subject to curfews and other restrictions. In Charleston and New Orleans, black sailors were imprisoned during the time their ships were in port to prevent them from making contact with local slaves. In 1859 South Carolina's legislature established the Committee on the Colored Population, which seriously considered enslaving all the state's free African Americans.

Given these circumstances, it is hardly surprising that many free blacks seriously considered leaving the South. Although some would cast their lot with those advocating immigration to Africa and the West Indies, the overwhelming majority of voluntary migrants moved into established African-American communities in the North.

GOING NORTH | Those northern cities closest to the South experienced the largest growth. By 1860 Cincinnati, just across the Ohio River from slaveholding Kentucky, was essentially a southern city in a northern state. Its black population was much smaller than that of New York or Philadelphia but it was overwhelmingly southern-born. Of Cincinnati's 3,700 African Americans, 70 percent were Southerners.

Interestingly, demographic studies show that African Americans in Cincinnati's black neighborhoods clustered together in a manner largely determined by the color of their skin. By 1860 mulattos, who made up more than half of the city's black population, were overrepresented in three of the five districts with the largest numbers of blacks. In two of those districts—a substantial distance from the worst areas of black poverty—they comprised 63 percent and 85 percent of the population. On the other hand, darker blacks constituted 60 percent and 70 percent in other, less attractive areas, and were concentrated most heavily in "Bucktown," a poor, undesirable neighborhood with little sanitation and a generally unhealthy environment.

FARTHER NORTH | In cities more distant from the South than Cincinnati, the number of southern-born blacks grew steadily during the antebellum years. By 1860, 65 percent of Detroit's African-American population had been born in the South. In other northern cities, too, blacks from the South were becoming a more significant proportion of the African-American population. In Boston, almost 30 percent of the city's blacks were southern migrants, as were more than half in Chicago, almost one-third in Philadelphia, and close to 40 percent in Buffalo. Migration from their southern homes was not easy, but as the antebellum period wore on, more and more African Americans made the move.

Some, like the Hodges family from Virginia, maintained households in both the North and South. In the early 1830s William Hodges, a free black man, left his home in Virginia bound for the North. He traveled all the way to Canada before

Country to City

Top: By the end of the 19th century, and despite the migration to the North, the West, and Southern urban areas, most African Americans remained in the rural South, working the land as tenant farmers or sharecroppers, like this family in front of a wooden house in Washington, D.C., or Virginia. *Bottom:* Even Southerners who had lived in cities faced the difficult task of trying to re-create familiar lifestyles in unfamiliar Northern surroundings. They depended on the experiences of those who had traveled ahead of them, and found jobs through a chain of contacts and references.

retracing his steps, finally settling in New York City. William kept in close contact with his brother, Willis, in Virginia through letters and messages delivered by friends. Shortly after William settled in New York, five of his nephews arrived and were enrolled in school, an opportunity they would have been denied in Virginia. Willis and his wife soon followed.

Their travel between their Virginia and New York homes was so frequent that various family members might be found living together in either location at any given time. They not only depended on one another for room and board during their extended stays, but William, who lived in New York semi-permanently, also helped other members of the family find employment. Willis remembered that his first impressions of New York came when his brother took him on a tour of the city, pointing out the various jobs available to blacks.

THE SEARCH FOR WORK | For African Americans, finding employment in northern cities was no easy task. Their job possibilities were limited by discriminatory labor practices demanded by European immigrants competing with blacks for skilled jobs. Racial limitations imposed on jobs in the North differed from those in the South, where bondspeople were forced to perform all types of labor.

Southern white men were expected to strive for the independence that landowning brought. If they could not all be planters, at the very least they were expected to be small farmers. Except in the few localities where European immigrants formed a substantial part of the southern population, all labor in the South was considered "nigger work," and free blacks were employed at many levels, even in skilled jobs. It was not unusual to find blacks working as carpenters, blacksmiths, and barrel makers in Charleston or New Orleans, especially prior to the late 1850s when foreign workers were less numerous in those cities. In New Orleans, one reporter observed, skilled work was performed by some white workers but also by a substantial number of African Americans, "and of the negroes employed in these avocations a considerable proportion are free."

In the North, however, African Americans were generally denied skilled jobs. Southern migrants were particularly disadvantaged since they were more likely than northern-born blacks to have job skills. Employment records for Philadelphia reveal that during the late 1850s, "less than two-thirds of [black workers] who have trades follow them" and "the greater number are compelled to abandon their trades on account of the unrelenting prejudice against their color." The situation in Boston, with its large immigrant population, was even worse. There, one foreign visitor reported seeing almost no black skilled workers in 1833. The few exceptions were "one or two employed as printers, one blacksmith and one shoemaker."

In New York City, although officials announced that they would "issue licenses to all regardless of race," they soon buckled under pressure from white workers to exclude blacks from jobs requiring special permits. African Americans found it almost impossible to obtain licenses as hack drivers or pushcart operators, denying them important opportunities to become small businessmen. Willis Hodges reported in the 1840s that in Virginia both enslaved and free blacks had trades and he "had expected to find the people of color in free New York far better off than those in Virginia." Instead, he found that "many tradesmen [he] knew from the South were cooks and waiters."

Cincinnati was no different. There, one white mechanic was reprimanded by the Mechanical Association for taking on a black apprentice, and a leader of another labor organization was called to account by his group for having helped a young black man learn a trade.

WORKING WOMEN | The rampant discrimination against black men in the labor markets of the North made it unlikely that a family could be supported on one salary. The domestic work open to African-American women was often steady, unlike the seasonal nature of many of the laboring jobs available to men. One attractive feature of domestic work in the homes of others, or of "taking in" washing or sewing at one's own home, was that such an arrangement allowed for the care of children at the workplace. Black women were often very influential within the household.

The story of Chloe Spear provides an interesting account of one African American "Wonder Woman." Born in Africa and enslaved in Boston until the end of the 18th century, Chloe married Cesar Spear, also a slave. After the family was freed, the Spears operated a boardinghouse in the city. In addition, Chloe did domestic work for a prominent family. While she was at work, Cesar saw to the cooking and other duties associated with the boardinghouse, but when she returned in the evening he turned the operation over to her while he was "taking his rest." After working all day, Chloe cooked dinner for her family and for the boarders and

Unskilled Labor

Two boys appraise the strawberries sold by an elderly man in Washington, D.C., 1900. Job openings for black men other than the traditional roles they had held for decades, such as waiters and servants, were rare in the North until the Great Migration. Most African-American children were denied access to public schools. In 1865 a committee appointed to consider the conditions under which African Americans lived in Washington, D.C., declared, unsurprisingly, that illiteracy was a significant impediment to progress.

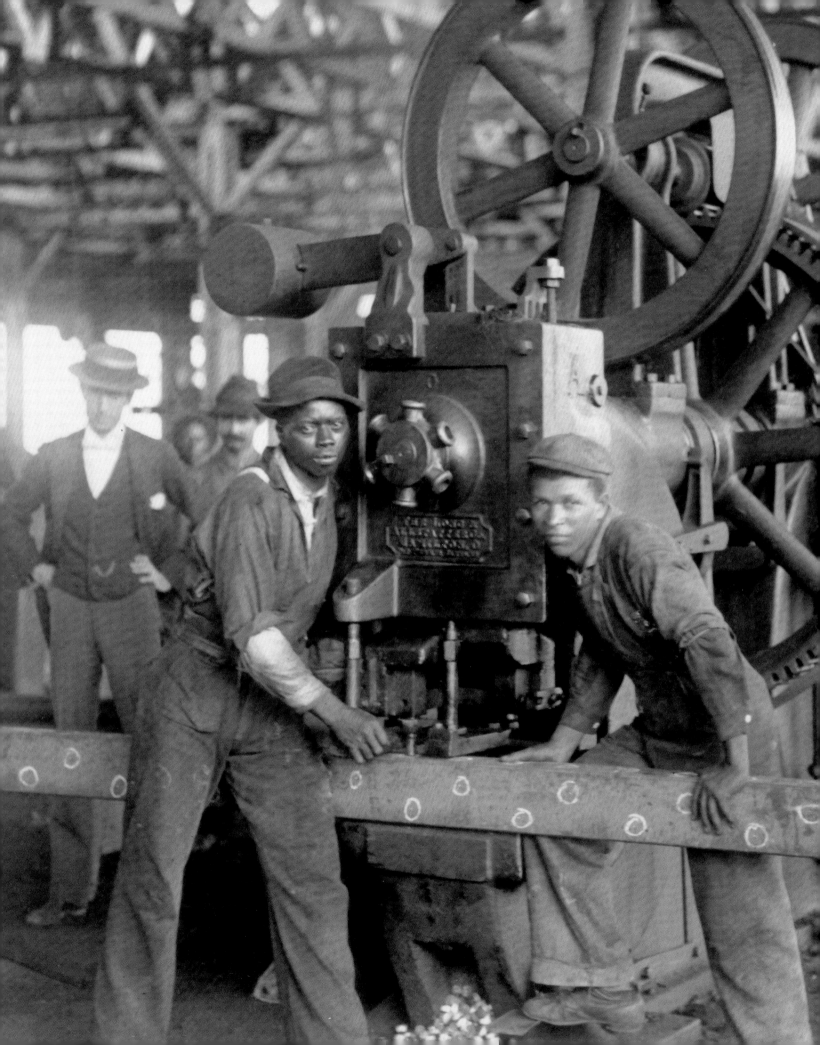

Skilled Labor

Young men operate a metal punching machine at a shipbuilding plant in Newport News, Virginia, ca. 1898. African Americans competed for jobs with European immigrants. Racial limitations reserved most of the jobs for whites, native or foreign. As a result, many African Americans who had been trained in skilled labor in the South worked at menial jobs in northern cities for little pay.

cleaned the house. In order to make extra money, she took in washing, which she did at night, setting up lines in her room for drying the clothes. She slept a few hours while the clothes dried, then ironed them and prepared breakfast for the household before going off to work for the day.

Although one might easily conclude that women like Chloe were cruelly exploited by their husbands, the reality was not quite so simple. Chloe did not routinely hand over her wages to her husband, as did most white working women of the period. She controlled her own money, as is usual among African women. At one point she decided to purchase a house despite the fact that the law prohibited married women from buying property in their own name. Chloe was forced to ask her husband to make the purchase for her. Told that it cost $700, Cesar determined that he could not afford it. "I got money," Chloe announced, and Cesar agreed to sign for the house.

Studies of the black family have long noted the increased independence and authority women exercised within the household because of their crucial role in the family economy. Chloe is an excellent example of the way African-American women asserted that role.

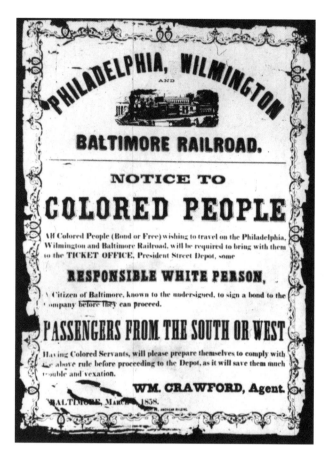

RACIAL RESTRICTIONS | Northern anti-black discrimination was hardly limited to matters of economics. Limits imposed on the basic civil rights of African Americans were, in some places, almost as debilitating as those they experienced in the South. Except in a few localities in New England, northern blacks were not generally allowed the right to vote, to serve on juries, or even to bring suits in courts of law.

In most northern communities, black children were denied public education or were segregated in underfunded, substandard schools. The public schools in Boston, integrated in 1855, and the black school system that functioned in Cincinnati in the 1840s were among the small number of exceptions.

Public accommodations, too, were segregated. In theaters, on trains and stagecoaches, in restaurants and hotels, African-American patrons were either relegated to inferior conditions or not admitted at all.

In some states the racial restrictions were more severe and all-encompassing. Oregon, Ohio, Indiana, Michigan, and Illinois either banned black immigration outright, imposed discriminatory state regulations, or required African Americans to post bonds that could amount to hundreds of dollars to ensure their "good conduct." Black migrants sometimes found ways to circumvent such legal constraints, but clearly northern migration posed considerable problems.

Not the least of these was the fact that no African American was free from slav-

Going North

Above: Without proof of their status—and even sometimes with proof—black people were vulnerable to slave catchers. In order to protect themselves and their passengers, railroads such as the Philadelphia, Wilmington, and Baltimore Railroad required African Americans to be accompanied by a white person at all rail depots.
Right: Although their legal status was often problematic in the North, and despite often harsh working conditions there, thousands of free people of color made the decision to emigrate in order to escape certain oppression in the South.

ery. Slavery reached out from the South to threaten all black people, not only fugitives. Even legally free blacks were in danger from kidnappers selling them into servitude. Some reports indicate that the majority of blacks captured as fugitives after the passage of the Fugitive Slave Act of 1850 were apprehended without the aid of legal authority and were denied any semblance of due process of law.

ORGANIZING RESISTANCE |

The vulnerability of free African Americans to kidnapping was perceived as being so great that several black leaders suggested that people of color carry weapons for self-defense. Members of one group arrested for carrying guns on Boston Common explained their actions by citing the need to protect themselves and other blacks from slave catchers. In New York black abolitionists such as Henry Highland Garnet and Samuel Ringgold Ward armed themselves; other leaders advised those threatened by slave catchers to "act as they would to rid themselves of any wild beast."

In their local communities, northern blacks made clear their intention to work for freedom and justice for themselves and those still in bondage. In cities such as New York, Philadelphia, and Boston, free blacks regularly called protest meetings to communicate their outrage and to plot strategy to deal with the evils of racial injustice. These town meetings were important forums for the interchange of ideas and provided a training ground for local black leadership. Black newspapers were filled with notices of community meetings called to discuss abolition, civil rights, educational issues, and general concerns of social and political reform.

Even in Cincinnati, where public protest was more restricted than in cities farther north or east, neighborhood meetings were important for reinforcing the conviction of the grass-roots community that the slave must never be forgotten and the fugitive must always be protected.

Although southern migrants often had friends and relatives living in the North, they were not always welcomed by the black population that had been

living there for generations. Sometimes black Northerners believed the newcomers to be unsophisticated, loud, superstitious, and uneducated. Many felt that the newcomers reinforced stereotypes of black people. In New York, elite African Americans founded the Sons of New York in 1884 to publicly mark their distance from the Southerners.

NEW HOUSEHOLDS | Often the problems faced by migrants to the North were simply too difficult to overcome. As many southern blacks left to make new lives for themselves, a few returned. One Virginian explained that she could not live in Ohio "in the least happiness or contentment." The South was an oppressive place for African Americans, but it was also home. "I feel this is my country," one free black Charlestonian told a foreign visitor, "leaving it will come hard." The thought of leaving loved ones and all that was familiar was enough to keep most free blacks in the South. Those who left would make every possible effort to re-create their familiar lives in unfamiliar places. These endeavors help to explain migration patterns.

The story of the Hodges family, discussed earlier, illustrates an important point about the pattern of black migration during the antebellum period. Like most migration, it was generally not random. Life for African Americans in the North was so difficult that without contacts and support it could be all but impossible. So blacks who had a choice of destination usually selected one where they could depend on contacts with friends and family. In a classic pattern of chain migration, they went where others they knew had gone before.

In the black communities of the North, the households of those who had been born out of state were likely to expand beyond the nuclear family to include boarders, family, and friends arriving from out of town. Boarding provided an important means for new arrivals to become acclimated to life in a new place. Through their hosts, boarders could be introduced to employment opportunities, social groups, the church, and friends. This network enhanced the mobility of poor people and provided financial assistance for the unemployed, while supporting those who faced discrimination and delivering newly arrived migrants from social isolation.

The Hodges household consisted mainly of family members, but migrants were almost as likely to seek the aid of friends or acquaintances. During the years before the American Civil War, one key characteristic of free black households was the significant proportion of the boarders who had been born in the same state as members of the host family. In over half the households that had boarders with listed occupations, at least one was employed in the same occupation as a member of the host family. Boarding also served an important function for the host family, providing necessary additional income from fees for household services like washing and ironing. In providing such amenities, many married women earned wages while working at home.

Women's Roles

Top: This portrait of six professional women—the Executive board of the Women's League in Newport, Rhode Island—was displayed as part of the American Negro exhibit at Exposition Universal, 1900, in Paris, France.

Bottom: Women sort tobacco at the T. B. Williams Tobacco Co., in Richmond, Virginia, 1899.

MAINTAINING COMMUNICATION | For migrants in the North, maintaining communication with enslaved family and friends in the South—a matter of critical importance—was a complicated proposition. Despite the difficulties, there was a steady stream of messages along an underground network linking those in and out of bondage. Black and white interregional travelers—many of whom would not have considered themselves part of an "underground"—were the means of transmission. In many instances, this communication was as simple as "telling of thems at the home place": spreading news or gossip about familiar people and places.

In northern communities where southern migrants clustered, African Americans expected newcomers to share their knowledge about family and friends. Black travelers were closely questioned. In antebellum Cincinnati, local blacks knew that the Dumas Hotel was a place to gather information on people and conditions in the South. Visiting slaveholders often lodged their personal servants at the Dumas. While the owners pursued their business in the city, their bondspeople sought the company of Cincinnati blacks. Information was regularly exchanged, and many migrants maintained contact with loved ones through this link. For 30 years Willie Mathis kept in touch with her mother, enslaved in Virginia, in this manner. Another Cincinnati woman used this communication service to smuggle letters to her children in bondage in North Carolina. During the antebellum decades, the Dumas became a kind of underground post office.

In Boston, much farther north than Cincinnati, there were fewer contacts to encourage large numbers of black migrants to settle. Yet many came despite the distance, for African Americans were not ignorant of that city's possibilities for freedom. Peter Randolph was born enslaved in Virginia. After he secured his freedom, he traveled with 66 others to Boston, led there by the underground communication network. "The name Boston," he explained, "always had a musical and joyous sound to the colored people of the South." Although several southern whites attempted to convince Randolph and his party that the North generally, and Boston in particular, was a dangerous place, southern blacks knew better. They understood, as one said, "that this city is foremost in advocating the Negro's cause and vouchsafing to him the immunities of citizenship."

Although Boston was far from being a promised land, the existence of an established and active black community also attracted migrants to the city.

Information Highway

Above: A carriage waits in front of the Union Hotel in Chattanooga, Tennessee, which catered only to African Americans. Hotels provided a place for the exchange of news and messages.

Right: The church was the cornerstone of free black communities. Religious congregations, like the Bethel African Methodist Episcopal Church in Chester, Pennsylvania, were often central in the formation of benevolent societies and political organizations.

African-American newcomers, barred from many city facilities, found support within this community. With hotels and white boardinghouses closed to them, job opportunities severely limited, and sections of the city unsafe for them, migrants relied on the established African Americans. They sought out friends and relatives in the area who provided housing and social contacts. Black migrants to antebellum Boston confronted many of the same problems as European immigrants and used many of the same coping techniques to aid their adjustment to urban life.

THE DEVELOPMENT OF NETWORKS | Black unskilled and semi-skilled workers who traveled frequently in search of jobs developed a network of acquaintances and contacts in Northern cities. By the 1850s a travel circuit had developed. For East Coast migrants, the circuit included Philadelphia, New York City, Providence (Rhode Island), New Bedford (Massachusetts), and Boston. Often an African-American worker was enticed from one of these cities to another by favorable reports from a friend who had gone before.

Down South, slaveholders were ever vigilant in attempting to isolate their chattel from "Northern information," but generally they were unsuccessful. African-American institutions, particularly churches, always suspect as centers of subversion, were closely watched. Despite the slaveholders' best efforts, however, southern black churches were an integral part of the interregional underground.

Even though Richmond's First African Baptist Church had a white minister (this was not an unusual situation; slaveholders hoped that white pastors could maintain control over their black congregations), its members kept in touch with those gone North through a clandestine mailing system based in the church. Several who had fled from bondage wrote back to their former comrades, giving information to help others follow their example. Messages and letters were brought to the church and distributed to enslaved and free blacks in the city. The system was shut down in the mid-1850s, after local slaveholders discovered it.

The efficiency of the underground network is exemplified by the case of Henry Williams, who escaped from slavery in Louisiana in the 1830s and traveled to Cincinnati, where he worked, maintained his freedom for a number of years, and met and married a woman from another town. Members of his church who knew that Williams was already married, and that his wife, still enslaved, was living in New Orleans, were outraged. They charged him with bigamy and desertion. The congregation demanded a signed release from her before they would sanction his new marriage. Henry faced a grave problem. How could a fugitive in Cincinnati contact his first wife, who was enslaved in New Orleans, to obtain a signed document? The underground communication network was the answer. A boatman who regularly traveled to New Orleans found the first Mrs. Williams and secured her "X" on the paper as well as her enthusiastic support for dissolving the marriage. The church then recognized Henry's second nuptials.

THE SAILORS | Black seamen and boatmen were vital message carriers. The tradition of African-American sailors dates back to colonial times, when blacks manned whaling ships and oceangoing merchant vessels as well as riverboats. In seaport and river port cities such as Boston and Cincinnati, the water routes offered an important source of income for black workers.

These mariners traveled frequently and were well versed in what one historian referred to as "travel craft"—the ability to seek out those with information vital to the survival of a black traveler in strange and possibly hostile places. Despite the efforts of authorities, many free sailors from the northern states, the West Indies, and England came ashore and spent time between voyages in black communities in southern ports. Some slaves also crewed on riverboats or coastal vessels. Contact between free and enslaved people was thus relatively easy, despite white Southerners' fears that it threatened their efforts to keep their

Water Ways

Top: African Americans found work on the seas and rivers beginning in the colonial period, when they served as crewmen on whaling ships and trade vessels as well as riverboats. During the 19th century, river transportation became increasingly important, and water routes in sea and river port cities like Cincinnati and Boston offered an important source of income. They also provided a valuable place and mechanism for the exchange of news and information.

Bottom: The steamer *Charles D. Shaw* sits docked at a landing along the Mississippi River.

bondspeople in ignorance. Seamen were pivotal to the operations of the interregional communication system.

Free blacks and runaways in the North depended on the sailors to bring information about family and friends whenever they came north, and to carry news back to the Southland. One Cincinnati woman kept in touch with her enslaved mother for more than three decades through messages smuggled by black boatmen. During those years she consulted her mother about her choice of a husband and informed her of the birth of her children. In 1843 the news of her grandchild's enrollment at Oberlin Collegiate Institute reached the proud grandmother in a Mississippi slave cabin, bound in body, she reported, but free in spirit.

CONSEQUENCES OF THE MIGRATION | By the end of the antebellum years, free African Americans in the urban North had established well-defined communities providing formal and informal supports and services not generally available elsewhere to African Americans. The institution of slavery was a focal point among a diverse black populace, even for those who had not personally experienced its horrors. Its presence profoundly shaped the relationships, activities, and ideas of the free black society.

The Civil War ended slavery, but the political and economic failures of the postwar period foreclosed the possibility for true freedom and brought a new structure of racial control. For northern blacks the demise of slavery meant fewer restrictions for southern relatives and friends, although they were far from totally free from the inhumane consequences of the South's peculiar institution.

Best and Brightest

After the abolition of slavery, some of the best educated and most gifted members of the African-American community, like these students from Howard University, moved to the South to participate in promised political and economic opportunities.

Many former slaves exercised their new mobility and migrated to the cities of the North and Midwest. Their numbers did not approach those of the World War I Great Migration, but they did significantly increase the urban black population of the North. Detroit's black population ballooned by two-thirds during the 1860s, with the vast majority of its new arrivals coming from the South. There were similar population explosions in Cleveland, Boston, New York, and Philadelphia.

The presence of slavery greatly complicated the lives of free blacks before the Civil War, and emancipation made its own demands. Urban African-American communities strained to cope with the needs of the incoming rural migrants. Northern white workers, uncomfortable with the growing black urban population and always sensitive to any increased occupational competition, resisted the hiring of African Americans in any skilled jobs. Northern society at first resisted the participation of black workers in the emerging factory economy, then limited the protections afforded them by labor unions.

STILL A SOUTHERN PEOPLE | So it was that economic and social pressures, aggravated by racial prejudice, continued to narrow opportunities and intensify differences within the African-American community. African Americans remained united in their commitment to racial progress, but their conflicts over means and even short-term ends became more visible. The fierce struggles between the forces of protest and those of accommodation symbolized by W. E. B. Du Bois and Booker T. Washington moved from the interior of black society to the public stage.

By the end of the 19th century the South had written its racial hostility and violence into its laws, with the blessing of the Supreme Court. Racial discrimination was codified in the South, and practiced almost as effectively by custom in the North.

Yet despite the thousands who migrated, blacks remained regionally stable. By the dawn of the 20th century, over seven million of the nation's almost nine million blacks lived in the South. African Americans remained a southern people. They were more likely now to live in the cities and small towns, but most were, as they had been for many generations, rural people working land they did not own—then as slaves, now as sharecroppers—bound by debt and legalized discriminatory practices.

The Westward Migration

The saga of African-American migration to the West begins in Philadelphia, where, in 1833, the Third Annual Convention for the Improvement of the Free People of Color considered the colonization of West Africa. After much deliberation, the assembly promoted immigration to Mexican Texas as a better alternative.

For more than a century to come, the twin themes of freedom and opportunity in the West struck a chord with many African Americans, propelling them toward the setting sun. Between 1860 and 1950, the black population of the western states grew from 196,000 to 1,787,000.

THE EARLY BLACK WEST | The first people of African ancestry to migrate into what is now the western United States originated from Central Mexico, to which 200,000 Africans were forcibly transported between 1521 and 1821. Beginning in the 1600s, the newcomers settled on the northern frontier of the Spanish colony, establishing a pattern that would continue into the 20th century.

Isabel de Olivera was typical of the hundreds of Spanish-speaking black settlers who founded and populated cities and towns from San Antonio to San Francisco. In 1781 they comprised a majority of the founders of Los Angeles. Olivera, one of the first inhabitants of Santa Fe in 1600, wrote:

> I am going...to New Mexico and have some reason to fear that I may be annoyed
> by some individual since I am a mulatto. It is proper to protect my rights in such
> an eventuality by an affidavit showing that I am a free woman, unmarried and
> the legitimate daughter of Hernando, a negro, and an Indian woman named
> Magdalena....I demand Justice.

When Mexico declared its independence from Spain in 1821—abolishing slavery and guaranteeing full citizenship rights to all, regardless of color—hundreds of free African Americans crossed the border into what was then Mexican Texas to seek

After a brief era of freedom during radical Reconstruction, Jim Crow laws throughout the South restricted African Americans' civil rights. Acts of violence and overt racism pushed some people west in search of greater freedom. Although life on the western plains had its own difficulties, many found that it offered them a new level of self-reliance.

the freedom denied them in the United States. But Texas revolutionaries crushed the aspirations of free blacks and fugitive slaves when they transformed the new Republic of Texas into a vast slaveholding empire in 1836. The days of freedom were over; for African Americans, that part of the West was no longer a safe harbor.

The first significant numbers of black Americans to enter the territory north of Texas did not do so by choice. Between 1830 and 1870, nearly 70,000 Native Americans were forcibly relocated from the South to Indian Territory. Their ranks included 10,000 blacks, some of whom were enslaved. At least 175 perished along the Trail of Tears.

THE FAR WEST | Whereas some African Americans had ventured into Oregon Territory as early as the 1840s, and Colorado Territory after the Pikes Peak gold rush of 1859, the vast majority moved to California. That state's gold rush, which began in 1848, stimulated migration from throughout the eastern United States. Between 1850 and 1860, 4,000 African Americans reached the Golden State. Half of that number settled in San Francisco and Sacramento, creating the first English-speaking black urban communities in the Far West.

Mifflin W. Gibbs arrived in San Francisco from Philadelphia in 1850 with only 60 cents in his pocket. After working as a well-paid bootblack, he and a partner opened a shoe store that became highly successful. In a 1902 autobiography, *Shadow and Light,* he recalled those early days:

> Thanks to the evolution of events and march of liberal ideas the colored men in California now have a recognized citizenship, and equality before the law. It was not so at the period of which I write. With thrift and a wise circumspection financially, their opportunities were good [but] from every other point of view they were ostracized, assaulted without redress, disfranchised, and denied their oath in court.

Other black migrants headed for the Mother Lode country, the gold vein stretching over four hundred miles along the western slope of the Sierra Nevada Mountains. Some African Americans struck gold. In 1851 miner Peter Brown wrote home to his wife in Missouri about his good fortune: "California is the best...place for black folks on the globe. All a man has to do is work and he will make money."

The abolition of slavery created the potential for mass African-American migration to the West. Few crossed the plains in wagon trains; they were more likely to take trains or steamboats. The vast majority, however, took the transportation most available to a newly freed people. They walked...into Texas, Indian Territory, and Kansas.

In Texas, agricultural workers made $20 a month—double their pay in Virginia, North Carolina, and Tennessee. Such an incentive attracted masses of

Gold Rush

These miners, photographed near Spanish Flat, California, in 1852,. were part of the California gold rush, which began in 1848 and stimulated a massive wave of western migration. Over the course of the next decade, four thousand African Americans arrived in California. Some were enslaved and accompanied their owners, while others were free men who hoped to strike it rich in the mines, or worked as cooks, stewards, and in other services. Letters home indicate that at least some of the migrants were motivated by more than personal financial gain. In 1851 Peter Brown wrote to his wife about his son, "I wish you to tell Peter to be industrious.... I am trying to make enough money to buy him when I get home."

people. In the last three decades of the 19th century, the African-American population of Texas more than doubled—from 253,000 to over 620,000.

African Americans, mainly from Arkansas and Tennessee, also migrated into Indian Territory, where they became farmers on land they could not legally own until 1889. In Indian-controlled areas, their status as intruders could subject them to expulsion. Despite these obstacles, the black population in Indian Territory would rise sixfold to 36,000 by 1900, outnumbering the Native Americans.

TO KANSAS | Kansas, which had been a sanctuary for fugitives during the Civil War, continued to loom large in the minds of many African-American Southerners. Between 1870 and 1890, some 30,000 migrants settled in the state. Kansas was the closest western state to the Old South that allowed blacks to homestead in the 1870s, and it became a magnet for land-hungry newcomers from Missouri, Virginia, Kentucky, and Tennessee, as well as such Deep South states as Louisiana and Mississippi.

The 1862 Homestead Act applied to Kansas and other western states and territories: Settlers—regardless of their race or gender—could pay a small filing fee and receive 160 acres from the federal government. In return, they agreed to reside on the land, and improve it over a five-year period. After six months, they could purchase the property for $1.25 an acre.

Another factor pulling black migrants to Kansas was the state's powerful abolitionist tradition. Here, John Brown had first battled to free slaves, and here the first black soldiers joined the Union Army. Kansas had welcomed the Emancipation Proclamation and was among the first to ratify the Thirteenth Amendment. "I am anxious to reach your state," wrote a black Louisianian to the governor of Kansas in 1879, "not because of the great race [for land] now made for it but because of the sacredness of her soil washed by the blood of humanitarians for the cause of black freedom."

After the Civil War, thousands of blacks relocated to areas free of racial restrictions and violence. The first of these "political migrations" was a mid-1870s exodus from Tennessee. It was led by Benjamin "Pap" Singleton, who recognized the limitations of Reconstruction-era political reform in the South. Singleton had escaped a dozen times during his years of enslavement, finally reaching Canada as a passenger on the Underground Railroad. In 1874, while working as a carpenter in Nashville, he distributed a circular, "The Advantage of Living in a Free State," encouraging migration to Kansas. At least 10,000 African Americans journeyed to the Sunflower State between 1874 and 1890, partly in response to his call.

In 1877 a white developer, together with six prospective black homesteaders from the South, founded the town of Nicodemus. They envisioned a self-sustaining, self-governing black agricultural community on the Kansas frontier. Named after a legendary African prince who purchased his freedom from slavery, the new town

Settlers

Top: Companies of African-American soldiers often remained together, establishing black towns and communities after the end of the Civil War. These buffalo soldiers, as they were called, and their wives were photographed in Montana around 1890.

Bottom: The journey to California was not an easy one. In order to cross the plains and the mountains, migrants faced hunger, drought, and disease. Free blacks sometimes signed on as servants with groups of white migrants to make the journey west. This picture was taken on the Overland Trail in Wyoming in the 1870s.

quickly captured the nation's attention. In July the first 30 colonists arrived from Kentucky. They were joined the following spring by an additional 150 men and women from Tennessee, Missouri, and Mississippi. Nothing in their experiences had prepared the migrants for life on the Kansas frontier. The flat, barren, windswept High Plains, known for blazing summer heat and bitter winter cold, were better suited to growing cactus than corn and wheat. One of the settlers, Williana Hickman, was dismayed to discover that the townsfolk lived not in houses, but in dugouts. "We landed and struck tents," she recalled. "The scenery was not at all inviting and I began to cry."

Despite their initial misgivings, Hickman and most of the early colonists stayed on. By 1880, 258 blacks and 58 whites resided in the town and the surrounding area. For African Americans across the country, Nicodemus became an important symbol of self-governance and economic enterprise.

But the town's prospects were always precarious and, in the 1880s, it underwent a steady decline. The winter blizzards of 1885 destroyed 40 percent of the wheat crop, and settlers began to leave. Two years later, the Missouri Pacific Railroad bypassed the town and, as was the case for hundreds of other communities cut off from the railway, Nicodemus's fate was sealed. After 1888 local boosters ceased trying to attract new settlers, and prominent citizens left the area.

In the summer of 1879, a few hundred blacks settled in Morris and Graham counties—the vanguard of some 6,000 Southern African Americans who would join the exodus to Kansas. Although the so-called Kansas Fever conjured up images of a leaderless movement of impoverished freed men and women, driven by blind faith toward a better place, it was a rational response to conditions in the South. When a St. Louis *Globe* reporter asked a woman with a child at her breast if she would return to her former home, she replied, "What, go back!...I'd sooner starve here."

But Topeka Mayor Michael C. Case spoke for many of his city's white residents when he refused to spend municipal funds to aid the "Exodusters," as they

1st Stone Church

J. WILLIAMS
GENERAL
MERCHANDISE.

CIGARS & CIDER.

All Colored People

THAT WANT TO

GO TO KANSAS,

On September 5th, 1877,

Can do so for $5.00

were called, suggesting the money would be better used to return them to the South. The Topeka *Colored Citizen,* on the other hand, celebrated the migration: "Our advice...to the people of the South, Come West, Come to Kansas...it is better to starve to death in Kansas than be shot and killed in the South."

The Kansas exodus ended almost as suddenly as it had begun. Its demise was the result of neither white opposition, nor of the advice of leaders such as Frederick Douglass that blacks remain in the South, nor of the machinations of swindlers who preyed on the people's gullibility. Rather, word filtered back that little free land remained and that many Exodusters were still destitute a year after their arrival. Although migration from Texas, Mississippi, and Louisiana continued after 1880, it never reached the level of the summer and the fall of 1879.

MIGRATION TO OKLAHOMA | Oklahoma Territory became the other major area for black migration. It was created in 1866 out of the western half of the original Indian Territory on land originally set aside for settlement by Native Americans, such as the Comanche and Cheyenne nations. Pressure from white prospective settlers persuaded the federal government to further reduce Indian lands and open the surplus to homesteaders. The famous April 22, 1889, "run" for land claims followed.

For many African Americans, Oklahoma Territory represented the possibility of creating towns and colonies where black people would be free to exercise their political rights without interference. Edwin P. McCabe, who as State Auditor had been the most powerful black man in Kansas, arrived in Oklahoma in 1890. Through his newspaper, the Langston City *Herald,* McCabe declared the Territory the "paradise of Eden and the garden of the Gods." To blacks growing restless under Southern segregation and lynch law, he added a special enticement: "Here the negro can rest from mob law, here he can be secure from every ill of the southern policies."

McCabe and his wife, Sarah, founded Langston City, an all-black community. It was named after John Mercer Langston, a black Virginia congressman who favored migration to Oklahoma and had pledged support for a black college in the town. The McCabes, who owned most of the town lots, immediately began to advertise for purchasers through the *Herald*'s network of readers in Kansas, Arkansas, Texas, Louisiana, Missouri, and Tennessee. By 1891, 200 people lived in Langston City, including a doctor, a minister, and a schoolteacher.

Langston City's fate depended largely on homesteading in the region. Nearly a year before the Sac and Fox reservation was opened to settlers, *Herald* agents spread the word throughout the South. Hundreds of African Americans arrived in time for the September 22, 1891 opening, many of them armed and reputedly ready to secure a home "at any price." Six months later, thousands of African Americans raced for the opening of the Cheyenne-Arapaho lands, and in 1893 many more staked claims in the Cherokee Strip.

Over time, a thriving farming population arose, which supported African-American business owners and professionals. By 1900 African-American farmers owned 1.5 million acres valued at $11 million. Black land ownership peaked at the turn of the 20th century. By 1910 it was in decline, and many of the children of the first generation of Exodusters now fell easy prey to the siren call of the cities.

The African-American migration to the Twin Territories produced 32 all-black towns. Boley, founded in the former Creek Nation in 1904, was the most famous. It was established by two white entrepreneurs—William Boley, a railroad manager, and Lake Moore, a former federal officeholder. They hired an African American, Tom Haynes, to promote the community. Booker T. Washington visited Boley in 1908. The town, he wrote,

> ...is striking evidence of the progress made in thirty years.... The westward movement of the negro people has brought into these new lands, not a helpless and ignorant horde of black people, but land-seekers and home-builders, men who have come prepared to build up the country....

Two years later, Boley's day in the sun was over. Agricultural prices plummeted; crops failed. In 1907 Oklahoma gained statehood, and the Democratic-dominated state legislature quickly disenfranchised black voters, and segregated public schools and accommodations. Jim Crow had come to Oklahoma.

MOVING FARTHER WEST | By the end of the 19th century, African Americans had established a number of agricultural communities in Dakota Territory and in Nebraska. Two hundred former Tennesseeans homesteaded in Harlan County, Nebraska, and in 1884 I. B. Burton, a successful farmer in Crete, Nebraska, published a letter in a Washington, D.C., newspaper: "A large company can emigrate and purchase railroad lands for about half of what it would cost single persons, or single families.... Windmills are indispensable in the far west, and one windmill could be made to answer four or five farmers each having an interest in it." Few African Americans answered Burton's call until the Kinkaid Homestead Act of 1904 threw open thousands of acres in northwestern Nebraska's Sand Hills region. By 1910, 24 families, most from Omaha, had claimed 14,000 acres of land in Cherry County. Eight years later, 185 African Americans homesteaded 40,000 acres around a small all-black community, aptly named Audacious.

Ava Speese Day wrote of her childhood in the Sand Hills: "The Negro pioneers worked hard....it was too sandy for grain so the answer was cattle....We [also] raised mules [which] brought a good price on the Omaha market." In the early 1920s, however, the state's black farm families began to leave the land and move on to cities.

In 1910 Oliver Toussaint Jackson, born in Ohio but by that time resident for

Midwest Settlement

Top right: The Oklahoma territory was created in 1866 in response to pressure from potential settlers for large tracts of land in the West. African Americans were among those who made a run to stake claims, like this family posed outside their dugout home near Guthrie in the Oklahoma Territory in 1899.

Top left: Unsettled western lands created the possibility of founding all-black towns where blacks could wield all of the economic, social, and political power. Boley, Oklahoma, was organized in 1903. This photograph depicts Boley's, town council, about 1910.

Right: The African-American population of Texas more than doubled in the last three decades of the 19th century, with citizens like the postmaster, his wife, and another resident of Littig, an all-black town outside Austin.

LITTIG, TEXAS
POST OFFICE

H 39481 Negro postmaster, with his wife, also pastor and district superintendent, Littig, Tex

25 years in Denver, made the last major attempt at black agricultural colonization on the High Plains. Inspired by Booker T. Washington's self-help philosophy, Jackson and his wife, Minerva, filed a "desert claim" for 320 acres in Colorado's Weld County, and the town of Dearfield was established. Within five years the colonists had claimed 8,000 of the county's 20,000 available acres. Dearfield's population peaked at 700 in 1921. But the lure of Denver jobs, the inability to obtain water for irrigation, and the post-World War I agricultural depression all led to the colony's demise. A bleak countryside did not help matters. One former resident recalled, "It was always the same...a lot of wind blowing...bad wind." Dearfield, like Boley, Nicodemus, and other black towns before it, slid into oblivion.

TO THE CITIES | Today, most African-American Westerners live in the region's cities. The origin of these contemporary communities lies with the rise of the black urban population during the 19th century as African-American men and women moved to Denver, San Francisco, Seattle, and Los Angeles in search of jobs in the urban economy.

By 1910 the combined black population of the five largest western cities was only 18,000—just one-fifth of the number living in Washington, D.C., at the time. In the big cities and smaller towns like Topeka, Kansas; Salt Lake City, Utah; Virginia City, Nevada; and Helena, Montana, the newcomers established churches, fraternal organizations, social clubs, and even fledgling civil-rights organizations. In their new hometowns, male and female migrants were employed as personal servants. Black men also worked as hotel waiters, railroad porters, messengers, cooks, and janitors. Some entrepreneurial African Americans operated barbershops, restaurants, and rooming houses.

Most black migrants to Colorado settled in Denver; in 1870, 56 percent of the state's African-American population lived there. One of the first was Barney Ford, who had come from Virginia in 1860. He worked as a barber and restaurant owner until he built the Inter-Ocean Hotel in 1874. For many years it was "the aristocratic hostelry of Denver." Ford later opened another hotel in Cheyenne, Wyoming. But most of the black men who came to fast-growing Denver were single laborers and construction workers. In the 1890s middle-class African Americans began to concentrate in the Five Points district, creating a stable, if increasingly segregated, community.

In 1900 black Denver boasted three newspapers, nine churches, one hotel, various restaurants and saloons, a funeral home, and a drugstore. Its professional class included two doctors, three lawyers, and numerous musicians. By 1906 Sarah Breedlove had arrived from Louisiana and married newspaper reporter Charles Walker. She became Madam C. J. Walker; her nationally marketed line of beauty products would make her one of the nation's most successful African-American entrepreneurs.

THE GOLDEN STATE | Established during the Gold Rush, San Francisco had the oldest black urban community in the West. But the number of African Americans in the city declined between 1890 and 1910 as many moved across the bay to Oakland, the city's first suburb. Most were laborers or domestic servants, but sailors, ship stewards, and dockworkers made for greater employment diversity than existed in inland communities. However, their meager wages did little to raise the overall prosperity, and most African Americans survived on the urban economy's edge.

Despite their financial difficulties, black San Franciscans created a model for organized African-American community life in the West. In 1865 they could learn the "fine art of dancing" for $3 a month at Seales Hall. Four decades later they could exhibit a flair for Shakespearean acting at Charles H. Tinsley Drama Club. These urbanites saw successful citizenship as linked to standards of Victorian civility and sought, through "refinement" and knowledge of the world, to gain the respect of their fellows, white and black.

By 1910 Los Angeles, with 7,599 African-American residents, had the largest black urban population in the West. The land boom of the 1880s had increased the city's population, allowing a few early settlers to reap immense profits. Bridget "Biddy" Mason was one of them. She had purchased a house on Spring Street in 1866 for $250; 15 years later she sold part of the property for $1,500. Mason established the city's oldest black church, First African Methodist, in 1872, and left behind a dynasty of African-American real-estate tycoons. Her son-in-law, Charles Owens, owned valuable parcels in downtown Los Angeles, and her grandson, Robert C. Owens, built a $250,000 six-story building in 1905 on the site of Biddy's original home. The *Colored American Magazine* designated him "the richest Negro west of Chicago." Robert C. Owens became a confidant of Booker T. Washington and a major contributor to Tuskegee Institute.

African-American Los Angeles grew rapidly during the 20th century's first decade. In 1903 the Southern Pacific Railroad brought 2,000 black laborers to break a strike of Mexican-American construction workers, doubling the size of the community. Intense interethnic rivalry resulted and, today, still lingers. Hundreds of black Texans also migrated to the area. Familial networks encouraged emigration. "We came here in 1902," declared a Tennessee couple. "We were doing pretty well, so we sent back home and told cousins to come along. When the cousins got here, they sent for their cousins. Pretty soon the whole community was made up of Tennessee people."

Urban boosters also helped attract new Angelenos. E. H. Rydall wrote in 1907, "Southern California is more adapted for the colored man than any other part of the United States [because] the climate...is distinctively African...this is the sunny southland in which the African thrives." The first black residential neighborhood began to evolve south of downtown, along Central Avenue. The migrants created a vibrant district, which eventually became known as the Harlem of the West.

Below, top: Although the story of homesteaders is more romantic, most black migrants moved to western cities where they found access to housing and jobs more readily than in other parts of the country. Some opened successful businesses like this barbershop.

Below, bottom: Madam C. J. Walker (1867-1919), a native of Louisiana, is perhaps the best-known of Denver's early 20th-century African-American residents. She launched a career making and marketing beauty products for African-American women.

Right: By the early 20th century, young people like these cyclists in Denver had fled from rural towns to western cities like San Francisco, Seattle, and Los Angeles.

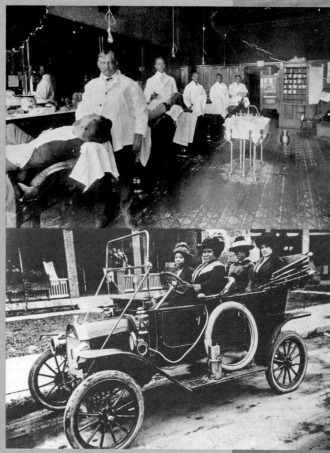

WORLD WAR II AND AFTER IN THE BLACK WEST | World War II initiated the largest migration of African Americans in the region's history. During the 1940s the West's black population grew by 443,000 (33 percent), with most of the newcomers settling in the coastal cities of California, Oregon, and Washington. The increase resulted, in the main, from the booming defense industries, which rescued black workers from decades of menial employment. Thousands more African Americans were stationed on military bases; after the war, many sent for their families and settled permanently. The World War II migration made the entire region younger, more southern, more female, and noticeably more black than ever before.

Getting to the Pacific coast in those days was not an easy task. Many migrants followed long, hot, dusty stretches of highway across Texas, New Mexico, and Arizona. Since few hotels would take them in, travelers took turns driving, and camped along the roadsides. Those making the trip by train faced three or four days on crowded, uncomfortable, and often segregated cars. But people were willing to endure these poor conditions because black workers could find decent-paying jobs in shipyards and aircraft factories all along the Pacific coast. However, they also encountered their share of problems, including unwarranted job transfers, anti-black remarks by supervisors and co-workers, and residential segregation. Fanny Christina Hill recalled her experience in the 1940s: "They did everything they could to keep you separated.... They just did not like for a Negro and a white person to get together to talk."

But black workers in the West Coast plants joined integrated unions, worked in the same buildings as whites, and lunched in the same cafeterias. For thousands of black women and men in skilled jobs, the defense industry work changed the quality of their lives. Fanny Christina Hill put it bluntly: "The War made me live better. Hitler was the one that got us out of the white folks' kitchen."

African Americans shared their nation's joy on V-J Day, 1945. But for many the celebration soon turned bittersweet. By 1947 thousands of blacks who had been "essential workers" during the war were unemployed and roaming the streets of Los Angeles, Oakland, and Portland. The postwar job outlook in Portland was so dismal that the black population declined by half between 1944 and 1947.

But in other cities black people prospered. In San Francisco African American men gained union membership and access to the skilled jobs those organizations controlled. Large numbers entered the construction trades and transportation, and a few obtained white-collar jobs in banks, insurance firms, and public utilities. Progress was slower for women; by 1950 more than half remained in domestic service, but a few were beginning to work as clerks, stenographers, and secretaries.

In Seattle, Boeing's black workforce kept growing. The Cold War required more military planes, and there was a great demand for commercial aircraft.

St. Augustine, Texas
Although agricultural towns like Dearfield, Colorado, and Nicodemus, Kansas, experienced short-term success, most of the all-black agricultural communities failed the test of time. By World War I many residents had given in to the lure of urban jobs.

Between 1945 and 1950, Seattle's black population increased by 5,000 people. By 1948 the median income of the city's African-American families was $3,334, only 4 percent below that of white families nationally.

Although African Americans continued to migrate westward after 1950, the region never again experienced the huge influxes of World War II. By 1965, the year of the Watts Uprising in Los Angeles, it was clear that racial discrimination in employment, housing, and public schools had made the region remarkably similar to the rest of the nation. Although many African-American Westerners saw their lives improved by the Civil Rights and Black Power movements, after Watts there was a palpable decline in optimism among both the middle and working classes about the region's potential for affording them opportunity and racial justice.

Even the most successful individuals now realized that thousands of other black people in South Central Los Angeles, Denver's Five Points, or Seattle's Central District faced a daunting task in overcoming both the physical and psychological barriers constructed by centuries of racism and poverty. These Westerners had finally abandoned the search for a racial promised land. Instead they chose political and cultural struggle because, for them, the West was the end of the line both socially and geographically. There was no better place to go.

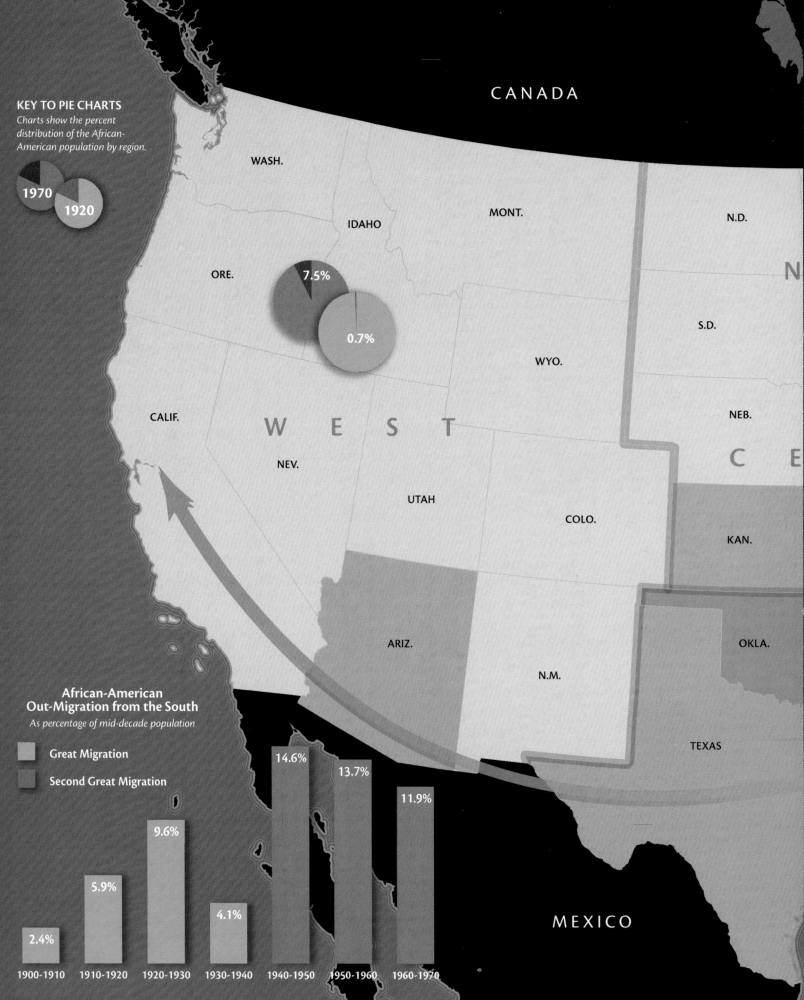

CANADA

WASH.

MONT.

N.D.

IDAHO

ORE.

7.5%

0.7%

S.D.

WYO.

CALIF.

W   E   S   T

NEB.

NEV.

C   E

UTAH

COLO.

KAN.

ARIZ.

N.M.

OKLA.

African-American Out-Migration from the South
As percentage of mid-decade population

Great Migration

Second Great Migration

TEXAS

MEXICO

2.4%

5.9%

9.6%

4.1%

14.6%

13.7%

11.9%

1900-1910   1910-1920   1920-1930   1930-1940   1940-1950   1950-1960   1960-1970

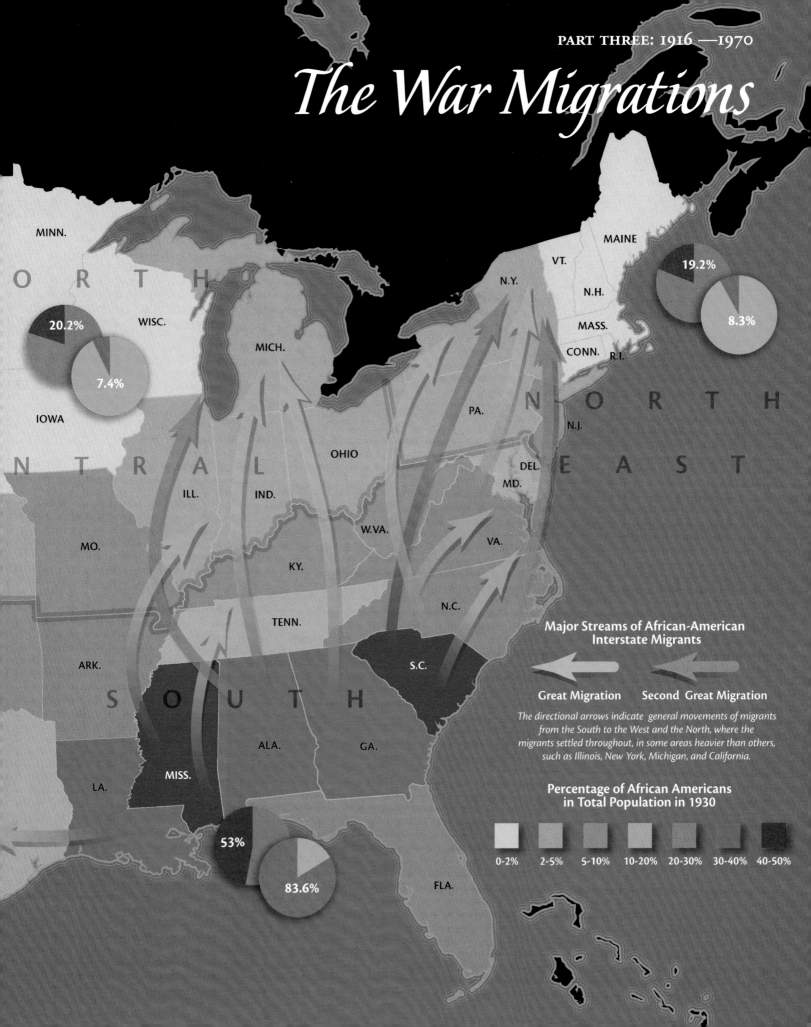

The War Migrations

Major Streams of African-American Interstate Migrants

Great Migration   Second Great Migration

The directional arrows indicate general movements of migrants from the South to the West and the North, where the migrants settled throughout, in some areas heavier than others, such as Illinois, New York, Michigan, and California.

Percentage of African Americans in Total Population in 1930

0-2%   2-5%   5-10%   10-20%   20-30%   30-40%   40-50%

The Great Migration

In the spring of 1916, the attention of the American press and public was focused on the Great War in Europe. Few noticed the tiny stream of Southern black men coming north to work on the Pennsylvania Railroad. But between 1916 and 1918 alone, nearly 400,000 African Americans—500 each day—took what they hoped was a journey into freedom.

The migration was a watershed in the history of African Americans. It lessened their overwhelming concentration in the South, opened up industrial jobs to people who had up to then been mostly farmers, and gave the first significant impetus to their urbanization.

In 1910 seven million of the nation's eight million African Americans resided below the Cotton Curtain. But over the next 15 years, more than one-tenth of the country's black population would voluntarily move north. The Great Migration, which lasted until 1930, was the first step in the full nationalization of the African-American population.

LEAVING THE SOUTH | Several factors precipitated one of the largest population shifts in the country's history. In 1898 the tiny boll weevil invaded Texas and proceeded to eat its way east across the South. Crops were devastated, thousands of agricultural workers were thrown off the land, and the long reign of King Cotton as the region's economic backbone was finally brought to an end.

Even more important was World War I. Since the 1850s, massive numbers of European industrial workers had been immigrating to the United States—by 1900, more than a million were arriving each year. The onset of war in Europe, in 1914, brought all that to a halt within three years.

Although the country did not enter the conflict until 1917, it had been supplying the European combatants since hostilities began. The cessation of immigration resulted in an acute labor shortage at a time when workers were needed to gear up the arms and war-supplies industries. The war created an economic boom, and

New York's African-American population stood at 91,700 in 1910; within ten years, it had reached 152,400, and by the time the Great Migration was over in 1930, there were 327,700 black New Yorkers. This couple in furs stands alongside their car in Harlem, New York, 1933.

an alternative supply of labor was needed to meet the increased demand. The South, with its surplus of workers resulting from agricultural disaster and chronic underdevelopment, clearly fit the bill.

The region in 1916 suffered not only from underdevelopment, but also from isolation. Its separation from mainstream America was the result of unique historical factors: the institution of slavery, its slow recovery from the devastating Civil War, and its overreliance on cotton as the region's economic engine. The South was behind the rest of the country at the start of Reconstruction, and its disadvantage only grew over time. It had fewer schools, lower literacy levels, and poorer basic services. The rural areas had slow and inadequate communication with the outside world. In comparison to their counterparts in the Northeast and Midwest, southern workers were grossly underpaid, their wages no more than two-thirds of those paid elsewhere in the country. Indeed, the region was more of a colony exporting raw materials than an equal trading partner to the more economically advanced North. Large numbers of skilled workers, white and black, were trapped.

MOUNTING VIOLENCE | In addition, the political and social climate was deteriorating. Between 1890 and 1910 most African Americans in the South had lost the right to vote through restrictive requirements such as property qualifications, poll taxes, literacy tests, and the "grandfather clause" that limited the vote to those whose grandfathers were registered voters, thus disqualifying blacks who had gotten the franchise only with the Fifteenth Amendment in 1870. The tightening of Jim Crow laws led many to leave the South, as illustrated in Alabamian Charles "Cow Cow" Davenport's "Jim Crow Blues":

> *I'm tired of being Jim Crowed, gonna leave this Jim Crow town,*
> *Doggone my black soul, I'm sweet Chicago bound,*
> *Yes, Sir, I'm leavin' here, from this ole Jim Crow town.*
>
> *I'm going up North, where they think money grows on trees,*
> *I don't give a doggone, if ma black soul should freeze*
> *I'm goin' where I don't need no B.V.D.s.*

Intimidation and outright violence were also used not only to disenfranchise the black community, but also to control and terrorize it. At least two to three people were lynched every week. Although lynching had been used for decades, it evolved in the late 19th and early 20th centuries, becoming more sadistic and exhibitionist. People were horribly tortured and mutilated for hours in front of huge crowds that included women and children.

Though economic, social, environmental, and political forces were crucial to

Land of Cotton

While other crops were economically significant, cotton was by far the South's and the country's most important staple crop. By 1860 cotton exports amounted to more than 50 percent annually of the dollar value of all United States exports. After the Civil War, the cotton-growing industry got on its feet again by development of a "cropping system." The planter gave each tenant a plot of land and a portion of the crop: half the crop, or less if the planter furnished the tools, seed, and mules. This group of African-American men, women, and children stand in a cotton field, some holding baskets containing handpicked cotton.

the migration, so too was the indomitable will of the African-American migrants—their burning desire to control their own destinies. The decision to pull up one's long-planted roots and journey into the unknown is not easily made. For southern migrants, it was a balancing act. Serious questions had to be answered: How bad is it here? How good is it there? Who in the family will make the journey? How will those left behind be cared for? How much will it cost? Where will I live?

MIGRATION FEVER | As reports spread of plentiful job opportunities that existed above the Mason-Dixon Line, the workers' situation began to change. They heard fantastic promises but were cautious and awaited reports from pioneers who went north to test the waters. One worker said, "Of course everything they say about the North ain't true, but there's so much of it true, don't mind the other."

Every conceivable method was used to draw the black labor supply from the South. Labor agents from northern companies stood on street corners offering train passes to the young, male, and strong. It soon sparked a migration fever. Black newspapers carried job advertisements touting good wages and other advantages of living in the North. They also published success stories about recent migrants already making more money than they had ever dreamed possible. Their letters confirming success were read out loud in churches, barbershops, and meeting halls. Southern blacks soaked up all the information available: Was this real? Would they pay? What was it like up North?

"TO THE NORTH"

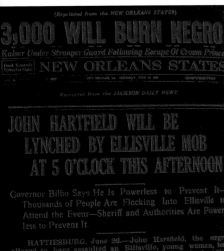

Still, not everyone wanted to go north, and in fact the migrants were not typical Southerners in many ways. Over half came from cities and towns and had long abandoned work on the land. The great majority departing from the Alabama steel towns of Birmingham and Bessemer were experienced miners heading for the coal fields of Kentucky, West Virginia, and Pennsylvania. Despite the rural nature of the South, the migrants came from a variety of nonfarming occupations. Surveys done in Pittsburgh and Chicago showed that only a quarter of the migrants in those cities came from agricultural backgrounds.

Rarely did young and old, able-bodied and dependent, parent and child migrate together. It was too expensive. Young men between 18 and 35 who had worked as unskilled industrial laborers were usually the first to go. Many were married and had children, and expected to reunite with their families as soon as they had "made their way."

The reasons for leaving varied: "freedom and independence," better wages, educational opportunities for their children. Still others intended to stay only long enough to save some money and return. One migrant, asked why she left the South, replied: "I left Georgia because I wanted better privileges." Did that mean mixed schools and association with white people generally? "No," she responded, "I don't care nothing about that, but I just want to be somewhere where I won't be scared all the time that something is going to break loose."

The migrants headed to the large industrial centers—Detroit, Pittsburgh, New York, and most of all Chicago. Leaving home was a wrenching experience, though mitigated by exhilaration as hope for the future in some instances drowned out the accustomed sounds of the past. A migrant from Gulfport, Mississippi, reported from Chicago, "I'm tickled to death over this place. Sorry I was not here years ago."

Though many influences surrounded them, migrants made their own decisions about when and where to go, and what type of job to take once they got there. They constantly attempted to control the world around them by negotiation, bargaining, and compromise.

THE JOURNEY NORTH | The journey north was made by train, boat, bus, sometimes car, and even horse-drawn cart. It was most often a long, grueling experience; the travelers confronted segregated waiting rooms, buses, and train coaches, as well as unfamiliar procedures and unfriendly conductors. Very little food or drink was available. Fares were expensive, deterring many would-be migrants from making the trip. Regular passenger fares—2 cents per mile in 1915—skyrocketed within three years to 24 cents a mile.

Getting to the "promised land" did not come cheap, so many migrants made the journey in stages, stopping off and working in places in the South, then continuing on their way. This so-called step migration could take a very long time. Painter Jacob Lawrence recalled that his family was "moving up the coast, as many families were during that migration....We moved up to various cities until we arrived—the last two cities I can remember before moving to New York were Easton, Pennsylvania, and Philadelphia."

During the early period, northern employers assisted the migrants with transportation. Their agents gave out travel passes whose cost was often deducted from future wages. These agents, who were paid a flat fee for each worker they produced, were selective, favoring those who appeared in good health, men over women, the young over the old.

The railroads, in dire need of workers to transport war materiel and maintain the rail lines, were among the first employers to recruit. In the summer of 1916, the Pennsylvania Railroad brought 16,000 southern African Americans north to do unskilled labor. The agents from the Illinois Central Railroad issued passes to bring workers to Chicago. Other industries central to the burgeoning war economy, such as the steel mills, made great and unprecedented promises to prospective African-American employees. These workers were poor and eager to take advantage of any opportunity. "Just give us a chance" was their common refrain.

So many Southerners made their way north on their own that employers soon cut back on travel passes. Meanwhile, local authorities were trying to deny the agents access to the black community. In some cases, their passes were not honored at the depots. On many occasions, travelers were pulled off trains to prevent them from leaving the South.

NETWORKS AND MEDIA | More influential than the agents in the long run were family and friends. Prospective migrants financed their tickets by selling all their possessions. When that was not enough, families pooled their resources to send one member. With the breadwinner gone north, other family members had to support themselves until the migrant made good. Many women provided family support by taking jobs as domestics. They also saved money to buy their own tickets. One wrote, "So many women are wanting to go...we can't get work here so much now, the white women tell us we just want to make money to go North and we do." Both parents sometimes went north while grandparents or other family members cared for their children.

Letters from family and friends already settled in the North provided specific accounts of jobs and housing, encouraging others to make the journey. A few dollars enclosed in the envelope lent further legitimacy to the writers' claims.

These letters were often read in churches on Sunday mornings. For many, the Great Migration was like a religious revival or the flight out of Egypt. Churches formed migration clubs to exchange information and facilitate passage north.

Moving North

Above: "Migrants came north in thousands, tens of thousands, hundreds of thousands—from the docks of Norfolk, Savannah, Jacksonville, Tampa, Mobile, New Orleans, and Galveston; from the cotton fields of Mississippi, and the coal mines and steel-mills of Alabama and Tennessee; from workshops and wash-tubs and brickyards and kitchens they came, until the number, by conservative estimate, went well over the million and a half mark" wrote James Weldon Johnson in *Black Manhattan.*

Right: Once a wealthy New York City suburb, by 1930 Harlem was a thriving black enclave in which two-thirds of the city's 328,000 African-American residents lived.

Leaders were chosen to correspond with northern industries, newspapers, and placement services on the entire group's behalf.

Many African-American newspapers were leading players in the epic drama that was the Great Migration. By the turn of the century, the black press was becoming a more effective weapon for the community in its struggle against racism. To respond to the demand of a growing racial consciousness, 50 new black periodicals were created. Some, like *The Urban League Bulletin,* were founded to respond to the migrants' needs. Established newspapers, such as the *Amsterdam News* in New York, covered issues vital to the newcomers. Robert Abbott's *Chicago Defender,* however, was the unquestioned star.

THE CHICAGO DEFENDER | The *Defender* emphasized southern racial injustice and provided African Americans in the region with information they could read nowhere else, including advertisements from employers. Its loud and unceasing advocacy of African-American migration infuriated white southern commercial and political interests. Police in several cities confiscated copies, but vendors responded by smuggling them in from rural areas. Pullman porters secretly delivered bales of papers on their trips from Chicago. Copies were mailed in packages that disguised their contents.

One Mississippi county declared the *Defender* German propaganda and banned it. All of this intrigue only added to the paper's popularity. Though circulation estimates vary, Abbott claimed that during the Great Migration the *Defender* sold 150,000 copies an issue, with a total readership far exceeding that number.

In January 1917 the newspaper created its own migration event. Banner headlines proclaimed, "Millions to Leave the South. Northern Invasion will Start in Spring—Bound for the Promised Land." The article promised reduced fares and special accommodations starting on May 15, 1917.

The Great Northern Drive never happened. The *Chicago Defender* was forced to declare that "there were no special trains scheduled to leave southern stations on May 15th, and that this date had been selected simply because it was a good time to leave for the north, so as to become acclimated." But the forces were already in motion. Thousands of migrants, managing to scrape together the money to pay full fares, boarded the northbound trains.

Newspapers

The *Chicago Defender* was the first African-American newspaper to have a circulation of more than 100,000. Its actual readership was probably five times higher. Flora Sengstacke, mother of Robert Sengstacke Abbott, founder and publisher of the *Defender,* holds a copy of the newspaper just off the press in 1921.

Macon Ga April 2 1918
To the Bethenlem Baptist Associa
tion reading in the chicaga
Defender of your help
securing positions I want
to know if it is any way
you can oblige me by
helping me to get out
there as I am anxious
to leave here + every
thing so hard here I hope
you will oblige in help
ing me to leave here
ans at once to 309
middle St Mr J. H. Adam

On April 22, 1918, Mrs. J. H. Adams, from Macon, Georgia, wrote to the Bethlehem Baptist Association of Chicago. She had read about the group in the *Chicago Defender* and hoped its members could help her "get out there as I am anxious to leave here." Black newspapers were a lifeline for potential migrants.

A NEW INDUSTRIAL LANDSCAPE | The Great Migration spurred a massive increase in the African-American communities in northern cities. In the decade between 1910 and 1920, New York's black population rose by 66 percent, Chicago's by 148 percent, Philadelphia's by 500 percent. Detroit experienced an amazing growth rate of 611 percent.

In the Motor City, Henry Ford started a small experiment to see if black workers could be used on the assembly line. In 1910 fewer than 600 of the more than 100,000 automotive workers in the United States were African American. By 1929 there were 25,000 and Ford employed approximately half of them.

Once settled, usually with the aid of family members or friends from "down home," migrants strove to achieve their vision of the American Dream. Long hours and several jobs were not unusual. The great majority were on the bottom rungs of the economic ladder. Many had been skilled craftsmen in the South but were barred from such jobs in the North by company policy, union regulations, or white-only traditions within various trades.

There was also a wide disparity in pay scales. In Alabama unskilled foundry workers earned $2.50 for a ten-hour day. The same workers in Illinois took home $4.25. As a result, southern migrants, at times unwittingly, worked for less than the going rate. White workers were decidedly unhappy at being undercut.

The newcomers entered a labor market at the rear of a delicately balanced ethnic employment line already sustained by low wages and vulnerable workers: the 25 million Europeans who had entered the country between 1871 and 1915, and their descendants. By 1910 the foreign-born made up a quarter of the nation's workforce. In many of the key industries, such as mining, clothing factories, steel mills, slaughterhouses, and packinghouses, they constituted a clear majority.

NEW JOBS FOR THE MIGRANTS | The arrival of masses of southern black workers changed the face of the industrial world. Employers' initial reluctance to tap this "inferior" stock was quickly erased. "If it hadn't been for the negro at that time," said a former official of the Carnegie Steel Company, "we could hardly have carried on our operations."

The migrants also became easy scapegoats. In the eyes of most whites, low wages, deteriorating factory conditions, unemployed white males, all had but one cause: Black workers had been brought in. The labor movement, which had been struggling over the years to organize foreign and native white workers, was

Left: The National Urban League was formed to counsel and assist migrants from the South by responding to their social and economic needs. This included locating housing and jobs. Here, young men wait for jobs outside the Chicago Urban League employment office.

Below left: The automobile factories in Detroit started to hire black men in 1916. By 1929, twenty-five thousand African Americans were employed at the assembly lines.

Below right: It was not rare for skilled southern workers to become laborers in the North. The former coal miner pictured was a janitor in Chicago, a tinsmith and a clergyman worked as laborers in the stockyards, and the owner of a café became an elevator man. This trend was common in other cities such as Detroit, Philadelphia, and New York.

overwhelmed with the introduction of southern black labor. Employers were quite simply able to operate as if the movement did not exist. From the beginning they had tried with varying success to discipline organized workers by breaking their strikes with cheaper newcomers. To protect themselves, unions in turn had welcomed the new labor to their ranks. Employers found at last, with black labor, a force that local unions were unwilling to absorb. American race prejudice was simply too big an obstacle to overcome.

The migration altered black employment patterns dramatically. Between 1910 and 1920 the number of African Americans in the manufacturing industries increased by 40 percent. In Chicago in 1910, 51 percent of the black male labor force was engaged in domestic and personal service, but ten years later that figure had been cut nearly in half. In 1910 only 67 blacks were working in the packinghouses of the Windy City; in 1920 there were nearly 3,000.

Wages varied by city, industry, and the worker's skill level, with the average migrant earning about $25 for a 48- to 60-hour workweek, while Pullman porters could take home as much as $35. Wages remained fairly constant during the migration period, but prices rose quite sharply in a war-related inflationary spiral. In 1919 the Bureau of Labor Statistics estimated that $43 was the weekly income necessary for a family of five to maintain an acceptable standard of living. Obviously, on the migrants' salary alone, most families could not achieve this standard.

Many had been shortchanged in wage agreements that they signed before leaving the South. Those who avoided that pitfall fared little better. Arriving in the North with few assets, they were in no position to bargain over wages. The high costs of food and lodging were sufficient incentives to force many to take the first available job.

After wages, the most common complaint among migrants was lack of opportunity for advancement. The foremen, they stated, favored white workers in the distribution of work, recognition of efficiency, and the opportunity to work overtime. This preferential treatment for whites cost the African-American workers dearly. The denial of promotions cost them even more.

The low wages paid to black men forced women into the workplace. In Chicago in the 1920s, over 85 percent of African-American women were on the work rolls—21 percent in manufacturing and 64 percent in domestic service. By comparison, only 31 percent of native-born white women held jobs.

HARD LIFE IN THE NORTH | The migration years saw the emergence of service organizations to provide aid and support to the newcomers, such as the National Urban League, founded in 1911 in New York. The Chicago Urban League opened its doors in 1917, and in its first two years some 55,000 migrants sought assistance in finding jobs and housing. The National Association for the

If You are a Stranger in the City

If you want a job   If you want a place to liv
If you are having trouble with your employe
If you want information or advice of any kin
CALL UPON

The CHICAGO LEAGUE ON URBAN
CONDITIONS AMONG NEGROES
3719 South State Street
Telephone Douglas 9098   T. ARNOLD HILL, Executive Secreta
No charges—no fees. We want to help YO

Educating Newcomers

Above: Organizations such as the Chicago Urban League took great pains to educate newcomers on correct decorum in public. Old-time residents feared a backlash on the whole community from any indiscretions by the migrants. They urged them to forget their "rural ways." The handbill urged strict observation of laws and customs and printed a list of 26 don'ts.

Right: World War I led to jobs that had been reserved for men becoming available to women. Most industrial jobs that women held during the early years of the Great Migration were handed back to men after the war. This photograph of women workers was taken in 1919.

Advancement of Colored People (NAACP) and similar organizations provided a needed lifeline for incoming migrants.

Besides the white-black competition for employment in the cities, there was also white-black competition for living space. Prior to the migration, African Americans were often dispersed in small clusters in several city neighborhoods, where they lived in relative obscurity and invisibility. But soon white opposition effectively closed the market to newcomers, thereby creating ghettos. Whites also fled the areas where black migrants concentrated "as if from a plague." City government, banks, and realtors conspired to keep African Americans' residential opportunities constricted.

On a single day in Chicago, real-estate brokers had over 600 black families applying for housing, with only 53 units available. When the migrants did find housing accommodations, they were usually dilapidated and barely habitable. Landlords maximized their profits by dividing larger units, with no alterations, into several tiny flats. Black neighborhoods became seriously overcrowded as a result. In Cleveland the population density in black areas was 35 to 40 persons per acre, while citywide it was only half that.

The combination of overcrowding, poverty, and poor access to quality medical treatment—even in the North there were few black physicians, and hospitals were generally segregated—ensured a variety of serious health problems in African-American communities. Working long, arduous hours in badly ventilated spaces, coming home to equally unhealthy conditions, getting insufficient rest and nutrition made migrants particularly susceptible to many infectious illnesses. African-Americans' death rates were consistently higher than those of whites. Children were even more at risk. A shocking number died before the age of ten; more than a quarter of these succumbed before their first birthday. The mortality rate for black infants was twice that of white babies. The deaths soared during the steamy summer months in overcrowded slums.

In some cities the migrants were removed from other sectors of the African-American community. The black elite sought to distance itself from the newcomers, citing their lack of education and rural background. Black migrants responded to social isolation by forming communities that were comprised of people from the southern areas they had left behind. In northern cities one could find blocks of people from the same general area of Georgia, Alabama, Mississippi, Louisiana, or the Carolinas. Throughout the urban North, the migration brought concentrations of African Americans, and the combination of concentration and hope produced vibrant black communities.

MIGRATION AND RELIGION | The church was the cornerstone of the community, providing not only guidance but also relief. Besides the established churches, small Holiness or Pentecostal storefront churches with highly emotional services developed during the migration. Their pastors were migrants themselves who worked during the day, and they catered mostly to the newcomers. By 1919 there were more than a hundred black storefront churches in Chicago, and in 1926, 150 blocks in Harlem counted 140 churches. They contrasted with the 45 more middle-class churches that had been prevalent in the northern black communities before the war. These more established churches grew rapidly too as Southerners became used to city ways and joined them in great numbers, leaving the storefront establishments to the new arrivals.

Other religious movements developed as well and recruited heavily in the migrant population. Their focus on racial consciousness and pride was a powerful magnet to the Southerners in search of new identities. Noble Drew Ali, originally Timothy Drew from North Carolina, organized the Moorish Science Temple of America in 1913 in Newark, New Jersey. Drew proclaimed himself a prophet ordained by Allah and mixed some Islamic tenets into his teachings. In 1915 Prophet F. S. Cherry from Tennessee established the Church of God, a Jewish movement in Philadelphia that still retained numerous Christian elements and taught that God, Jesus, and other biblical figures were black. The Nation of Islam was established in 1931 in Detroit by Wallace Fard Muhammad—believed to be from Pakistan. He was succeeded in 1934 by Elijah Poole, a migrant from Georgia who became Elijah Muhammad.

Migrants also followed charismatic leaders, such as Father Divine and Daddy Grace. Father Divine, a Southern migrant, established the Peace Mission Movement in Brooklyn around 1912. Calling himself God, he preached racial and gender equality and counted tens of thousands among his followers. Bishop Charles M. Grace, known as Sweet Daddy Grace, was born in the Cape Verde Islands, off Senegal, and migrated to Massachusetts in 1903. He founded the United House of Prayer for All People, a Pentecostal church, around 1919.

What the Southerners found in these movements, according to African-American anthropologist and Harlem Renaissance activist Arthur Huff Fauset, was a response to their particular needs as migrants:

> It must come as a great relief as well as release to such people to enter into the spirit of a group like one of the holiness cults, with its offer of assurance through grace and sanctification, and the knowledge that they will be aided not only in their efforts to support their customary burdens, but that in addition they will be equipped to measure arms with the white man, something they scarcely dreamed of doing previous to their advent into the North.

THE RED SUMMER | The first years of the Great Migration would see an unprecedented wave of mob violence sweep the nation. Twenty-six race riots—in cities large and small, North and South—would claim the lives of scores of African Americans. But the migrants did not instigate this bloody wave of lawlessness; it was, in most cases, directed at them.

The so-called Red Summer of 1919 actually began two years earlier in East St. Louis, Illinois, in July 1917. It was the only one of the battles to be directly linked to racial conflict in the workplace, but white workers' fear of job competition was likely behind all of them. The East St. Louis riot began after African-American workers were hired to break a strike at an aluminum plant. A delegation of trade unionists met with the mayor and demanded that black migration to the town be stopped. As they left the meeting, they were told that a black man had accidentally shot a white man during a holdup. In a few minutes, the rumor spread that the shooting was intentional and involved an insulted white woman, then white girls.

Mobs quickly took to the streets, threatening and attacking any blacks they could find. The local police made no attempt to control the situation. Some of the whites later drove through the main black neighborhood firing indiscriminately into homes. Before the rampage ended, 48 African Americans were dead, hundreds injured, and more than 300 buildings destroyed.

Chicago's turn came on July 27, 1919, as the temperature soared into the nineties. Several black children drifted into waters off a public beach, by custom reserved for whites. Stones were thrown at them and one child drowned. A crowd of blacks and whites gathered at the scene. When a black man was arrested on a white's complaint while a white man, identified by black witnesses as a suspect, was not, blacks attacked the arresting white officer and the riot was under way. The

Church Aid

Churches sent letters to northern industries, asking for assistance to move and work. One such letter was sent from Mobile, Alabama, on April 21, 1917: "Dear Sirs: We have a club of 108 good men wants work we are willing to go north or west but we are not able to pay rail road fare now if you can help us get work and get to it please answer at once. Hope to hear from you."

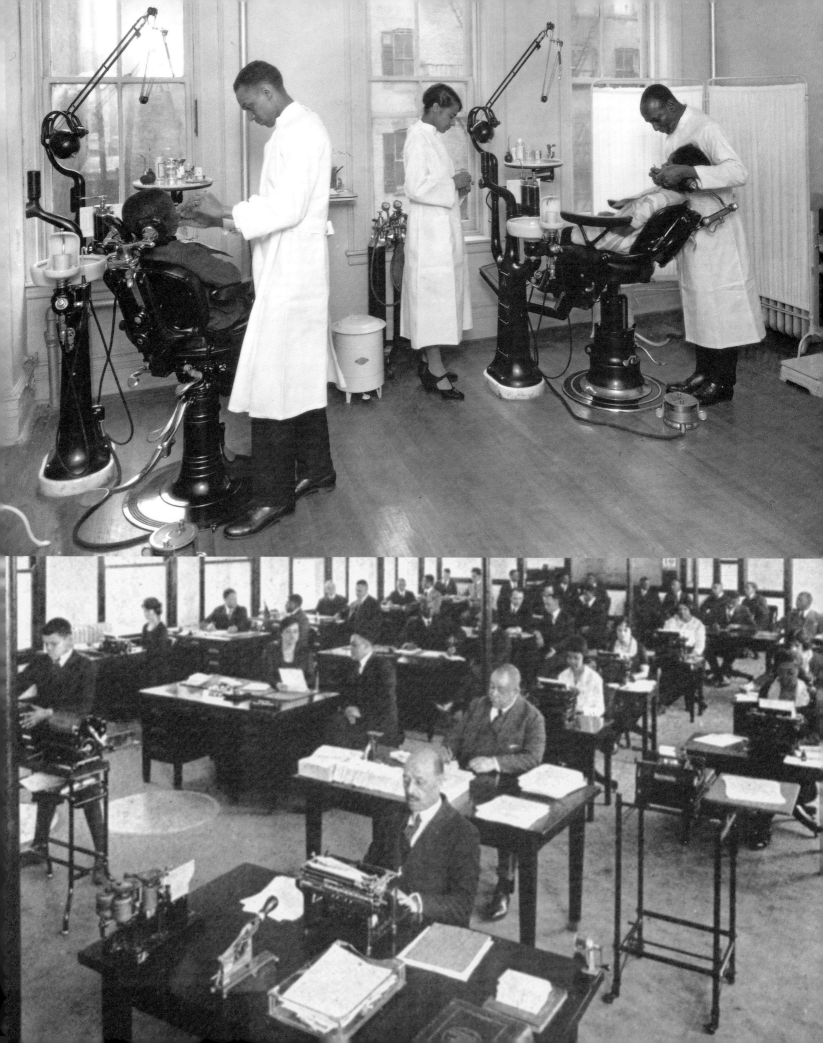

Career Opportunities

Left: A new professional elite developed during the migration. It was made up of men and sometimes women who achieved status by virtue of their education and training. The migration greatly expanded the market for African-American businesses. In New York, black ownership rose from 12 percent in 1915 to 40 percent in 1928. The most successful black businesses were ones in fields where whites would not serve blacks: restaurants, insurance, funeral homes, tailor shops, beauty shops, health care, and saloons.

Above: The Harlem Renaissance flourished from the 1920s to the 1930s. For the first time, African-American literature, music, and visual arts entered mainstream America. In this 1924 picture, from left to right, are: Langston Hughes, Charles S. Johnson, E. Franklin Frazier, Rudolph Fisher, and Hubert T. Delany.

violence was confined mainly to the south side of the city, where 90 percent of the African-American population lived.

In the course of several days of rioting, both blacks and whites were beaten. Thirty-eight people were killed, 23 of them black, and 537 were wounded; most of the one thousand families left homeless were African Americans. Although the other riots during that terrible summer varied in ferocity, it was made abundantly clear that race mattered very much in urban America.

Two years after the Red Summer, a riot erupted in Tulsa, Oklahoma. On May 30, 1921, Dick Rowland, a young black man accused of sexually assaulting a white woman in an elevator, was arrested. On May 31 the *Tulsa Tribune* published a fictitious news story stating Rowland scratched the woman's hands and face and tore at her clothes. By 10:30 p.m., a mob of nearly 2,000 white people surrounded the jail, ready to lynch the man. In hopes of defending him, a group of blacks, who were previously turned away, returned to the jail to assist the sheriff. But before they could return to Greenwood—a predominantly black community that achieved such levels of wealth that it earned the reputation as the "Negro Wall Street of America"—the Tulsa Riot began. In its aftermath, more than 300 African Americans were murdered and nearly 6,000 were imprisoned. Half of Tulsa's black population, and as many as 2,500 people, left town, some temporarily but many definitively.

THE QUEST FOR POLITICAL POWER | Their painful experience of disenfranchisement in the South, coupled with their belief in the power of the ballot, led many migrants to register to vote almost immediately after arriving in the North. Having received so little benefit from their tax dollars for so long, African Americans now sought political representation. Members of this new electorate brought with them bitter memories of political exclusion. Some had witnessed firsthand the violence and intimidation used against would-be black voters; many others had been told of them. Most, if not all, of these negative events were perpetrated under the auspices of the Democratic Party. A laborer originally from Alabama told an investigator that he could never vote for a Democrat as long as he kept his memory.

Their loyalty to the Republicans, however, did little at first to advance the interests of black migrants. But Republicans were more likely to field strong black candidates in predominantly African-American districts. The migrants firmly believed that electing such candidates was the key to achieving power, even if, as was often the case, the candidates were selected by a white political machine.

Chicago was one of the first cities where African Americans attained a measure of political influence, as a number of black politicians rose to prominence. Perhaps the most outstanding was Oscar DePriest, who became Chicago's first black councilman in 1915. In 1928 DePriest became the first black elected to the United States House of Representatives in the 20th century, a defining moment in African-America's political history. In 1935 Arthur W. Mitchell, a white Democrat, defeated him. This election signaled the beginning of the seismic shift of blacks' political allegiance from the party of Abraham Lincoln and emancipation to that of Franklin D. Roosevelt and the New Deal.

Black Nationalism, spurred in particular by Marcus Garvey, became an important part of the sociopolitical landscape. Garvey had formed the Universal Negro Improvement Association (UNIA) in his native Jamaica in 1914 and brought it to New York three years later. He drew his following largely from the lower end of the economic spectrum—people who believed that middle-class black leaders had no concern for the masses. A large part of his followers were Southern migrants. Besides advocating going back to Africa, Garvey and the UNIA promoted economic independence

and racial pride, crucial issues to people who had faced contempt, violent racism, and socioeconomic dependence in the South, and were determined to improve their lot in the North.

LEGACIES | Though they faced discrimination, exclusion, and violence, African-American migrants never stopped moving forward. In 1890, 63 percent of all black male laborers worked in agriculture. By 1930 only 42 percent did so. During that period, the number of African-American schoolteachers more than doubled, the number of black-owned businesses tripled, and the literacy rate soared from 39 to 85 percent.

Many newcomers discovered their entrepreneurial talents as storeowners, real-estate brokers, funeral directors, and providers of various skilled services to their community and to the larger population. The large numbers of migrants resulted in the formation of new institutions. By the mid-1920s, there were over 200 black hospitals and 25 black nursing schools in the United States.

Power to the People

The UNIA became the largest mass movement in African-American history, with members throughout the Caribbean, Africa, South America, and Great Britain. UNIA parades in Harlem attracted thousands of marchers and spectators who took pride in the strength, discipline, and display of power of "the New Negro."

Under the banner of black self-help, several social service organizations were founded to aid migrants and, more generally, uplift the black community from the inside. Many northern churches also established recreation centers and welfare agencies to respond to the needs of their members.

A new spirit prevailed in the arts as well. Mamie Smith from Cincinnati did one of the first commercial recordings by a black artist. Her "Crazy Blues" sold two million copies and she earned nearly $100,000 in royalties. Her success ushered in an era of "race records" and recognition on the part of the recording industry that a significant market existed within the black community. Race records quickly became big business.

The 1920s saw the emergence of the New Negro Movement, later called the Harlem Renaissance. Writers, poets, painters, musicians, and sculptors took some of their inspiration from the lives and struggles of the newcomers to the North. But, as Langston Hughes wrote, "The ordinary Negroes hadn't heard of the Negro Renaissance. And if they had, it hadn't raised their wages any." Nevertheless, the movement was a reflection of the racial consciousness and pride that people felt in the urban North, and it produced important works in all facets of the arts.

In the wake of the 1921 Tulsa Race Riot, at least two thousand African Americans left Greenwood, temporarily or permanently. In search of the administration of justice, the Oklahoma legislature in 1997 created the 1921 Tulsa Race Riot Commission.. The 11-member committee identified survivors, created a historical account of the riot, and favored recommendations for reparations.

Many scholars have noted that African Americans seemed to leave the South uncounseled by the black leadership. Although Booker T. Washington died in 1915 and did not see the mass exodus, it is clear from his pronouncements that he would have opposed it. He often said, "the Negro is at his best in the South" and would find there greater economic opportunity and a higher moral life. The *New York Age* warned skilled southern workmen "to think carefully" before migrating where skilled jobs were hard to get. Professor Kelly Miller, of Howard University, declared, "The Negro's industrial opportunities lie in the black belts."

Yet ultimately, leaving the South was not about economic opportunity or living a "higher moral life." Most migrants paid dearly, in some coin or other, for their departure. The Great Migration was about African Americans starting over and making sacrifices for future generations. As W. E. B. Du Bois concluded, the journey north represented not the end of a struggle but only its beginning.

The Second Great Migration

1940 TO 1970

The dramatic exodus of African Americans from countryside to city and from South to North during World War I and the decade that followed brought with it major changes in all dimensions of African-American life—economic, political, social, and cultural. The Great Migration was, up to that point, the largest, voluntary internal movement of black people ever seen.

Somewhat ironically, the Great Migration's sequel—during and following the Second World War—has not been given its own title by scholars. It is in fact often considered to be merely a continuation of the earlier movement following a momentary pause during the Depression. In many ways, however, this second huge exodus from the South deserves a separate identity; it was larger, more sustained, different in character and direction, and it precipitated an even more radical and lasting transformation in American life than its better-known predecessor.

THE NUMBERS | Between 1910 and 1940 roughly one-and-a-half-million black Americans left the South for northern cities, but during the decade that followed the Crash of 1929, this emigration slowed to a trickle. However, with America's entry into World War II looming on the horizon, the exodus of blacks from their southern homeland resumed. Between 1940 and 1950 another one-and-a-half-million African Americans left the South. The migration continued at roughly the same pace over the next 20 years. By 1970 the geographic map of black America had fundamentally changed. Roughly one of every seven black Southerners pulled up stakes and headed north or west. Both their places of origin and destination shifted from earlier patterns.

The western states, especially California, witnessed an explosive growth of their African-American populations. In 1930 some 50,200 African Americans lived in Los Angeles, San Francisco, and Oakland; 20 years later the three cities' combined black population had soared to 254,124. Altogether, 339,000 African Americans moved to the western half of the country during the 1940s, in contrast to a mere

The demand for labor—particularly in the booming war industries—provided new employment opportunities for African Americans during World War II. African-American women especially benefited from growing employment opportunities; during the war the percentage of black women with industrial jobs rose from 6.5 percent to 18 percent. Shown here are women welders at the Landers, Frary, and Clark plant in New Britain, Connecticut, 1943.

49,000 in the previous decade. Over the 30-year course of the migration, arrivals to the West remained constant; those to the Northeast steadily increased while those to the North Central region decreased considerably.

Most of the migrants to California came from southwest and central states like Louisiana, Texas, Arkansas, and Oklahoma. Almost three times as many African Americans left this region between 1940 and 1950 as did during the previous 30 years. The South Atlantic states, however, remained the most frequent point of origin for migrants, contributing from over a third to 40 percent of those leaving the South in each decade. This is particularly striking, given that Delaware, Maryland, the District of Columbia, and Florida usually had net gains in their black population. Thus the combined totals for the region actually mask the fact that the two Carolinas and Georgia experienced a virtual hemorrhage of their black citizenry. Well over half a million African Americans left those three states in each of the three postwar decades.

The centuries-long era during which black Americans had lived mostly in the rural South and worked primarily in agriculture was over. By the end of World War II, the number of African Americans living in cities exceeded those in rural areas, and by the time the migration concluded in 1970, African Americans had become a more urbanized population than their white fellow citizens. By 1950 most blacks no longer worked in agriculture or as domestic labor—the occupations that had always characterized their existence in America—and the population was more evenly distributed throughout the nation.

OUT OF THE SOUTH | As with most migrations, there were several factors that drew African Americans out of the South and into cities throughout the nation. The most important was the massive collapse of southern agricultural employment. The principal factors contributing to this economic disaster were great declines in the prices of sugar, tobacco, and especially cotton coupled with the negative effects of federal policies designed to rescue southern planters (at the expense of the workers) and the restructuring of commodity production that followed.

With the onset of the worldwide depression, cotton prices fell from 18 cents a pound in 1928 to less than 6 cents a pound in 1931. Despite crashing prices, demand was suppressed further by continued high production that bloated surpluses; in the face of the price collapse, farmers harvested a record crop in 1933. Cutting production seemed to be the only solution. The Roosevelt administration achieved this by paying farmers to reduce the land planted and by buying up surpluses already on the market. Although the U.S. Supreme Court declared the initial program, the Agricultural Adjustment Act, unconstitutional, a revised system was put into place during the late 1930s that achieved the same ends.

Farm owners now received direct subsidies for taking land out of production,

Hitching North

During the Depression, the migration out of the South was insignificant. Finding work anywhere was a challenge. Trapped in the South, African Americans often could rely only on day work. They traveled great distances for a day or a few weeks of work as cotton or strawberry pickers. These migrant workers were traveling north from North Carolina to harvest potatoes.

as well as so-called parity payments that reimbursed the difference between their cost of production and the market price of their product. The owner's tenants and sharecroppers were to share in the benefits of crop reduction. Subsidies were to go to tenant farmers who rented the land and to the sharecroppers in proportion to their claims on the total crop. In practice, however, most tenants and croppers were excluded from most if not all of these subsidies. After a political struggle, the planters succeeded in reducing or eliminating payments to croppers and sometimes redefined their tenants as croppers.

The New Deal's intended rescue of southern agriculture set in motion its permanent transformation. The reduction in acres planted meant that fewer workers were needed to make a crop. This initial reduction was made worse by mechanization. For the longest time, southern planters—in control of a captive, cheap, and intimidated labor pool—had little reason to mechanize; but now, with subsidies providing the capital and parity payments guaranteeing a profit, they found the move to mechanized production relatively easy and attractive. They began to use

tractors. As a result, cotton land planted during the 1930s decreased, while production—using fewer laborers—increased. Increasing yields from greater mechanization and intensive use of fertilizers made this possible. Although labor needs ballooned at harvest time, they could be met by turning former tenants and croppers into temporary wageworkers.

One displaced cropper, Mae Bertha Carter, remembered, "I didn't stay on the farm too long after that. When those mechanical cotton pickers came in was about the time we were told to leave the farm." Another Mississippian, Maud Jones, recalled those days:

> It seemed like all the jobs that came through then, the white had them all and there wasn't anything for the black people to do but still go back to the field. They didn't go to school to cook for a tractor driver, so they just didn't stay here to do it.

Between 1930 and 1950, the number of southern tenant farmers was cut roughly in half, while from 1940 to 1950 the number of tractors tripled. In addition, many planters began to use the mechanized cotton picker. The need for laborers at harvest time was thus drastically reduced. A social organization of production—the sharecropping and tenant system—that was almost a century old was eliminated. By 1940, moreover, the United States was no longer producing the majority of the world's cotton; competitors in India, Brazil, and Egypt increased their respective market shares. Indeed, by the 1950s the South was no longer the dominant source of cotton even within the U.S.—production had shifted to California and Arizona. For many Southerners, it was time to go.

Legendary blues singer Koko Taylor grew up chopping cotton in the Mississippi Delta. She was one of the many thousands who didn't stay:

> When I was 18 years old, I left Memphis, my husband and I. And we got the Greyhound bus up Highway 61 and headed north to Chicago. He didn't have no money and I didn't have no money. We had one box of Ritz crackers that we split between us. With no money, nowhere to live, no nothing; we was just taking a chance. And I figured, "If he got enough nerve to take a chance with nothin', I have too." So that's what we did.

FLEEING RACISM | Besides a dire economic situation, Southerners, as they had done during the Great Migration, were also fleeing Jim Crow. Rev. James McCoy, pastor of New Mount Pilgrim Mission Baptist Church in Chicago, originally from Mississippi like his large congregation, recalled:

The Changing South

Top, left: Due in part to the implementation of New Deal agricultural programs that attempted to limit production and reduce agricultural acreage, sharecroppers were ousted from the land they had worked. Their number had peaked in the early 1930s, reaching 776,000, but by mid-decade the number was declining.

Top, right: Many agricultural workers did not have the resources to rent land for farming and thus worked as day laborers, migrating from farm to farm. These vegetable pickers are waiting to be paid after a day's work near Homestead, Florida.

Bottom: Because of increased world production and the onset of an international economic depression, American production of cotton was facing collapse. The need for laborers, like this sharecropper and his wife in Mississippi, steadily decreased as a result of mechanization, improved methods of irrigation, seed genetics, and more effective pesticides.

We suffered. We didn't have. We worked land that we thought we owned and after a while found out that we didn't own it. We could go to town and we had to wait until everybody else passed by and then we could walk on the street. It was a suffering life. If we walked up to a counter we had to wait until everybody else was gone...then we could buy what we wanted and paid more than anybody else. And it was always a problem in our way of life. We suffered to get this far.

Although lynching had greatly diminished by 1935—there were 18 lynchings that year—violence was still prevalent in the South. People were threatened, beaten, fired from their jobs, and publicly humiliated. A letter published in the *Chicago Defender* stressed:

> Dear Sir, I indeed wish to come to the North—anywhere in Illinois will do so long as I'm away from the hangman's noose and the torch man's fire. Conditions here are horrible with us. I want to get my family out of this accursed Southland. Down here a Negro man's not as good as a white man's dog.

With little hope of redress in the justice system, African Americans were at the mercy of abusive employers, landlords, and almost anyone bent on depriving them of their rights. Notwithstanding the Fifteenth Amendment of 1870 that guaranteed African Americans the right to vote, the vast majority were effectively disenfranchised by restrictive rules that applied only to them. Rigid segregation in public spaces, with its cortege of "Whites Only" and "Colored" signs on water fountains, restroom doors, hospital wards, in transportation and housing, was a constant humiliation and a reminder that blacks were second-class citizens.

Compared to the South, the North—although segregated in practice if not by law—appeared appealing. World War II veteran John Wiley was working in Memphis at the U.S. Army Depot. On the segregated bus home from work one day, a white man demanded his seat. Wiley refused. The other black riders loudly voiced their support:

> The bus driver told him [the white man] 'You ought to come up here to the front 'cause you gonna get in a whole lot of trouble'. I said, 'He sure gonna get in a lot of trouble! I was so angry at them. I had a switchblade knife in my pocket. I went home and told my wife....We left the next day and came here to Chicago and I've been here ever since.

The Klan and Jim Crow

Above: The Ku Klux Klan—in its various incarnations throughout the late 19th and 20th centuries— used terror and intimidation to enforce its ideals of white supremacy and to punish anyone viewed as a threat to those ideals. During the civil rights movement, many Klan-affiliated groups emerged, gained support, and became increasingly violent in their efforts to suppress African Americans and civil rights advocates. These Klansmen walk in downtown Montgomery, Alabama, during the bus boycott in 1956. *Right:* Motivation for African

Moving North or West, people hoped, was leaving behind violence, hard labor, and lack of opportunity. As Claude Brown put it in his autobiography, *Manchild in the Promised Land:* "Going to New York was good-bye to the cotton fields, good-bye to 'Massa Charlie,' good-bye to the chain gang, and, most of all, good-bye to those sunup-to-sundown working hours. One no longer had to wait to get to heaven to lay his burden down; burdens could be laid down in New York."

INTO THE NORTH AND WEST |
Southerners were not only pushed out of the South, they were also pulled to the North and West by the particular

Americans to leave the South was also provided by Jim Crow, the legal and customary system through which racial segregation was enforced, particularly in the South. Jim Crow—which began to develop after Reconstruction and intensified in the 1890s—encompassed the segregation of public spaces and facilities, discrimination in employment and housing, and disfranchisement through poll taxes and literacy tests. Signs such as the one pictured above were daily reminders to African Americans of their unequal status.

economic climate created by the Second World War. Indeed, although black tenant farmers and sharecroppers had migrated to southern cities and towns in the late 1930s, there had not been any significant movement out of the region during that time. The net African-American out-migration from the South during the 1930s was only 347,500, scarcely more than a fifth of what it would be in the following decade. The 1940s movement happened in part because of the tremendous expansion of industrial production during and after World War II.

Industrial mobilization began even before America's entry into the war in 1941 following Pearl Harbor. The Lend Lease program to supply Great Britain led to dramatic increases in production as early as 1940. Once the United States became engaged in a two-front war against Japan as well as Germany, production shifted into high gear. In addition to the normal needs for munitions, clothing, food, and training facilities, the naval war with Japan spurred increased shipbuilding and the production of naval materiel, much of it channeled to and through Pacific Coast ports. Lured by the promise of industrial jobs and opportunities for greater social equality, more than 700,000 African-American civilians left the South during the war. Established industrial hubs—such as Detroit, Chicago, Pittsburgh, and New York City—attracted many.

In California, the destination of vast numbers of black migrants, federal spending grew from $1.3 billion dollars in 1940 to $8.5 billion in 1945. The federal government accounted for about 45 percent of the state's personal income during the war, compared with just 8.5 percent ten years earlier. West Coast aircraft plants increased their work force almost 15 times; in 1940 they employed 36,848 workers, by V. J. Day, nearly 475,000 were working on the assembly lines.

Although Pacific coast shipyards accounted for more than half of all vessels built during the war, the South, long a major training ground for military forces and the site of numerous bases, also began to produce armaments and warships. Production at southern textile factories, oil refineries, steel mills, and seaports was also boosted by the war. But even this substantial improvement in the region's economy could not stop the tide of black migrants.

African Americans were not exactly welcomed with open arms in northern and western industrial centers, but the South, in comparison, was more deeply racist and hostile. For example, Bell Aircraft opened a huge factory on the outskirts of Atlanta. It employed 35,000 workers but only 2,500 of them were black, and just 800 had skilled positions. The rest were relegated to jobs as janitors, cafeteria workers, and other industrial equivalents of domestic labor. In the western shipyards, by contrast, men and women in greater numbers could find skilled work.

Friends and family members, who had already made the trip north or west and had found better jobs there than the South had to offer, enticed those who had not moved yet to follow them. Letters came back home with descriptions of the riches that could be found above the Mason-Dixon Line:

> Hello Dr., my dear old friend. These moments I thought I would write you a few facts of the present conditions in the North. People are coming here every day and finding employment. Nothing here but money—and it's not hard to get. I have children in school every day with the white children. However are times there now?

But it was not only the prospect of employment, the desire to escape the drudgery of agricultural labor, or the need to escape racism that pulled the migrants northward. There was also the siren song of the bright lights and the big city. Vernon Jarrett, veteran columnist for the *Chicago Tribune,* and himself a migrant, recalled:

> Radio had a tremendous impact in terms of making people dream of going North one day. You heard music coming from the Grand Terrace Café...Earl "Fatha" Hines, Duke Ellington...Cab Calloway...the young Count Basie. Chicago—this was a place where black people could talk back to white people—and could vote. We read the *Chicago Defender* and we would have great dreams and great fantasies about this place, this Mecca of human rights and civility. And of course, much of this was exaggeration, but it was the kind of exaggeration

Western War Workers
Richmond, California, in the San Francisco Bay area, drew thousands of migrants during World War II. Richmond was home to the shipyards of Henry J. Kaiser. Destination communities in the West—unlike Northern cities—had not experienced large influxes of black migrants prior to World War II. This couple settled in Oakland.

When the United States entered World War II at the end of 1941, President Franklin D. Roosevelt's administration needed to mobilize industry for the war effort. More than $100 billion in government contracts was awarded in the first six months of 1942, increasing job opportunities in northern and western cities. Over one million African-American civilians entered the workforce during the war years, like this man working on a B-52 bomber, right.

Bottom left: The expanding wartime economy also created some non-factory, white-collar jobs for African Americans. These office workers are selling war bonds in Brooklyn, New York.

Bottom right: Industrial jobs in the North were particularly appealing to young African Americans, who found opportunities for employment through government training programs, like those sponsored by the National Youth Administration.

people needed to maintain hope in this country and their own lives.

Segregated residential patterns in Northern cities spawned flourishing institutions in black neighborhoods, including a thriving nightlife. On the musical front, rhythm and blues, born in the late 1940s of the fusion of blues, jazz, boogie-woogie, and gospel, was popularized by southern migrants such as Muddy Waters, who moved from Mississippi to Chicago in 1943; Bo Didley, who left Mississippi in 1935 and also settled in Chicago; and Ray Charles, who migrated from Georgia to California. R&B, an urban music, flourished on the South Side of Chicago, Los Angeles Central Avenue, and Harlem, the neighborhoods that were home to the old and new migrants.

Working Women

Left: Of the approximately one million African Americans who found work during the war years, 600,000 were women. The proportion of African-American women in industrial occupations almost tripled during the war, rising from 6.5 to 18 percent. Los Angeles-area aircraft plants were among the first to offer employment to African-American women, such as this one working at the Long Beach plant of the Douglas Aircraft Company.

Above: The Housewives' League of Detroit was founded for the purpose of keeping money in the black community and using economic power to obtain jobs for African-American workers.

THE MIGRANTS | The sheer magnitude of the second migration and its duration suggest that a wide range of social classes, age groups, and economic levels were drawn into it at different times and places. There are strong indications, however, that as is usually the case, the second Great Migration was selective—drawing on that part of the black population best disposed to take and benefit from the risks associated with leaving home for an unfamiliar city.

It appears that the initial wartime migrants were more likely to be urban and/or wage laborers rather than simple "peasants turned city-ward" as they were often characterized. The displacement of tenants and sharecroppers during the 1930s had already moved thousands of black families into urban wage labor and often sent them to live in the cities. The southern urban black population had grown tremendously over the preceding decades. During the 1920s alone major metropolitan areas like Atlanta, Birmingham, Houston, and Memphis had experienced growth rates ranging from 41 to 86 percent. Even in Mississippi, still the most rural southern state, the black urban population had increased from 5 to 7 percent between 1890 and 1940. The black populations in Louisiana and Oklahoma, two major sources for the western migration, were substantially urban by 1940 (52 percent and 47 percent, respectively).

The migrants were largely people who had already made the transition to urban life or at least to wage labor and who were generally better educated than their nonmigrating neighbors. In addition, given the increase in the northern urban population due to the Great Migration, potential migrants probably had access to many more informal networks of communication about jobs than in the 1910s and 1920s. Many migrants already had kinfolk in the northern and western cities that could provide both information about jobs and support.

World War II had a significant impact on gender relations and the status of women, black and white. For black women its impact is especially marked because of their significant—though still limited—recruitment into the defense industries and their rejection of private domestic labor.

Black women migrants during the First World War were unlikely to be recruited for industrial labor; indeed, many moved from southern household help to the same jobs up North. By contrast, the federal censuses of 1940 and 1950 show a nationwide reduction in the number of blacks employed in domestic labor from 24 percent to 15.1 percent.

For southern women the change was even more dramatic. In many cities the proportion of the black female labor force confined to private domestic work exceeded 70 percent. These numbers plunged by the postwar period—in Atlanta, from 70 percent in domestic labor in 1940 to 50 percent ten years later. Although this change often simply meant doing the same kind of labor in nondomestic settings (from laundress to working in a commercial laundry, for example), it still meant better wages and benefits, and sometimes unionization.

In the first years of the migration, men were twice as likely to travel to the more distant destinations than women, who tended to stay closer to the South. But it was a temporary phenomenon because over the entire period of the second migration, migrants were more likely to be married than nonmigrants. Just as during the Great Migration, people used various strategies including wives following husbands, wives and husbands migrating together but leaving their children in the care of parents until they got settled, and single women joining kinsmen in distant cities.

Bright Lights, Big Cities

Above: Segregated residential patterns in northern cities spawned flourishing African-American institutions in black neighborhoods, including a thriving nightlife. Pictured is the bar at Palm Tavern on 47th Street in Chicago.

Right: The housing crunch in northern cities, along with the segregation and discrimination facing African Americans attempting to find places to live, led to extremely crowded conditions, such as those pictured in this Washington, D.C., apartment in 1942.

THE IMPACT OF THE MIGRATION | The impact of the second Great Migration was much less dramatic than in earlier years, perhaps because its demographic effect was less spectacular. Despite the new westward push of the second migration, the cities that had been the principal destinations of the earlier exodus—New York, Chicago, and Detroit—were also the principal goals of migrants in the 1940s.

But the percentage increases in the black populations of these cities was smaller the second time around. Moreover, African-American communities and their social infrastructures were already well established in these northeastern and midwestern communities.

Western communities, on the other hand were usually experiencing a large influx of African Americans for the first time, and they arrived as part of a vast shift of the general population. Eight million Americans moved west of the Mississippi after 1940, half of them to the Pacific coast. There were 171,000 African Americans in the West in 1940 (1 percent of the total population) but 620,000 by 1945. Between the spring of 1942 and 1945 alone, 340,000 African Americans settled in California.

On the labor front, shop floor conflicts with unions and the development of housing discrimination unfolded much as they had in the East and Midwest during the years of the Great Migration. Meanwhile, in the East, riots and "hate-strikes" erupted in numerous cities across the nation, such as Chicago and Harlem in 1943.

Many features of these labor and housing conflicts were different in the West because of the magnitude of the war effort and the new federal role in the economy. For example, the San Francisco shipbuilder, Kaiser, experimented with new production techniques and labor management policies. Some of these—such as prefabrication, which reduced the skill levels needed by those entering the work force—benefited both African Americans and women. Even when employers like Seattle's aircraft manufacturer Boeing Company and Atlanta's Bell Aircraft remained committed to discriminatory hiring, the federal government's interest in sustaining wartime

Protest

Left: African Americans, like these in Stuyvesant Town, New York City, regularly protested the discrimination and segregation they faced when looking for decent housing. In 1957 New York was the first state to adopt a fair-housing ordinance; but it had little influence on the overall situation.

Above, left: In 1940, only an estimated 3 percent of voting-age African Americans in the southern states were registered to vote; by 1968, this number had grown to 62 percent. The Voting Rights Act passed in 1965 banned literacy tests and gave the federal government power to oversee registration and elections. Along with increasing the number of African-American voters, the Act contributed to a large increase in black elected officials.

Above right: Angry demonstrators during Harlem riots, 1964.

production often made it an ally of African Americans pushing for change.

In 1941 A. Philip Randolph's March on Washington Movement had forced President Roosevelt to issue an executive order mandating an end to racial discrimination in defense industries and setting up an agency, the Fair Employment Practices Committee, to enforce it. Though the enforcement mechanism was weak, the agency's hearing and complaint process did provide a forum for black political mobilization that would bear dividends in future years.

In the case of housing discrimination, however, the federal role was decidedly negative. The government was deeply implicated in policies that restricted the ability of African Americans to obtain mortgages outside of black neighborhoods. It also turned a blind eye on segregation in much of the temporary housing constructed during the war to shelter defense-related production workers. And, finally, government policies and financing played a major role in stimulating the expansion of the suburbs and "white flight" in the postwar era. This flight was described by Ruth Wells:

> Realtors would move in a black person with a lot of children. And so the white people in the neighborhood would see all these little black kids running around and they didn't like that....People are frightened...and they didn't give them very much for their houses, but they went up on the price—sometimes double— when they get ready to sell it to the blacks.

FROM COUNTRY TO INNER CITY | The pervasive demographic changes that came with the migration transformed both the character and representation of the race problem in America and, as a consequence, the image of African Americans.

Since the arrival of the first Africans, the black presence in America has been framed as a problem—a labor problem, a social problem, a political problem. For the first three centuries, when most African Americans lived in the South and earned their livelihood from agriculture, the so-called Negro Problem was distinctly southern and linked to the backwardness of the southern economy and society. Blacks were backward because the South was backward, or the South was retarded because of deficiencies in African-American character and culture. Either way it was a regional problem.

With the urbanization of the African-American population and its spread all over the country, the "problem" became a national one, and its terms of reference began to change. In popular speech as well as in literature and art, in sociological and historical work, black urban life became the dominant setting and motif.

In a very brief time, the now familiar image of a black inner-city core surrounded by a white suburban ring emerged as the dominant pattern of American life. Thus did the "ghetto" become dominant in scholarly and creative literature by the 1960s—the term "inner city" being a virtual synonym for black people.

Although this rural to urban shift was evident even during the Great Migration, there were decisive changes in its character and nuances during the post-World War II era. Unlike the earlier urban expansion, this one was generally portrayed negatively, by blacks as well as whites. The novelty, excitement, and creativity of black urban life that figured so prominently in the literature and art of the Harlem Renaissance, for example, gave way to themes of deterioration. The visual and literary images were now accented in emotional tones of lament, loss, and despair.

The magnitude of change is made clear by the fact that the very nature and terms of discussion of what had once been referred to as "the Negro Problem" were radically altered. Black life and racial conflicts now were characterized with phrases such as, "the rise of the ghetto," "the problem of the inner cities," "urban disorders," and "the underclass."

But in contrast to this view, black urban communities across the country became centers of political and cultural activity. The New Deal coalition formed in the late 1930s, the civil rights movement of the 1950s and 1960s, the various liberation struggles of the late 20th century, all were grounded in the social and political ferment of these new urban societies.

THE LEGACIES | The vast remapping of black living space and work in the United States was the dominant and lasting consequence of the second Great Migration. These changes contained the seeds of extraordinary political transformations as well. Cities, south as well as north and west, provided a more favorable breeding

ground for political mobilization—both inside and outside the established political system—than rural regions.

Eventually, white flight to the suburbs combined with black migration to the urban areas produced African-American political majorities or large pluralities in several key cities. This laid the basis for the election of numerous African-American mayors, state legislators, and congresspersons.

There is ample evidence of increased political consciousness among southern migrants even before voting barriers fell later in the century. Migrants were already politically aware, if not active, prior to leaving the South and, as in the Great Migration, many registered to vote as soon as they reached their destinations.

Despite several postwar recessions, the military mobilizations of the Korean War and the Cold War caused the western and some midwestern states to remain economically attractive to African Americans for two decades after V. J. Day.

The substantial urban concentrations of black Americans were no doubt instrumental in changing marketing strategies for commercial goods and cultural products. For better or worse, the representation of African Americans in the nation's everyday life—in the media and culture—would be radically different at the end of the 20th century than at its beginning. The changes in African Americans' self-perception created by this new reality ultimately formed the basis for the various political, social, and cultural movements that reshaped black citizenship in the 20th century.

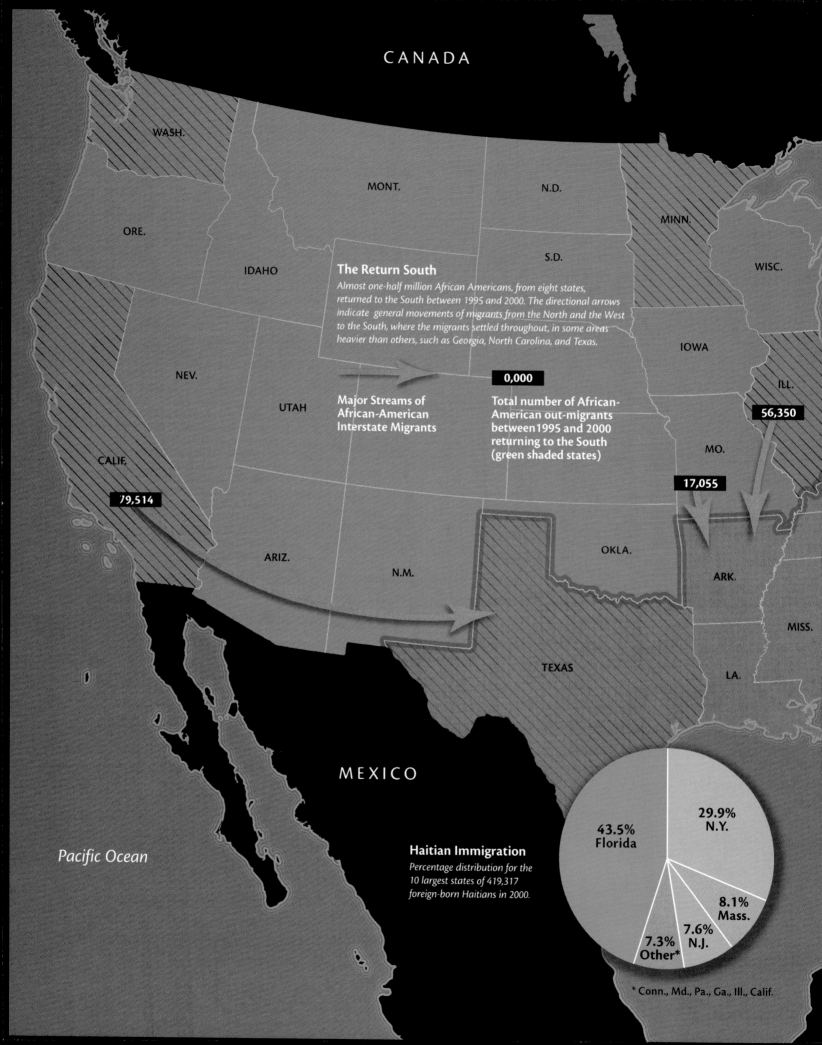

CANADA

WASH.

MONT.

N.D.

MINN.

ORE.

IDAHO

S.D.

WISC.

The Return South

Almost one-half million African Americans, from eight states, returned to the South between 1995 and 2000. The directional arrows indicate general movements of migrants from the North and the West to the South, where the migrants settled throughout, in some areas heavier than others, such as Georgia, North Carolina, and Texas.

IOWA

NEV.

0,000

ILL.

UTAH

Major Streams of African-American Interstate Migrants

Total number of African-American out-migrants between 1995 and 2000 returning to the South (green shaded states)

56,350

MO.

CALIF.

79,514

17,055

OKLA.

ARK.

ARIZ.

N.M.

MISS.

TEXAS

LA.

MEXICO

Pacific Ocean

Haitian Immigration
Percentage distribution for the 10 largest states of 419,317 foreign-born Haitians in 2000.

43.5% Florida

29.9% N.Y.

8.1% Mass.

7.6% N.J.

7.3% Other*

* Conn., Md., Pa., Ga., Ill., Calif.

Contemporary Migrations

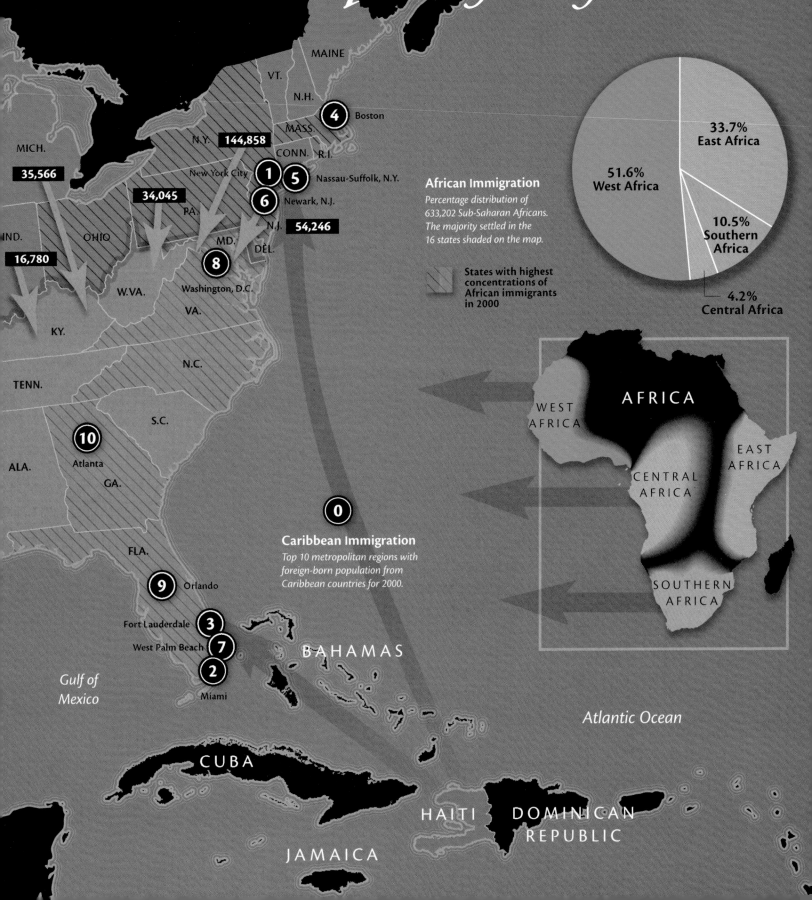

MAINE

VT.

N.H.

MASS.

CONN. R.I.

4 Boston

MICH.

35,566

N.Y. **144,858**

New York City **1** **5** Nassau-Suffolk, N.Y.

6 Newark, N.J.

PA.

N.J. **54,246**

IND.

16,780

OHIO

MD.

DEL.

8

W.VA.

Washington, D.C.

VA.

KY.

N.C.

TENN.

S.C.

10

Atlanta

ALA.

GA.

FLA.

9 Orlando

Fort Lauderdale **3**

West Palm Beach **7**

2

Miami

Gulf of Mexico

BAHAMAS

CUBA

JAMAICA

HAITI

DOMINICAN REPUBLIC

Atlantic Ocean

0

Caribbean Immigration

Top 10 metropolitan regions with foreign-born population from Caribbean countries for 2000.

African Immigration

Percentage distribution of 633,202 Sub-Saharan Africans. The majority settled in the 16 states shaded on the map.

States with highest concentrations of African immigrants in 2000

33.7% East Africa

51.6% West Africa

10.5% Southern Africa

4.2% Central Africa

AFRICA

WEST AFRICA

CENTRAL AFRICA

EAST AFRICA

SOUTHERN AFRICA

Caribbean Immigration

The journey of Afro-Caribbean peoples to the United States started a long time ago when enslaved Barbadians were taken by their British owners to South Carolina during the 17th century. Indeed, most of the earliest Africans to arrive in what would become the United States were seasoned men, women, and children from the Caribbean. This first, involuntary migration was followed by a large influx of people from the British West Indies at the turn of the 20th century. A third wave made its way between 1930 and 1965; and the fourth movement is still going on. The impact of these migrations upon American society, and especially upon African America, has been profound.

Revelers at Carnival display Caribbean flags in creative ways. The revelers "show" the flags of the countries from which they migrated, or with which they identify. Some show two flags simultaneously, indicating their special ties to the countries their flags represent. The American-born children of the immigrants are among the most enthusiastic participants in this ritual and wear the flags of their parents' nations.

THE COLONIAL PERIOD TO 1900 | Caribbeans and African Americans were brought together in Britain's North American colonies, in the North as well as in the South. Barbadian slaves—many of them born in Africa—constituted an important portion of the black population of Virginia and the Chesapeake, and Barbadian interests developed South Carolina, which in the 18th century extended and broadened its trading relations with other Caribbean colonies. Jamaica soon surpassed Barbados as a market for Carolinian products. The degree of intercourse between the two areas was enormous, and the significant influence of the Caribbean on South Carolina endures to this day.

Well into the 18th century, the majority of slaves in the North had either lived or were born in the Caribbean. In New York, with the North's largest enslaved population, people from the Caribbean continued to outnumber Africans brought directly from the continent. Though people of West Indian origin gained a reputation for rebelliousness after a revolt in New York City in 1712, and laws placed higher duties on them, the imbalance continued. One estimate puts the ratio of enslaved Caribbeans to Africans at three to one between 1715 and 1730. Of slaves introduced by New Yorkers between 1715 and 1741, the largest number came from Jamaica, followed by Africa, Barbados, and Antigua.

Caribbeans also figured prominently among the free people of color in the North. Prince Hall, who is believed to have been from Barbados, established black freemasonry in the United States and was a distinguished leader of Boston's African-American community during the 18th century. Denmark Vesey, who was born in Africa or the Caribbean and had been enslaved in the Virgin Islands and Saint Domingue, in 1822 organized an elaborate slave uprising in Charleston, South Carolina, that was eventually betrayed before it could be launched.

John B. Russwurm, of Jamaica, and his African-American colleague Samuel E. Cornish started *Freedom's Journal,* the first black newspaper, in 1827. As late as 1860 one in five black Bostonians had been born in the Caribbean islands.

The Caribbean population in the United States was relatively small during the 19th century but it grew significantly after the Civil War. The foreign-born black population, which was almost wholly Caribbean in origin, increased by 500 percent between 1850 and 1900, from 4,000 to more than 20,000.

Distinguished Caribbean migrants populate the annals of 19th century black America. A significant number were skilled craftsmen, scholars, teachers, preachers, and doctors. Jan Earnst Matzeliger, the inventor of a revolutionary shoe-making machine, had migrated from Suriname. Edward Wilmot Blyden, a major contributor to black nationalism, was born in the Virgin Islands. Joseph Sandiford Atwell, a Barbadian, became the first black man after the Civil War to be ordained in the Episcopal Church, and Bert Williams, the famous comedian, was born in Antigua.

Robert Brown Elliott, U.S. congressman and state attorney general of South Carolina; W. E. B. Du Bois; poet, songwriter, and activist James Weldon Johnson and his brother John Rosamond Johnson; and poet and educator William Stanley Braithwaite were among some of the most distinguished sons and daughters of these early immigrants.

LEAVING THE CARIBBEAN | What was new in the early 20th century was, therefore, not the Caribbean presence itself but its scale and visibility. The significant growth in Caribbean presence in the early part of the century is easily explained. It lay in the increasing economic hardship and disenchantment in the British West Indies and the simultaneous expansion of the U.S. economy (especially during the First World War and the 1920s) with its relatively high wages and growing employment opportunities.

The British Caribbean experienced a catastrophic decline in its sugar economy, the mainstay and primary employer in the region since the 17th century. The British colonies found themselves unable to compete against cane sugar from Cuba and Brazil and sugar beets produced in Europe. Between 1840 and 1900 the price of Jamaican sugar had dropped almost 80 percent. The number of sugar estates on the island fell from 670 in 1836 to just 74 by 1910, drastically reducing the number of

workers employed in the industry. Though banana cultivation expanded rapidly, it could never make up for the shortfall created by the collapse of the sugar economy.

Barbados' ruling class managed to break the fall of King Sugar on Barbados but it did so on the backs of black Barbadians by instituting a mercilessly exploitative system remarkably similar to that which prevailed during slavery. A similar dynamic enfolded in St. Kitts, Nevis, Montserrat, and Antigua. The death rate, especially infant mortality, soared on these islands. Malnutrition was commonplace and outright starvation was not unknown. As one petitioner to the British government put it in 1899, "Her Majesty's black and colored subjects in the West Indies have had to choose between a death from starvation in their native islands and suffering ill-treatment as immigrants in the Dominican Republic because their native islands are merely Islands of Death."

The gravity of the situation was compounded by a series of natural disasters that contributed to emigration. Hurricanes, floods, and droughts afflicted the islands with unusual frequency and intensity between 1880 and 1920. Jamaica's capital, Kingston, and surrounding areas were devastated by a massive earthquake in 1907. The colonial authorities had the means to ease the impact of these catastrophes, but, especially in Barbados, they made little effort to alleviate the suffering of the people.

The structure and oppressiveness of colonial rule on the islands took its toll on the aspiring black middle class as well as the workers and peasants. They became increasingly dissatisfied. Black teachers received meager salaries and no pensions at the end of their careers. Those few who made it into the civil service were locked down in low-level jobs, well below their capabilities. To make matters worse, in 1911 the Jamaican authorities decided to scrap competitive civil-service examinations. They were replaced by an undemocratic appointment system that

Afro-Caribbean Migrants

Left: When the banana industry declined in Jamaica at the beginning of the 20th century, the center of banana production shifted to Central America—Costa Rica, Guatemala, and Honduras. As this change unfolded, Afro-Caribbeans migrated to these countries.

Inset, left: Jamaican sugar production could not compete with the cheaper versions from Cuba and Brazil. The drop in production led to a migration of Jamaican sugar-cane workers to Cuba, while others left for the United States.

Above: By the 1930s, the great majority of Afro-Caribbean children had been born out of wedlock. Infant mortality rates were staggeringly high, wrought by poverty, malnutrition, venereal and childhood diseases, overcrowded living conditions, and neglect. This epidemic of child deaths visited havoc on families.

favored whites and the light-skinned. There were strong and loud objections, but they were ignored.

THE CENTRAL AMERICAN ROUTE | Though the working and emerging middle classes both had strong motivations to migrate, they did not move to the United States in equal numbers. The majority of immigrants headed for Central America. They labored on the construction of the Panama Canal and the huge banana plantations being developed by the United Fruit Company in Costa Rica, Guatemala, Honduras, and elsewhere in the region. They also migrated in large numbers to Cuba to work on the sugar plantations, and to a lesser extent to the Dominican Republic and Puerto Rico where sugar production was expanding rapidly. In all of these destinations they were subjected to rank discrimination and ill treatment.

Conditions were especially bad on the Panama Canal, where the hardships of Jim Crow policies were augmented by malaria, yellow fever, ghastly accidents, and a high death rate. Workers endured the privations of exile because wages were higher. They sent money home to their loved ones, made frequent visits, and bought land on their native islands. In the end, however, most settled in the lands of migration.

The dispersal of Caribbean people was facilitated by a remarkable network of transportation. Since the 17th century, Bridgetown, Barbados had served as the first port of call for British ships crossing the Atlantic. By the beginning of the 20th century, shipping networks extended from Bridgetown to all parts of the world. It was therefore not just the intolerable conditions on Barbados nor the opportunity for work abroad that resulted in the extraordinary migrant stream from the island. An indispensable element was its working class's unique access to relatively cheap transportation to a bewildering variety of different points on the globe.

Jamaica had also benefited from an extensive shipping network. At the end of the 19th century this was augmented by the development of the banana trade with the United States by what would become the United Fruit Company. Its banana ships always made room for passengers. Boston was their first port of call; later New York, Philadelphia, Baltimore, New Orleans, and other ports were added. This facilitated greater and cheaper access for immigrants from the island to the U.S. in the late 19th and early 20th centuries.

TO THE UNITED STATES | The stream of migrants to the United States was relatively small compared to the flow to Central America and Cuba. For whereas 108,000 entered the United States from the entire Caribbean region between 1899 and 1932, it took only two islands, Jamaica and Barbados, to supply more than 240,000 laborers to Panama between 1881 and 1915. The migration to the U.S. was also distinct in another important respect. Those who immigrated to this country were disproportionately literate and skilled, with a significant number being professionals or white-collar workers.

The number of black people, especially Caribbeans, who migrated to the United States increased dramatically during the first three decades of the 20th century, peaking in 1924 at 12,250 per year and falling off during the Depression. The foreign-born black population increased from 20,000 in 1900 to almost 100,000 by 1930. Over 140,000 black immigrants passed through United States ports between 1899 and 1937 despite the restrictive immigration laws enacted in 1917, 1921, and 1924. The wave of black humanity entering the United States was focused on the northeastern coast and broke mainly on the shores of Manhattan. Tens of thousands came through Ellis Island, though the voluminous literature on that legendary port of disembarkation takes scant notice of this fact.

From the end of the 19th century up to 1905, South Florida was the migrants' primary destination. There was a large wave of migration from the Bahamas and a smaller flow of black cigar makers from Cuba. New York was the second most popular state for settlement, followed closely by Massachusetts.

But Florida's preeminence was soon surmounted by New York, and the number headed for Massachusetts dropped sharply by 1920. During the peak years of migration—1913 to 1924—the majority made their way to New York City, settling primarily in Manhattan and Brooklyn. By 1930 almost a quarter of black Harlem was of Caribbean origin. Less than a decade later, New York's *Amsterdam News* informed its readers that with the exception of Kingston, Jamaica, Harlem was the largest West Indian city in the world.

The first cohort of 20th century Caribbean immigrants to the United States was not only more literate and skilled than their compatriots left behind but was also more educated and skilled than the European immigrants who entered the country at the same time. Moreover, they were more literate than the native-born white population in the United States.

It was this wave that laid into place the institutional infrastructure of Afro-Caribbean life in New York City and elsewhere in the nation. It has been estimated that by the 1930s a third of New York's black professionals—including doctors, dentists, and lawyers—came from the ranks of Caribbean migrants, a figure well in excess of the group's share of the city's black population. Furthermore, the Caribbean newcomers accounted for a disproportionately large number of New York's black businessmen and women.

A study of the entries in *Who's Who in Colored America,* covering the period 1915–1932, yields a remarkable number of black migrants. In 1930, though only 0.8 percent of America's black population was foreign born, 6 percent of those

PHOTOGRAPH OF BEARER.

SIGNATURE OF BEARER.

A Female Migration

Afro-Caribbeans seeking to enter the United States were required to obtain permission from American consulates in the Caribbean (*above*). But with American society having what was termed the Negro Problem, the United States government was hostile to black immigration. Its consulates in the Caribbean erected barriers to Afro-Caribbean immigration, and they succeeded in keeping large numbers of people from migrating. The American policy was a contributing factor in the selective character of Caribbean immigration.

listed in the book were immigrants. Over 8 percent of doctors, 4.5 percent of lawyers, more than 14 percent of businessmen, 4.5 percent of clergymen, over 3 percent of professors, and 4 percent of writers/authors had come from the Caribbean.

Among the sons and daughters of this generation of Caribbean migrants is a phalanx of distinguished African Americans: Malcolm X, Louis Farrakhan, Harry Belafonte, Colin Powell, St. Clair Drake, Cicely Tyson, Vincent Harding, Robert Moses, Shirley Chisholm, Margaret Walker, Kareem Abdul-Jabbar, Audre Lorde, Michelle Wallace, Paule Marshall, Sonny Rollins, Rosa Guy, June Jordan, and Lani Guinier.

SHUTTING THE DOOR | The second decade of the 20th century, in contrast, would see a deliberate attempt to block the entry of black people into the United States. Despite the dramatic fall in immigration following the outbreak of World War I, by the end of 1914 Congress was debating legislation that would drastically restrict newcomers. Senator James Reed of Missouri secured quick passage in the Senate of an amendment to the bill excluding members of the "black or African race" from entry into the country. The African-American press was unanimous in its condemnation of the measure and the National Association for the Advancement of Colored People voiced its strong opposition.

The greatest opposition to this piece of legislative racism came from Booker T. Washington. He was uncharacteristically passionate and combative on the question and, to his credit, pulled out all the stops to kill the amendment. He mobilized his influential network of powerful supporters, white and black—the "Tuskegee Machine"—and personally waged a campaign in the major newspapers against the measure. Washington vigorously reminded Americans of the indispensable labor that Afro-Caribbeans had performed in building the Panama Canal. They should not now be slapped in the face, he said, and told they cannot enter this country. He organized a massive lobbying campaign and even such black opponents of his usually accomodationist positions as W. E. B. Du Bois, and co-founder of the NAACP and newspaper editor William Monroe Trotter joined forces with him on this issue.

The Immigration Act of 1924 drastically turned the tide of Caribbean immigration to the United States. It plummeted from 10,630 in 1924 to only 321 in 1925. Primarily aimed at restricting non-white and Southern and Eastern European

Above: Women were well represented among Afro-Caribbean immigrants. In the first decade of the immigration they were the minority, but as time went by they equaled and surpassed the men in number. Tens of thousands of seamstresses and dressmakers, clerks, housewives, and domestics filled the ranks of the immigrants. More women settled in the Northeast than in Florida. These women have just arrived at Ellis Island from Guadeloupe, French West Indies.

633

Freshly Squeezed
SUGAR CANE JUICE & WATER COCONUT

Change and Continuity

In the 1920s immigrants from the Caribbean accounted for a disproportionately large number of black entrepreneurs in New York City; today they are no less dominant a presence among black businesspeople than they were in the period 1900-1952. Indeed, they are the majority of black entrepreneurs in several areas of the city. They own shops and restaurants; construction, realty and shipping companies; transportation vans, taxis, bakeries, beauty parlors, and barbershops.

Left: A patron comes out of a Rastafarian restaurant in Brooklyn, New York.

Above: Norris Keel, a Trinidadian, has been a "street entrepreneur" for over 20 years. He migrated to the United States for more opportunities and as a way to help his family in Trinidad.

immigration, the law stipulated an immigration quota system of 2 percent of the foreign-born for each nationality enumerated in the 1890 census.

Northwestern Europe was favored in this system, and those from the European colonies could only enter under the designated quota allotted to their colonial masters. Thus those from the British Caribbean entered under the British quota set at 34,007 in 1925. Although Britain consistently underused its quota by several thousands, the Caribbean migration was nonetheless kept low, never rising in the late 1920s and 1930s to the levels reached before the 1924 legislation.

During the Depression, due to economic hardship and an even more restrictive immigration policy, more Caribbean people returned to the islands than entered the United States. Despite all this, the black population of foreign origin and their American-born offspring grew from 55,000 in 1900 to 178,000 in 1930. Migrants from the islands together with those of Caribbean origin coming from Central America made up over 80 percent of the total.

NEW WAVES | The level of Caribbean immigration picked up after the United States entered into the Second World War in 1941. Almost 50,000 Caribbeans (black and white) settled in the country between 1941 and 1950. They took advantage of the rapidly expanding war economy and postwar economic growth. Beginning in 1943, thousands of migrant workers were brought from the region to work in American agriculture to help the war effort. Florida's sugar plantations were their primary destinations, but they were soon dispersed to other states and sectors of the American economy.

By war's end over 40,000 workers from the Bahamas, Jamaica, Barbados, St. Vincent, St. Lucia, and Dominica were working in the United States. They labored in nearly 1,500 localities in 36 states. Some 16,000 worked in industrial occupations. For some, especially those in Florida, conditions were intolerable. Many ignored the no-strike clause in their contracts and engaged in other forms of open resistance, sometimes with success. Some broke their contracts and fled from their assigned jobs.

Jamaican tobacco workers in Connecticut took flight to New York and Boston rather than return to their native land after their contracts expired in 1950. Others were able to transform their status from migrant worker to immigrant and remain legally in the country. Many, however, returned to the Caribbean and then made their way back to this country as bona fide immigrants rather than contract laborers.

Though originally intended to alleviate the alleged wartime labor shortage in Florida agriculture, the Caribbean program continues to this day. In 1989 some 14,000 Caribbean migrant workers labored on American farms.

The postwar flow of Caribbean immigrants suffered a major setback with the passage in 1952 of the Immigration and Nationality Act—the McCarran-Walter Act. Though allowing a passageway for drastically reduced numbers of Caribbean farm workers to enter the U.S., the bill closed the door to virtually every other would-be black immigrant. The law had the desired effect of retarding the rate of Caribbean immigration to the U.S. Thousands still came but they were overwhelmingly the close relatives of people already living in this country, rather than new immigrants as such. The migration stream was now diverted to Britain, which was to receive approximately 300,000 Caribbean immigrants between 1948 and 1966.

In 1964 Lyndon Johnson was elected president in a landslide; the Democrats took control of both houses of Congress. As a senator from Texas, Johnson had voted for the McCarran-Walter Act, but as President he made good on his campaign promise to continue John F. Kennedy's efforts to reform the immigration laws. Johnson linked the Civil Rights Act of 1964 and the Voting Rights Act of 1965 to a new and more equitable immigration policy.

The new, liberalized immigration law—the Hart-Celler Act, as it is commonly known—was passed in September 1965 and went into full effect on July 1, 1968. It marked a major turning point in U.S. immigration policy and launched a new wave of immigration from the Caribbean. For those who sought better opportunities abroad, it was especially welcomed, because beginning in 1962 Great Britain began to systematically block their entry. Caribbeans now headed north to America.

RECEPTION AND ADAPTATION | In 1900 Florida—with the highest concentration of black immigrants—had less than 22 percent of them. New York State followed with 17.3 percent, and Massachusetts with 17 percent. But by 1910 the process of concentration had begun, with New York leading the way with almost a third (32 percent) of black immigrants. In 1920 more than 43 percent of black immigrants lived there, rising to 59 percent by 1930 and over 61 percent a decade later. New York appears to have served as a magnet for those who had previously resided in other states. It was in the 1920s, then, that New York became preeminent as a destination for Caribbeans, a position it would maintain for more than half a century.

The explanation of New York's rapid preeminence, though multifaceted, is not hard to find: improved and cheaper transportation from the Caribbean to the city accompanied by extensive advertisement in the islands and news reports on immigrant life in the United States (the *Jamaica Times* was especially attentive to this subject). One immigrant writing in Harlem's *Amsterdam News* in the 1930s went so far as to claim that "Seventh and Lenox Avenues were as well known to people in Kingston, Jamaica; Bridgetown, Barbados; Port-of-Spain, Trinidad; and other West Indian capitals, as to the people of Brooklyn. Everybody wanted to get to New York."

The reception, perception, reaction, and adaptation of Caribbean immigrants have undergone changes since the migration flow began in earnest at the end of the 19th century, but there has also been remarkable continuity.

One of the constants is the perception of the immigrants; because their skin color is seen as black, they are placed in the same category as African Americans. This has made them subject to the same disabilities as their American counterparts: the racial discrimination and violence, especially in the South, and the routine humiliation of daily life. There were, however, especially in the Jim Crow South, bizarre exceptions allowed to black immigrants.

Greeted with the words, "What you damned niggers want here?" Trinidadian airman Hubert Julian and his group were, in the end, treated royally at a Texas gas station in 1931. They had passed themselves off as Ethiopians. The teenage Sidney Poitier was dealt with indulgently by the racist Miami police when they realized he was a black foreigner. But in 1963, at a drive-in hamburger joint near Fort Benning, Georgia, a black Vietnam veteran and army officer was quizzed by the waitress: "Are you Puerto Rican?" "Are you an African student?" Colin Powell answered, "I'm a Negro. I'm an American. And I'm an Army officer." He was refused service and sent to the Jim Crow window at the back.

But their nationality, especially in the South, could also bring negative and special attention to Caribbean immigrants. In Miami the authorities branded them as troublemakers. And as early as 1908, one of the city's judges praised the police for altering the views of "Nassau Negroes who upon arrival here consider themselves the social equal of white people."

In the 1920s the Ku Klux Klan targeted them, especially the supporters of Marcus Garvey's Universal Negro Improvement Association (UNIA). In 1921 the Klan kidnapped the vice-president of Coconut Grove's UNIA branch, Rev. R. H. Higgs, and released him only after he had promised to go back to his native Bahamas.

Each generation of Caribbean immigrants has expressed shock at encountering American racism. And it frequently led to their radicalization. Many have figured prominently in radical and dissenting movements, stretching from the 18th century to the present. But others, though relatively few in number, have also been broken by the encounter, literally driven mad by American racism, some even to suicide.

The immigrants' relations with African Americans have drawn much attention. In general, the tensions have been overstated at the expense of the genuine collaboration that also existed. There was definite tension, especially during the "Garvey Must Go" campaign of 1922-23, and tensions between these two elements of the African Diaspora still exist. But there has also been a remarkable level of collaboration and cooperation between them. African Americans and Afro-Caribbeans married one another, shared their culture (including cuisine, music, and sartorial tastes), learned to live with one another, and joined forces in the various political movements to fight racist and class oppression.

CHANGE AND CONTINUITY | With the exception of Cubans, Caribbean immigrants have made New York State and New York City their principal destinations and sites

of settlement in the U.S. Cubans, following trends established as long ago as the 1870s, have made Florida, and Miami in particular, their primary home. Florida, however, has grown increasingly popular among Haitian and Jamaican immigrants. Nevertheless, more than half of Barbadian, Guyanese, Haitian, Jamaican, and Trinidadian immigrants have settled in New York, especially Brooklyn and Queens.

Today, there are between 2.6 and 3 million Caribbeans (of all races) in the United States, or 1 percent of the total population. More than 72 percent of Afro-Caribbeans are foreign-born, and they represent 4.6 percent of the black population. Entrepreneurs continue to flourish in the community, and the 2000 census shows that the median household income of Afro-Caribbeans is $40,000. Although it has decreased since 1990, it is still higher than the African-American median household income, but is now lower than the income of immigrants from Africa.

From the early days of Caribbean immigration, West Indian music, including soca, calypso, and reggae, has had a profound impact on popular music. Other aspects of Caribbean culture such as food and Carnival have also entered mainstream America. In the last two decades, Carnival, which started in Harlem in 1950, has become a regional event. The first celebration takes place in Atlanta on Memorial Day weekend, and over the next five months events are held in other cities. The largest one, which takes place in Brooklyn, New York, on Labor Day, draws hundreds of thousands of revelers and spectators. These spectacular public events, which generate millions of dollars in revenue, are the clearest expression of the development of strong Caribbean communities and a defined Afro-Caribbean identity.

Haitian Immigration

Between the 1700s and 1809, following the successful slave revolt and the independence of Haiti under the leadership of Toussaint L'Ouverture, large numbers of Haitians of African descent migrated to the United States. Although many put down roots in New York, Maryland, Pennsylvania, South Carolina, and Georgia, the vast majority settled in Louisiana. Their activism had profound and enduring repercussions on the politics, culture, religion, and racial climate of the state. Several generations later, new waves of Haitian immigrants arrived on American shores. Their preferred destinations, this time, were New York and Florida. Like the first immigrants, they encountered suspicion, discrimination, and a particular kind of prejudice; but also, like their predecessors, the Haitians who migrated in the past 30 years came with a strong sense of self-esteem and a deep pride in their history and culture.

FROM SAINT DOMINGUE TO LOUISIANA | The revolution in Saint Domingue unleashed a massive multiracial exodus: The French fled with the slaves they managed to keep; so did numerous free people of color. In addition, in 1793 a catastrophic fire destroyed two-thirds of the principal city, Cap Français (present-day Cap Haïtien), and nearly ten thousand people left the island for good. In the ensuing decades of revolution, foreign invasion, and civil war, thousands more fled the turmoil. Many moved eastward to Santo Domingo (present-day Dominican Republic) or to nearby Caribbean islands such as Jamaica and Cuba. Large numbers of immigrants, black and white, found shelter in North America, notably in New York, Baltimore (53 ships landed there in July 1793), Philadelphia, Norfolk, Charleston, and Savannah, as well as in Spanish Florida. Nowhere on the continent, however, did the refugee movement exert as profound an influence as in southern Louisiana.

Between 1791 and 1803, 1,300 refugees arrived in New Orleans. After future emperor Napoleon Bonaparte sold the colony to the United States in 1803 because his disastrous expedition against Saint Domingue had stretched his finances and military too thin, events on the island loomed even larger in Louisiana.

Toussaint L'Ouverture was responsible for the only successful slave revolt in the world. It led to the establishment of the first black republic and the second independent country in the Americas. In Little Haiti, the predominantly Haitian neighborhood in Miami, elementary school students dress up as Toussaint L'Ouverture to commemorate Haitian Independence Day.

In January 1804 an event of enormous importance shook the world of the slaves and their enslavers. The black revolutionaries crushed Napoleon's army—which counted mercenaries from all over Europe—and proclaimed the nation of Haiti (the original Indian name of the island) the second independent nation in the Western Hemisphere and the world's first black-led republic. Following the event, the number of immigrants to Louisiana increased and then skyrocketed between May 1809 and June 1810, when Spanish authorities expelled thousands of Haitians from Cuba, where they had taken refuge several years earlier. Nearly 90 percent of them settled in New Orleans. The 1809 migration brought 2,731 whites, 3,102 free persons of African descent, and 3,226 enslaved refugees to the city, doubling its population. Sixty-three percent of the Crescent City's inhabitants were now black. The multiracial refugee population settled in the French Quarter and the neighboring Faubourg Marigny district, and revitalized Creole culture and institutions. New Orleans acquired a reputation as the nation's "Creole Capital."

Haitians exerted an enormous influence on 18th- and 19th-century Louisiana. Those who settled there, as voluntary immigrants or slaves, brought additional African cultural and religious elements to the black community. Congo culture was reinforced, and Louisiana saw the influx of people from the Bight of Benin (Fon, Yoruba) who were numerous in Saint Domingue but hardly represented in the United States. Black Haitians introduced a new musical and dance tradition to Louisiana; they also brought dances and rhythms they had learned in Cuba. This rich African, Haitian, and Afro-Cuban heritage mixed with the local African-American productions to give Louisiana a distinctive musical experience that culminated in the creation of jazz.

Haitians exercised their influence on religion as well. They brought Vodou, which became hoodoo or voodoo in Louisiana, and in 1842 native New Orleanian Henriette Delille, a freeborn woman of Haitian descent, founded the second Catholic religious order of African-American women in the United States, the Sisters of the Holy Family. Mother Mary Lange, a Haitian refugee, founded the first order, the Oblate Sisters of Providence, in Baltimore in 1829.

Southern architecture owes a lot to the Haitian immigrants. The shotgun house evolved in Haiti from a West African—Yoruba, according to many scholars—house design in which two or more rooms were constructed in a straight line back from the entranceway on the street. New Orleans shotgun houses, which first appeared in the city after the massive 1809 immigration of Haitian refugees, have dimensions quite similar to shotgun houses in Haiti.

The refugee population reinforced a brand of revolutionary republicanism that impacted American race relations for decades. With an unflagging commitment to the democratic ideals of the revolutionary era, Haitian immigrants and their descendants appeared at the head of virtually every New Orleans civil-rights campaign. Their leadership role in the struggle for racial justice offers dramatic evidence of the scope of their influence on Louisiana's history. For generations Haitian émigrés and their descendants demanded that the nation fulfill the promise of its founding principles.

THE NEW TRENDS OF HAITIAN MIGRATION | Since the establishment of the first black republic in the world, Haitians who have migrated to the United States have

Free Persons of Color

Left: In the three-tiered racial order of colonial Saint Domingue, free people of color occupied an intermediate status between slaves and whites. The white elite denied their assimilation into the colony's social and political life. They suffered the added humiliation of a dress code designed to emphasize their inferior status.

Right: Black units—which counted many Haitians in their ranks— engaged in combat at Port Hudson and elsewhere in the South faced a grave danger not shared by their white comrades. After the January 1, 1863, Emancipation Proclamation authorized black enlistments, Confederates responded by declaring no black soldier would be allowed to surrender. News reports of Confederate atrocities against black soldiers circulated in the press in the following weeks.

been victims of negative stereotyping; no contemporary immigrant group has encountered more prejudice and discrimination. The story of Haitians in the United States in the 20th and 21st centuries is not one of unrelenting sadness, however. Many, if not most, struggle against prejudice and prevail. They have a strong sense of self-esteem and are proud of their heritage, as is evident in the innumerable community organizations that promote Haitian theater, music, stories, art, religion, cuisine, and the Creole language. Thus for many Haitian immigrants, life in the United States is a conflict between pride in their roots and prejudice against blacks in general and Haitians in particular.

Haitians have a long history of migration and temporary sojourns in other countries. More than one million are estimated to live in the Dominican Republic, where many serve as contract laborers harvesting sugarcane.

The children of Haiti's middle and upper classes have traditionally attended schools in France; political opponents have tended to leave the country after power changes hands. But for a long time, few Haitians came to the United States. In spite of the popular image that all immigrants want to come to America, the reality is that immigrant flows are directed toward the countries with which they have the closest cultural, political, and economic ties. Haiti's links and largest immigration flows have traditionally been to France, along with French-speaking African countries and Canada.

The Coast Guard's resolve to prevent Haitians from attaining refuge on U.S. soil is mirrored by the desperation that forced so many people to leave. These refugees look out defiantly on a Coast Guard ship in August 1987, after having been intercepted at sea. A large part of the discrimination against Haitians came in the form of special attention from the Coast Guard and INS. Haitians were virtually singled out from among other Caribbean islanders fleeing their homelands. Coast Guard officials and the INS worked harder to repatriate Haitian immigrants than immigrants from other countries, including Cuba and the Dominican Republic. Between 1990 and 1995, close to 72,000 Haitians were intercepted at sea.

Until the late 1950s, only about 500 Haitians permanently immigrated to the U.S. each year, while another 3,000 came temporarily as tourists, students, or businesspeople. The origin of the Haitian immigration to the United States can be traced to the assumption of absolute power by President François "Papa Doc" Duvalier in 1957. The United States became more involved in Haitian affairs, and the candidates for emigration began to focus on the U.S. With the U.S. 1965 Immigration Act, which permitted family members to bring close relatives, more people entered the country. Nearly 7,000 Haitians became permanent immigrants every year, and another 20,000 came with temporary visas. But it was during the late 1970s and early 1980s that Haitian immigration entered the American public consciousness as boatloads of people washed onto South Florida's shores.

FROM HAITI TO THE UNITED STATES | President John F. Kennedy thoroughly deplored Duvalier's infamous corruption, brutal human rights violations (carried out by the infamous Tontons Macoutes), and tyrannical oppression of his political enemies, an all-inclusive group that ranged from trade unions and churches to the Boy Scouts. For a brief time, the U.S. actively encouraged Haitians to immigrate.

The first to leave were members of the upper class who directly threatened the Duvalier regime. Around 1964 the middle class began to leave the island. The 1965 Immigration Act permitted legal residents to bring close relatives, and the northward stream broadened.

In September 1963 the first boatload of Haitian refugees landed in South Florida. They asked for political asylum, but the INS summarily rejected the request and the boat was sent back to Haiti. The incident was a preview of the epic to come. By the late 1970s, crude sailboats, often nearly overflowing with refugees, began to arrive regularly. Though there were tales of boats that never made it, enough arrived to cause concern among South Florida officials. The desperate plight facing many Haitians began to make media headlines. Haitian advocates argued that they were fleeing legitimate political persecution and at least deserved a chance to make their case. Repeatedly, the INS used its resources to turn them back.

François Duvalier's death in 1971 brought no appreciable change in Haiti's despotic political conditions. His 19-year-old son, Jean-Claude (nicknamed "Baby Doc"), succeeded him as president-for-life. With the murderous assistance of the Tontons Macoutes, he perpetuated the reign of terror. In February 1986 anti-government demonstrations finally toppled his regime, and Baby Doc fled to France with an estimated $120 million.

With Duvalier out, the Haitian masses rejoiced in the belief that democracy would finally come. The flow of refugees into South Florida noticeably declined, although the United States continued to interdict boats and detain their passengers in the ongoing effort to deter Haitians from coming to this country. Even with a new regime, the economic and political conditions did not improve in Haiti. Repression and corruption continued under what Haitians refer to as "Duvalierism without Duvalier." From Jean-Claude Duvalier's fall until December 1990, the country experienced four military coups and a fraudulent election. Human rights violations, desperate poverty, and government corruption remained an integral part of everyday life. As a result, the number of Haitians seeking refuge in the United States climbed.

Haitians' hopes rose again with the election of President Jean-Bertrand Aristide in December 1990. The activist Catholic priest's victory caused a substantial drop in the exodus of refugees. But the return of democracy and the associated decline in Haitian "boat people" proved all too brief. On September 30, 1991, after just eight months in office, Aristide was overthrown in a military coup. In the aftermath, soldiers beat, tortured, or murdered the ousted president's supporters, who had been arrested and imprisoned without warrants. Haitians again began to leave for the United States: 38,000 in the first eight months following the coup.

A PARTICULAR PREJUDICE | The treatment of Haitian refugees represents a continuing bias in U.S. policy, especially in contrast to the way their Cuban counterparts are handled. The Coast Guard has attempted to intercept boats before they left Haitian waters; a disproportionate number of undocumented Haitians who made it to U.S. shores were incarcerated; and requests for political asylum have been met with the highest rejection rate of any national group.

Repeatedly, local South Florida and national officials have identified Haitians as a health threat: In the 1970s, tuberculosis was allegedly endemic among them. In the early 1980s the Centers for Disease Control identified Haitians as one of the primary groups at risk for AIDS. In spite of Haiti's removal from that list, the Food and Drug Administration in the late 1980s refused to accept the donation of blood from individuals of Haitian origin.

When Congress passed an immigration law that permitted many Central Americans to obtain legal immigration status, Haitians were left out. Later, when a law was passed specifically for Haitians, the INS delayed issuing regulations on who could qualify.

When Haitians began landing in South Florida with stories of political repression and were then denied refugee status, their plight became a public issue, especially when contrasted to the very favorable treatment of the Cubans. Although some Cubans espoused the Haitians' cause, most remained silent. African Americans were, and remain, the only ethnic group to consistently support the rights of Haitians coming to Miami.

Haitian advocates did, however, gain some short-term benefits for limited numbers of people. In 1980 Haitians who arrived before October 10 of that year were granted the same terms as Cubans who had come to the United States before that date. After that, newly arrived Cubans retained their privileges, while Haitians faced renewed discrimination.

In 1982 a U.S. federal court ordered the release of a group of Haitian refugees who had been detained by the INS. Later arrivals, however, were detained and returned. In 1994 Haitians were detained in Guantanamo Naval Base and seldom turned over to relatives in the U.S., while Cuban detainees were almost always released. In 2002 Haitian refugees who had a credible fear of persecution if returned to their homeland were not released on parole, although this was standard practice for other nationalities.

POLITICS OR ECONOMICS? | The INS, citing Haiti's abysmal poverty, maintained that its citizens were not fleeing persecution; they came because they wanted jobs. Haitian advocates, pointing to the ubiquitous and brutal repression of the Duvalier regimes and most of its successors, asserted that Haitians were true refugees. In a fundamental sense, both sides were right. Immigration and refugee laws, however, presume that individual migrant motivations can be separated.

Historically, immigrants came—or were recruited—to take jobs that Americans either did not want or could not fill. Recruitment is no longer necessary, but the majority of immigrants to this country have been most directly motivated by economics. Many others came primarily because relatives had migrated earlier and they wanted to reunite with their families. Family reunification drives American immigration policy; once an immigrant flow begins, the momentum of reunification usually keeps it going. The last major category of immigrants is political refugees.

Haitians combine all of these motivations. Many of those who first fled François Duvalier's regime were escaping persecution. They initiated a Haitian diaspora that spread to Africa, France, Canada, the Bahamas, other parts of the Caribbean, and the United States. Many also had politically influenced economic reasons, as Papa Doc's policies affected everyone's economic security.

But the ultimate causes of the migration mattered little to American policy makers determined to deter Haitians from coming to South Florida, the focal point of Caribbean immigration since the Cuban Revolution.

South Floridians assumed that the "boat people" were uneducated, unskilled peasants who were likely to be disease-ridden. Although these stereotypes were eventually disproved, they still persisted and moved South Florida's leaders to pressure the INS into a consistent, resolute policy against Haitian refugees.

A PROFILE OF THE HAITIAN IMMIGRANTS | The 2000 U.S. Census found approximately 750,000 Haitians residing in this country. This figure, however, reflects an undercount by as much as 50 percent in some neighborhoods. Florida, with 268,000 Haitians, has more than one-third of the nation's total.

The second largest concentration, 180,000, is found in New York. Massachusetts, primarily Boston, has a significant community of some 50,000 Haitians. The remaining population is spread thinly throughout many states.

Although Miami is the closest city to Haiti and possesses a similar climate, the legacy of segregation still prevailed, and most Haitians who arrived in the 1960s

Haitian Leaders

Top: Haitian-born Joe Celestin became the first black mayor of North Miami on May 22, 2001. The city became the second South Florida municipality to elect a majority Haitian-American city council. Celestin's election underscores the fact that African Americans and Haitian Americans in North Miami are striving for similar political goals.

Bottom: Fred St. Amand and his daughter Sandra are members of the growing community of Haitian entrepreneurs who own and operate businesses primarily serving the Haitian community. Haitians have become active in the economic life of their neighborhoods, both in the U.S. and Canada.

settled in the northeastern United States and French Canada, where racism was less severe. A large Haitian community began to emerge in New York, along with others in Chicago, Boston, and Montreal.

The immigrants encountered the problems and difficulties common to many new arrivals, compounded by the fact that the Haitians were "triple minorities": They were foreigners, spoke a language (Haitian Creole) that no one else did, and they were black.

Many of those who came temporarily subsequently overstayed their visas, thus becoming undocumented immigrants. As the government and Haitian advocates fought during the 1980s over the rights of the newcomers to remain in this country, a South Florida Haitian community was emerging. Its focal point, known as Little Haiti, lies just north of downtown Miami and has become the center of Haitian life in the United States.

The Haitian population in South Florida is overwhelmingly composed of recent arrivals—nearly two-thirds of the foreign-born Haitians in Miami came in the 1980s, with 40 percent arriving between 1980 and 1984. Only 7 percent of Miami's Haitians reported in 1990 that they had arrived prior to 1970.

It is a youthful population: Nearly 42 percent were between 30 and 44 years old, while close to 20 percent were 14 years old or younger. However, the number of Haitian births in Miami held steady at 2,000 per year in the 1980s and early 1990s, a rate comparable to the broader population growth. Thus, the Haitian population is growing more from immigration than from new births in this country.

Refugees in South Florida found that anti-Haitian prejudice and discrimination created barriers to finding employment. Except for low-wage, dead-end jobs, there were few opportunities for the refugees. A 1983 survey showed that more than one-third had never worked since coming to this country. Nearly 30 percent of the males and more than 70 percent of the females were unemployed. But the situation improved, and by the 1990s Haitian unemployment rates, though still high, had begun to approximate those of African Americans. Businesses realized that Haitians would work cheaply and without complaint.

Beginning in the 1980s many of the first wave of immigrants who had settled in the Northeast and Canada moved to Florida; they diversified the economic mix

Cultural Life

Above: With roughly 50,000 Haitians in the metropolitan area, Boston has one of the largest concentrations of Haitians in the U.S. outside of South Florida and New York. Here, a youth rally at the Temple Baptist Church in Dorchester celebrates Dr. Martin Luther King, Jr.'s birthday. Such activity is indicative of the general move by Haitian-American youths to associate with African Americans and the history of struggle against racial prejudice in America.

Right: The Papaloko Band performs at the Tap Tap Restaurant in Miami during a Haitian Carnival night celebration. The proud tradition of art and performance continues to maintain a strong presence in Haitian communities.

by adding a component of entrepreneurs, professionals, and other middle-class Haitians.

THE HAITIAN SOUL: RELIGION AND CULTURE | To cope with their constant confrontation with prejudice and discrimination, most Haitians turn to the internal strengths of their culture. They recall Haiti's extraordinary, revolutionary history. They turn their gaze toward heaven and attend church more frequently and in greater numbers than any other contemporary immigrant group. They extol their world-famous art and music, as well as their African- and French-influenced cuisine.

Haitians are devout Christians. Surveys have shown that nearly 75 percent of recent immigrants to South Florida attend church at least once a week. In a striking departure from the denominational makeup of Haiti, where some 80 to 85 percent of the residents are Catholic, nearly 40 percent of Haitian Americans are Protestant. Storefront churches abound in Little Haiti, and a few Protestant congregations have had explosive growth. One Baptist church has converted a huge, former textile plant in Little Haiti into an impressive house of worship.

Religious communities provide a social support system for fellow immigrants. In rural Haiti, Vodou ceremonies draw families—immediate and extended—together. They help individuals cope with growing up, becoming ill, getting cured, and eventually dying. The religion provides avenues for prestige, an informal criminal justice system—through its rituals, those who behave improperly can be chastised and disciplined without recourse to police and courts—and the opportunity to participate in a multitude of ceremonies involving music, dance, skits, and crafts. It has been said that the Vodou temple in Haiti is "sanctuary, clubhouse, dance hall, hospital, theater, chemist's shop, music hall, court and council chamber in one."

In the United States, Christian congregations fill many of those roles and more. When an immigrant is sick or in dire straits, fellow parishioners may gather at the person's house to pray together and/or informally contribute money to help. Churches formally aid with charity and other services, and pastors and priests command great respect.

Haitian music has become part of the American pop culture scene. By far the most popular Haitian musician in this country is Wyclef Jean, the Grammy-winning, chart-topping singer, composer, and arranger who has been referred to as the "hip-hop Amadeus." His former multiplatinum band, the Fugees, chose their name as an abbreviation for "those from refugee camps." Jean has also been honored for his continuing efforts in support of musical education and expanded opportunities for underprivileged children. Haitian visual artists are now firmly established in major collections in the United States, and their works are bringing high prices at the leading auction houses.

FAMILY LIFE AND THE SECOND GENERATION | The family is the primary foundation for Haitian life in the United States. In fact, families sponsor and organize the migration. Once here, émigrés are expected to maintain and reinforce kinship ties back home. Actually, the refugees' financial support for family in Haiti may well contribute to their poverty in this country. Shirking these obligations shames both the immigrants and their relatives in the homeland. Nuclear families often expand to include more distant relatives and even former spouses. Children may often live with those relatives or with others not related by blood but still regarded as kinfolk. Children are at the core of Haitian life, greatly appreciated and linking families and households. Although most Haitians arrive in the United States with little money, nearly all have "social capital"—networks that can provide such resources as housing, employment, and knowledge of the local rules of survival.

A new group is emerging in the Haitian-American community: the second generation. They are a diverse group, with different stories, strategies, and identities. Sadly, some have internalized the stereotypes that cling to their community.

Some children and adolescents commit a form of cultural suicide by hiding their Haitian roots, claiming they do not know their native language. They are likely to have conflicts with their parents over their efforts to Americanize and, like American youngsters, they struggle for independence. For adolescent females, these battles can be particularly difficult. In traditional Haitian families, parents exercise nearly absolute control over their daughters, especially concerning expressions of sexuality.

Haitian parents, like other immigrants, view education as a path for their children to improve their lives. Many Haitian children do indeed excel. Second- and first-generation Haitian immigrant youth have flourished at the nation's elite universities. Language and cultural differences, however, often deter parents from directly participating in school activities. They frequently lack enough English to help with homework; groups like Parent Teacher Associations are unknown back home.

Nevertheless, parents constantly tell their children that they expect them to succeed academically. For middle-class students, the rewards of schooling are self-evident. It appears to those from a poor or working-class neighborhood, however, that white Americans will get all the good jobs, that blacks and Latinos do not have

Protesting INS Policy
Haitian-Americans demonstrate at the Immigration and Naturalization Service building on October 31, 2002, in Miami, Florida. Miami's Haitian community is protesting current INS policy that sends most Haitian refugees back home without any administrative hearing. The issue has come to the fore after more than 200 illegal migrant Haitians were taken into custody when their 50-foot freighter ran aground near the Ridenbacker Causeway in Miami.

the same opportunities. Believing that school is not worth the effort, an unfortunately large number of minority youths adopt an adversarial stance toward education. While many Latinos and African Americans do extremely well in school, others have given up hope.

Haitian youths in inner cities are often caught in this cultural vise. Their parents insist that they excel in school and maintain their Haitian heritage. At the same time, many of their African-American peers demean Haitian culture and maintain that racism blocks success for all blacks, regardless of academic achievement. Haitian youths must try to balance the expectations of their parents with the harsh realities of prejudice and discrimination that they confront. Some commit cultural suicide, but many more adopt dual identities, being American among peers and Haitian among family.

As Haitians pass through adolescence they become both more American and more Haitian. They dress in American styles, eat American food, and speak English. At the same time, as they mature, they often prefer to identify not as American or even African American, but as Haitian American or even simply as Haitian. They rediscover a pride in their Haitian roots.

Return to the South

1970 TO PRESENT

In the first six decades of the 20th century, one of the most significant demographic shifts in the history of the United States occurred: the movement of millions of African Americans from the rural South to the urban North. By 1970, however, this shift had begun to reverse—the number of return migrants eclipsed the number of departing African Americans. During the 1970s, the South added two million African Americans to its population, more than tripling the figure for the previous decade. The 1980s and 1990s would bring even more substantial return migration and population retention. Pictured is Stephanie S. Hughley (originally from Ohio), executive producer of the National Black Arts Festival. She is seated next to a drum from Ghana in her office in Atlanta, Georgia.

In the early 1970s the migration trend of the previous five decades began to reverse. African Americans were returning to the South. After decades of mounting migration north and west, the rates had actually begun to slow in the 1950s. But it was not until the late 1960s that the number of African Americans moving to the South eclipsed the number leaving. Since then, black migration to the South has continued to grow.

Many migrants—a majority of them college educated—seek economic opportunities in the reascending southern economy. Some want to escape deteriorating conditions in Northern cities, and others return to be nearer to kin, to care for aging relatives, or to retire in a familiar environment with a better quality of life than the urban North. All, in some way, reclaim the South as their home, the place that African Americans built and where their roots run deep.

A CHANGING TIDE | Despite the migration of 1.5 million African Americans to northern cities during the Great Migration, on the eve of World War II the black population remained largely southern and rural. Within two decades, however, its demographics changed dramatically. In 1940 only 23 percent of African Americans lived outside the South; by 1970 this figure had more than doubled, rising to 47 percent. But return migration had already started. It actually occurred throughout the 20th century. Even in the 1930s approximately one African American migrated from North to South for every four heading north. This number slowly evened out: from 1955 each five-year period saw 100,000 black Northerners relocating to the South. By 1970 there were more people returning to the South than leaving it.

Although many people moving to the South in the 1960s and 1970s had never lived there, overall this movement was indeed a *return* migration. Approximately two-thirds of the African-American migrants who moved to the South between 1965 and 1970 were going back to the region of their birth.

The trend continued in the 1970s: From 1975 to 1980, at least 41 percent of African Americans going south were return migrants, whose destinations included large cities as well as a wide range of smaller urban communities and rural regions. What these figures fail to show, however, is the number of "non-return" migrants—northern-born people moving to places in which they had strong and lasting kinship networks. In other words, they were the children and grandchildren of the Southerners who had left the South during the Great Migration and World War II.

The patterns of migration back to the South confirm the extent to which African-American migrants—both return and non-return—followed familial paths. The geographical patterns that had dominated the first two Great Migrations were shaped in large part by regional railroad routes and chain migration. Many African Americans who migrated north in the first half of the 20th century chose their destinations according to where they had access via local railroads and where other family members and friends had migrated before them. Dwayne Walls, in *Chickenbone Special,* recounts an old quote about the African-American residents of a rural community in North Carolina: "These people know only three places to go: Heaven, Hell, and Baltimore."

As migrants returned south, many followed the same paths that their predecessors had carved out when they migrated north. Despite the rise of the automobile, they moved along the old railroad routes: from eastern cities toward the Carolinas; from Ohio and Michigan cities toward Alabama; from Chicago toward Mississippi; and from Los Angeles toward East Texas.

But not all African-American migrants were returning home. Some were actually born in the North and were seeking economic opportunities rather than familial ties. They headed in large numbers for rapidly growing metropolitan areas, and only 16 percent went to less economically promising, more rural areas; in contrast, 45 percent of return migrants ended up in nonmetropolitan areas.

Nevertheless, coming home to family remained one of the most important factors pulling African Americans to the South. In a 1973 survey of return migrants to Birmingham, Alabama, the majority of respondents (52 percent) cited various kinship and family reasons, the single most important of which (cited by 12 percent of returnees) was to care for an ill or aging parent or relative. In a distant second, they mentioned various economic reasons (almost 20 percent) as the impetus for their return. Non-family social reasons (16 percent) and health/climate reasons (12 percent) also influenced decisions to return south.

THE NEW SOUTH: JIM CROW DISMANTLED | Among the most important factors contributing to the reversal of emigration out of the South were the political and social changes that culminated in a number of Supreme Court decisions and federal actions in the 1950s and 1960s. Although African Americans would continue to

face discrimination, violence, and other obstacles, actions taken by the federal government to formally dismantle Jim Crow generated change in many southern communities and sparked hope for a brighter future for the region.

The formal and informal segregation, discrimination in employment and housing, denial of civil rights, and outright violence that African Americans faced in southern communities had provided a major "push" factor during the first half of the 20th century. It was not merely custom, but also state and municipal laws that systematically excluded blacks from workplaces, public spaces, voting booths, and schools.

And it was the political awareness and activism among Southerners that brought about immense political and social transformations. The swelling ranks of the civil rights movement in the South during the 1950s and 1960s bolstered the assault on segregation with sit-ins, protests, voter-registration drives, and boycotts.

In the late 1960s, ever increasing numbers of African Americans chose to fight these battles in political arenas. Before the passage of the Voting Rights Act, a total of 72 African Americans held elected offices in the 11 states of the old Confederacy. Just five years later, that number increased almost tenfold: In March 1971, 711 African Americans held elected offices in the same states.

Tommy Dortch, a young man with political aspirations, moved back to the South in order to pursue a political career, explaining to the magazine *Ebony* in 1973: "I left the South like everybody else—looking for my future in the North…but it did not take me long to realize that, politically, I could get elected easier in the South and be more effective."

The promise of life in the South without the obstacles of the segregationist and discriminatory laws of the past—and the reality that informal but entrenched discrimination existed in the North—made the South an enticing destination.

Etta Willis, who left San Francisco for Mount Olive, Mississippi, described the improvement in Southern conditions in an interview with the *San Francisco Chronicle:*

> You don't have the racism here that you used to have; frankly I have experienced less racism here than I did in San Francisco. The racism in San Francisco is very hard to detect, but it's there. It's here too, but not like that. If someone doesn't care for you they tell you to your face, and I can't think of a time that's happened since I came back.

The Urban Landscape

Above: Opened in 1941, the Kingsborough housing project in Brooklyn, New York, was plagued by gang activity by the 1990s. No site captured the perils of urban life more than the public housing projects of the inner cities. Begun as an effort to alleviate some of the abhorrent conditions of crowding in northern cities—a particular plight of African Americans whose housing options were restricted by discrimination and segregation—many public housing projects became hotbeds of drugs, violence, and gang warfare.

Right: Carmen Johnson, born in Detroit and raised in California, moved to Atlanta in 1990. In 2001 she opened a real-estate franchise. Here, she consults with Valmond G. Aguilera, a businessman and former New Yorker.

Additionally, many of the humiliating social customs that had prevailed in the South decades earlier had begun to fade by the 1970s. Earnest Smith, who left Mississippi for Chicago in 1944, recalled the time before he left the South as one filled with discrimination, segregation, violence, and the embarrassment of answering to the term "boy." Smith and his wife moved back to Mississippi in 1970 and found a more hospitable environment. In a 1971 interview with *Ebony* magazine, Smith observed:

Everybody's been wonderful.... White folks used to always hurry you up or curse at you when I left [in the 1940s]. Now they stop you on the street to say "Hello" and some of 'em call you "Sir." And they say "yes ma'am" and "no ma'am" to my wife and call her "Miss Smith." Things changed so much, one guy come here from Chicago and brought his white wife.

Similarly, Elijah Davis, who moved back to Jackson, Mississippi, in 1970 after living in Gary, Indiana, for 20 years, remarked: "Before I left here years ago, there were places you couldn't go, places you couldn't eat at, and you couldn't make a decent living. But I can live in peace here. I can walk anywhere in town without fear."

That is not to say that African Americans in the South did not face obstacles, continued discrimination, and violence. Many of the same problems persisted; however, it was clear to all in the 1970s that something had indeed changed forever.

If the civil rights movement had not succeeded in creating a just and harmonious world, it had fostered important, tangible, and lasting changes in the social and political fabric of the nation—particularly in the states of the South.

FROM THE RUST BELT TO THE SUN BELT | At the same time, conditions in the North were starting to deteriorate. The economic boom in cities of the Midwest, Northeast, and West—spawned particularly by World War II—had come to a grinding halt by the early 1970s. Many of the factories and plants that had lured African Americans from the South during and after the war were abandoned in the wake of a globalizing economy and the oil crisis of the early 1970s. The new economic order literally destroyed communities and eliminated hundreds of thousands of manufacturing jobs.

For instance, in Detroit—the heart of the nation's auto manufacturing—jobs were cut by more than half in the 30 years following the end of World War II. In

1947 the city harbored 3,272 manufacturing firms, which employed approximately 338,400 people; in 1977 the number of firms had withered to 1,954 employing 153,300 people. As manufacturing companies increasingly sought cheaper labor and resources in offshore sites, the region previously known as the heartland of American industry was transformed into America's Rust Belt.

But the Rust Belt was not the only region in the country to experience economic transformation during this period. As manufacturing declined in the Northeast and Midwest during the 1970s, it grew in the states of the South and West. In 1963 the "east north central" region (primarily Michigan and Illinois) produced 30 percent of the nation's manufacturing output, while the South produced 21 percent, and the West 14 percent. By 1989, however, the east north central's manufacturing output had been cut almost in half, and the output of the South and West grew to 29 percent and 18 percent, respectively. Lured by cheaper—and nonunion—labor, less expensive land, temperate weather, tax breaks, and

Coming Home

Thelma Wallace Williams poses with heirloom quilts in front of her family home in Natchez, Mississippi, March 1993. Thelma began spending summers here in 1933, and continued to come back every summer through college. Thelma then received her master's degree in chemistry and embarked on a teaching career, retiring after 25 years at New York Technical College. After her husband's death other government incentives, manufacturers were increasingly choosing the Sun Belt states of the South and West as sites for new production facilities.

The migration deluge from the South had hit Los Angeles late, compared to the great cities of the East Coast and Midwest. But beginning in the 1940s, upwards of 300,000 African Americans poured in, pulled by the industrial boom that accompanied the Second World War. After the war, they stayed.

Now, more than a few migrants and their descendants are packing their bags. Over a five-year period in the early 1990s, spurred in large part by California's sagging economy, some 103,000 African Americans relocated to the South.

Thus, for those seeking job opportunities there was a curious symmetry between the original Great Migration and the return migration. Both involve (for many people) pushes at the origin and job prospects at the destination.

The economic draws of the South extended beyond manufacturing employment. African Americans were also drawn to an overall lower cost-of-living in the region, as well as thriving middle-class communities and career opportunities. As John Ash told *Ebony* in 1973, after moving to Atlanta from Los Angeles: "The high cost of land and high property taxes in California made Atlanta very attractive to us…. It just seemed as if we could get more for our money by settling here."

During the 1990s, Atlanta, which some called the Harlem of the nineties, was the favored destination of the returnees. It gained close to 160,000 black residents in six years. They saw the city as a new promised land, with unlimited opportunity, a great place to raise their children. Washington, D.C., and the metropolitan areas of Houston, Miami, Dallas-Fort Worth, Norfolk, and Orlando all saw a large black population gain during the nineties.

THE URBAN CRISIS | More tangible than the economic upturn and growing job opportunities in the South in the 1970s were the deteriorating physical and social conditions of the central cities of the North and West. During the 1960s the problem of the "ghetto"—urban decay, inner-city poverty, and unrest—appeared urgent. The decade saw a resurgence of urban uprisings in African-American neighborhoods, generally in response to manifestations of discrimination.

Hundreds of disturbances occurred throughout the 1960s in black urban neighborhoods, the most significant of which occurred in the Watts district of Los Angeles in 1965, in Newark and Detroit in 1967, and following the assassination of Dr. Martin Luther King, Jr., in cities across the country in 1968. This inner-city turmoil troubled many, including the residents of affected neighborhoods.

Earnest Smith, who moved from Mississippi to Chicago in 1944, commented after his move back to the South in 1970: "For the first 20 years, life in Chicago was real nice…. But the last five years was when I come to gettin' scared. They killed [Dr. Martin Luther] King and the people started tearin' up the place. Crime

in the mid-1980s, Thelma moved back to Natchez. She directs Project Southern Cross, which as part of its program operates the Mostly African Market, a gallery and store across the street from her home. *Above:* In the top row, center, is Margaret Page (1860-1940), Thelma Williams's grandmother, and one of three children born to a mixed union. She is pictured with her four daughters.

Black Southern colleges and universities continue to flourish, with many graduates deciding to stay in the South for professional opportunities. Pictured (left) is a group commencement exercise for Spelman College, Morehouse College, and Atlanta University.

Below: In 1962 James Meredith became the first African American to enroll at the University of Mississippi after suing for admission. On September 30, 1962, President John F. Kennedy sent 23,000 federal troops to squelch the rioting of about 3,000 white protesters. Two people were killed and 160 were injured. Meredith sits among fellow students at the graduation ceremonies on August 18, 1963. In May 2002, his son Joseph graduated as the top doctoral student from the University of Mississippi business school almost 40 years after his father became the first African American to attend Ole Miss.

in Chicago got so bad that I got scared and started carryin' a gun." To many, both the physical and social foundations of many urban African-American communities appeared to be crumbling in the late 1960s.

Issues concerning urban decay and poverty were of great interest to federal policy makers in the 1960s. Even before the "urban crisis" was on the national radar, President Lyndon B. Johnson declared a War on Poverty in his state of the union address in 1964. After the Watts riot, the problem of the ghetto and African-American poverty became the most urgent of domestic issues.

Despite all of the attention urban decay, unrest, unemployment, and poverty in the ghetto received in the 1960s, the programs spearheaded by the government were largely ineffective and highly criticized. When Richard Nixon was elected President in 1968, he dismantled virtually all of Johnson's War on Poverty programs.

African-American migration from the urban North to the South accelerated in part because of the dismal conditions faced by inner-city communities, but the South faced comparable problems. Rural poverty, for instance, was (and remains) one of the most entrenched economic problems in the United States. Nevertheless, the future of the urban North grew less and less promising for African Americans.

THE SOUTHERN BRAIN GAIN | Demographic studies have shown that migrants tend to have higher levels of education than nonmigrants, and so did African-American migrants from the South to the North. This is often not the case, however, in return migration. Return migrants generally have lower education levels than those who stay at their destinations—perhaps because of the fewer employment opportunities afforded those with lower education levels.

But this characterization may only be relevant for those who return soon after they had left in the first place. Demographers who have specifically studied the return migration to the South have found that the conventional wisdom does not hold: African Americans moving back south generally had higher occupational and educational status than non-migrants. They, on average, had higher incomes and occupations than the overall African-American population of the South. Unlike the previous migration from south to north, which included many agricultural workers, the net migration rates for African-American migration south were higher for those with college degrees or at least some college than for those with lower education levels.

Today, 50.5 percent of African Americans moving south have a college education. Some southern states have indeed experienced a "brain gain," attracting

Young Professionals

Above: From left to right: Eric Smith of Cleveland, Ohio; Dave Richburg of New York; Jefferson L. Clay II of Detroit; and Diana Richburg of New York work on business plans in Buckhead, Atlanta. Smith does a brisk business selling insurance and investment products from his Decatur, Georgia home and website.

Right: From left to right: Emily Murray, age 19; Rosa Benitez, age 18; and Tek Smith, age 17, clean dental tools with a BioSonic cleaner, as part of a Dekalb County, Atlanta health career course offered to high school students in preparation for jobs after graduation, or for two- or four-year health-related vocational programs.

thousands of black college graduates. Between 1995 and 2000, Georgia—particularly Atlanta—Texas, and Maryland had a particularly large influx of college-educated African Americans. New York was the top "brain drain" state, losing more than 18,000 African-American college graduates in that five-year period. Interestingly, as noted by demographer William H. Frey, "The major 'brain gain' states are distinct from those gaining the most white college graduates. Although southern states such as Florida, North Carolina, Georgia, and Texas are among the largest white gainers, the top ten list also includes six western states. Comparatively, then, the South appears to exert a stronger "pull" on highly educated blacks than it does on their white counterparts." Among the top ten gainers of black college graduates, only two (Arizona and Nevada) are not southern states.

This specific migration has contributed greatly to the growth of the middle class in many southern cities. Several elected officials, such as Atlanta Mayor Shirley Franklin and former Houston Mayor Lee Brown, are returnees.

Although the collective characteristics of the migrants can provide a glimpse into the range of factors prompting them to return to the South, the migration itself is distinguished by the diverse backgrounds and motivations of its participants. The personal decisions they make are of great importance in understanding their move; however, there are also several broad social, political, and economic transformations that assure a more promising future for African Americans in the South.

FAMILY MATTERS | Among the most influential factors prompting African Americans to migrate to the South was family. A 1973 survey of return migrants to Birmingham, Alabama, found that more than half of the respondents had moved back for reasons regarding their families. Many were, in fact, returning to take care of aging relatives. Thus it appears that return migration to the South was not just a nostalgic homecoming; it was a family strategy.

Asked in 1971 why African Americans were returning to the South, Atlanta businessman Jesse B. Blayton replied, "Grandma is here.... Most American blacks have roots in the South. The liberation thinking is here. Blacks are more together. With the doors opening wider, this area is the Mecca."

Even for those migrants who had never lived in the South and did not have specific family obligations to fulfill, a sense of family history could prove enticing. Author and poet Maya Angelou returned in the early 1980s to Winston Salem, North Carolina. Discussing African-American return migration, Angelou wrote:

The answer to the question "Why are so many young Black people moving South today?" is that the American South sings a siren song to all Black Americans. The melody may be ignored, despised or ridiculed, but we all hear it…. They return and find or make their places in the land of their foreparents. They find and make friends under the shade of trees their ancestors left decades earlier. Many find themselves happy, without being able to explain the emotion. I think it is simply that they feel generally important.

Since the early 1970s, when social scientists began studying African-American return migration, many debates as to the primary causes of the movement have taken shape. While some geographers, economists, and demographers have focused on economic factors, anthropologist Carol Stack, in her book *Call to Home,* has taken a more ethnographic approach that stresses the importance of kinship networks and long-term, multi-generational family bonds.

Stack found that children often served as a bond between northern and southern branches of a family: Some northern-born children moved to the South to be cared for by grandparents; others spent summers and holidays visiting southern relatives; and a substantial number moved South as adults to help care for elderly kin.

In light of these family strategies, the migration back to the South in the 1970s is not surprising: Individuals who migrated as young adults in the 1940s and 1950s were returning home to care for aging parents. But there is also something else: The feeling that by returning south African Americans are claiming back their heritage.

Actor Morgan Freeman, who was born in Tennessee and grew up in Mississippi before moving north and west, has gone back to the place of his childhood. As he explained, "This is home. This is where my roots are.... [W]e built the South, and we know it. What I own in the South isn't because I went and bought it. What I own is my place here, because my mother, my father, my grandmother, my grandfather, my great-grandmother...all the way back to my great-great-great-grandmother, who happened to be a Virginian—that's where they had the farms."

THE LEGACIES: A NEW GREAT MIGRATION? | While African-American return migration to the South may have caught social scientists by surprise in the 1970s, it was not merely a blip on the radar. The South continued to register a net gain of African-American migrants through the 1970s and 1980s, and in-migration increased dramatically in the 1990s. In the first half of the decade, the South recorded a net gain of 368,000 African Americans, compared with a gain of 97,000 in the first five years of the previous decade.

In this same period, 65 percent of the nation's black population growth took place in the South. The most recent census data, for the years 1995 to 2000, reveal a continuation of this trend: Approximately 680,000 African Americans moved South and 330,000 moved out, for a net gain for the region of 350,000.

Enough time has passed since World War I and the great surge in African-American migration from South to North to comprehend the momentous transformations this demographic shift wrought. It has been barely three decades since the flow of the Great Migrations reversed itself. This trend is far from over, as the net migration to the South continues to grow in the 21st century. While social scientists, and the migrants themselves, attempt to understand the push-and-pull factors shaping such a demographic shift, the full impact of this movement is yet to be realized. The return of African Americans to the South may yet rank among the nation's great migrations.

Whatever its causes and effects may be, after "generations of separation and decades of forgetfulness," as Maya Angelou observed, many African Americans have found "that they can come home again."

New Foundations

VIPs sign cement pavers, which became part of the foundation of South Dekalb Medical Center's new hospital. Hospital officials and supporters attended a ceremony in which they poured the foundation for their new hospital, the first full-service hospital in South DeKalb County, Georgia.

African Immigration

Over the past 30 years more Africans have come voluntarily to this country than during the entire era of the transatlantic slave trade that transported an estimated half a million men, women, and children to these shores. But this contemporary migration—although larger in strictly numerical terms, and concentrated over a much shorter period—forms only a trickle in the total stream of immigrants to the United States.

Nevertheless, small as it is still today, the African community has been steadily and rapidly increasing. Sub-Saharan Africans have recently acquired a high level of visibility in many cities. Close-knit, attached to their cultures, and prompt to seize the educational and professional opportunities of their host country, African immigrants have established themselves as one of the most dynamic and entrepreneurial groups in the United States.

Africans are traditionally family-oriented. The extended family—not the individual or the nuclear family—is the basic unit that makes up society. However, in the United States African families are generally nuclear, composed of parents and their children. But as increasing numbers of Africans become American citizens, more family members have the option to immigrate. The Ahonkai family, originally from Nigeria, has settled in Philadelphia.

WHO ARE THE MIGRANTS AND WHY DO THEY COME | Immigration from sub-Saharan Africa dates back to the 1860s when men from Cape Verde—then Portuguese-controlled islands off the coast of Senegal—made their way to Massachusetts. They were seamen and most were employed as whalers. Women soon followed, and after the demise of whale hunting, Cape-Verdeans worked mostly in textile mills and cranberry bogs.

A small number of African students sent by Christian missions and churches to historically black colleges and universities were also present from the end of the 19th century. The trend continued in the early 20th century. Nnamdi Azikiwe, the first Nigerian president, and Kwame Nkrumah, Ghana's first president, both studied at Lincoln University and pursued graduate studies at the University of Pennsylvania.

Traditionally, Africans had primarily migrated to their former colonial powers—Great Britain, France, and Portugal—and more than a million Africans presently live in Europe. But beginning in the late 1970s, these countries froze immigration due to economic slowdowns. The United States became an option.

At the same time, increasing numbers of students and professionals decided to remain in America due to political and economic problems on the continent.

Concurrently, the mounting debts, sluggish growth, exploding populations and high unemployment at home were pushing many Africans to seek their fortunes elsewhere. In the 1990s, emigration was also spurred by the Structural Adjustment Programs imposed by the International Monetary Fund and the World Bank, which resulted in cuts in education and health services, the discharge of public servants, private sector bankruptcies, and a decrease in middle-class standards of living within African nations. In addition, in 1994 more than a dozen French-speaking countries devalued their currencies by 50 percent; a restructuring of the public sector, numerous layoffs, more bankruptcies, and fewer prospects for college graduates were the consequences.

Emigrants were not only pushed out of their countries, they were also pulled to the United States. A number of favorable immigration policies enabled them to make the journey in much greater numbers than before.

THE NUMBERS | Census Department estimates of immigrants—particularly those without documentation—are traditionally unreliable. For example, the 1990 census counted 2,287 Senegalese, even though various studies showed at least 10,000 living in New York City. The 2000 census reports between 511,000 and 746,000 sub-Saharan Africans, with West Africans (36 percent) in the lead, followed by East Africans (24 percent). About 6 percent of the sub-Saharan Africans are South Africans, many of whom are white. A small percentage of East Africans are of Asian origin.

Nationwide, 1.7 million people claim sub-Saharan ancestry. Africans now represent 6 percent of all the immigrants to the United States. It is a recent phenomenon; about 57 percent immigrated between 1990 and 2000. People of sub-Saharan African ancestry now represent almost 5 percent of the African-American community. Those who were actually born in Africa form 1.6 percent of the country's black population. Over the past ten years, this group has increased 134 percent.

Africans are dispersed throughout the country, and in no state are they fewer than 150. New York has the largest African community, followed by California, Texas, and Maryland. However, the District of Columbia, Maryland, and Rhode Island have the highest percentages of Africans in their total populations. With 136,000 officially recorded immigrants, Nigerians are the number-one sub-Saharan African community; Ethiopians (69,500) and Ghanaians (65,600) come far behind.

Although media coverage of African immigrants is most often devoted to the refugees, they represent a minority of the African community. From 1990 to 2001, 101,000 African refugees—10 percent of all refugees who entered the country—were admitted to the United States. More than 40,000 were Somalis,

New Immigrants

By the end of the 19th century, men and women from Cape Verde arrived in great numbers. Their immigration continued until the restrictive laws of 1921 closed the door to non-Europeans. Between 1860 and 1920, about 20,000 Cape Verdeans made their way to New Bedford, Massachusetts. They worked in the textile mills and the cranberry bogs. These immigrants arrived in New Bedford on October 5, 1914. The 155 passengers had come from Fogo Island.

and close to 21,000 came from Ethiopia, while 18,500 arrived from the Sudan.

Africans are highly urban; 95 percent live in a metropolitan area and, like most immigrants, they tend to settle where other countrymen have preceded. A few Senegalese put down roots in New York in the early 1980s; today most Senegalese can still be found there. A large number of Nigerians reside in Texas—their homeland is a major oil producer and they have experience in that industry. Washington, D.C., the headquarters of the World Bank, the International Monetary Fund, and other international organizations, has attracted large numbers of highly educated Africans.

The Twin Cities, St. Paul and Minneapolis, have America's largest Somali population, estimated at 30,000. Many are refugees relocated directly from camps in East Africa. But the overwhelming majority—attracted by job opportunities, family reunification and educational possibilities—are now coming in a secondary migration from Texas, Virginia, and California.

Because sub-Saharan Africans live in higher-income and more highly educated areas than other people of African descent, they are largely segregated from African Americans and Caribbeans. Although this trend is somewhat in decline, it still holds true for New York and Atlanta, two cities where Africans are quite numerous.

Left: Africans have adopted the American tradition of national parades. Every year on September 27, Nigerians in New York gather to celebrate the independence of their homeland. The parade is the occasion for myriad Nigerian groups to come together in a cultural and social celebration of their country. The parade is also a way to affirm the community's presence and strength in the host nation.

Above: The lives of African immigrants are marked by ceremonies, such as baptisms and weddings, that are always big events in Africa. Although many expatriates return home to get married in elaborate ceremonies, increasing numbers have their weddings in the United States as there are now enough religious leaders, family members, and compatriots to make the elements of the ceremonies authentic.

THE BRAIN DRAIN | For a significant number of Africans, the United States is not their first migration country; many have come from Europe, the Middle East, the Caribbean, and other nations in Africa. These are motivated expatriates, adaptable risk-takers always in search of better opportunities and with a wealth of experience acquired at home and in their countries of first immigration. Besides their migration experience, the most significant characteristic of the African immigrants is that they are the most educated group in the nation. Almost half have bachelor's degrees or higher compared to 26 percent of native-born Americans. Contrary to popular belief, the most substantial part of African emigration is thus directly linked to the "brain drain," not to poverty. In fact, 98 percent are high school graduates.

Sub-Saharan nations bear the great cost of forming students who will continue their education in the West and may not return home during their most productive years. As renowned Nigerian computer scientist Philippe Emeagwali puts it: "The African education budget is nothing but a supplement to the American education budget. In essence, Africa is giving developmental assistance to the wealthier western nations which makes the rich nations richer and the poor nations poorer."

According to the United Nations Economic Commission for Africa and the International Organization for Migration, 27,000 intellectual Africans left the continent for industrialized nations between 1960 and 1975. While 40,000 followed them from 1975 to 1984, between 1985 and 1990 the figure skyrocketed to 60,000, and has averaged 20,000 annually ever since.

At least 60 percent of physicians trained in Ghana during the 1980s have left their country, and half of Zimbabwe's social workers trained in the past ten years are now working in Great Britain. To fill the shortage of professionals, about 100,000 non-African expatriates work on the continent at a cost of $4 billion every year—a figure that represents a large part of the aid directed toward Africa and ultimately goes back to the industrialized countries when expatriates send their pay home.

This substantial brain drain is a significant obstacle to development, but African expatriates stress that poor economic conditions and political repression are often responsible for their leaving. They also point out that low salaries, lack of adequate equipment and research facilities, and the need to provide for their extended families are the reasons for their emigration, not individualistic motivations.

Besides professionals who work in the United States, more than 32,000 under-graduate and graduate students from sub-Saharan Africa are enrolled in American universities. They pump more than half a billion dollars into American universities and the general economy each year. As a point of comparison, the total U.S. economic aid to sub-Saharan Africa is slightly more than $1 billion annually.

A significant proportion of African immigrants have "made it" in this country. Besides a few millionaires, 38 percent hold professional and managerial positions. The Africans' average annual incomes are higher than those of the foreign-born population as a whole. More than 45 percent earn between $35,000 and $75,000 a year, and—because of the immigrants' disproportionately high education levels—exceed the median income of African Americans and Caribbeans.

The fact remains, however, that the Africans' income levels, high though they may seem, do not mirror their academic achievements. As the most highly educated community in the nation, they should occupy many more top-level professional and managerial positions. There are several reasons for this. Degrees earned overseas are sometimes not readily transferable, so the immigrants must enroll in school once more, holding low-wage jobs to pay for their schooling. "It is at times degrading when you come here and find that all the education you have from home does not mean anything here. It is a shock. We had to start over from nothing," sums up a Sudanese social worker in Philadelphia.

Others, though possessing outstanding qualifications, cannot find adequate employment because of their status as undocumented aliens. Finally, the Africans must confront the same problems as other people of color—racism and job discrimination that result in lower incomes, the employment of overqualified people in lesser positions, and the lack of adequate promotion.

Although unemployment is rare among Africans, poverty does exist, particularly among the undocumented who are underpaid and live precarious, stressful lives. But poverty is usually mitigated by solidarity and communal life, as compatriots take care of one another.

A CLASS OF ENTREPRENEURS | The African presence has become highly visible on the streets of more than a few American cities—Harlem is the prime example. In the area around West 116th Street—called Little Senegal—Africans, mostly from French-speaking nations, own most of the stores. Philadelphia has over 20 braiding salons owned by African women. This follows a long-held West African tradition. Women have always formed a dynamic entrepreneurial group; in many countries they control the markets and also engage in long-distance commerce.

In the United States, vendors of both sexes roam the country bringing African arts and crafts to local fairs, flea markets, and African-American cultural events. From the time of the transatlantic slave trade, African arts and crafts transmitted and transformed over several generations have been at the core of African-American culture. Today, traditions developed and modernized in Africa and brought here by the immigrants are infusing a new dynamism into the cultural productions of the African-American community.

Some highly educated immigrants, realizing that their limited English proficiency and their foreign degrees would make it difficult to get the American jobs they coveted, have opened businesses as a second option. This entrepreneurial spirit is deeply ingrained in Africa, where the informal economic sector is particularly dynamic. To be one's own boss is a common aspiration, and Africans in the United States make the most of the opportunities offered by a free-market economy. These entrepreneurs do not look for a job; they come to create one. From information technology to the oil industry, they have established several successful companies.

They are also a major force in the revitalization of some inner-city neighborhoods. Without help from banks, and using their own money augmented by communal rotating savings, they have opened stores, car services, and restaurants that provide needed services to the community.

FAMILY LIFE: CONTINUITY AND CHANGE | Africans are traditionally family-oriented. The extended family is the basic societal unit. Respect for the elders, cohesion, unity, and solidarity are values held dear by Africans. Emigration, however, transforms the family. The extended unit is left behind and only the immediate relatives can expect to migrate. Nuclear families are created in the United States as émigrés marry locally and have children.

The percentage of African women in the migration is rising, and there is a significant new trend of women coming to this country on their own. Some are single,

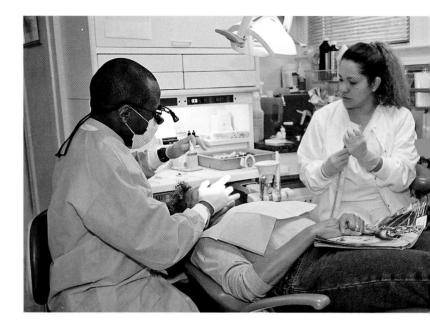

The Brain Drain

Above: The brain drain consists of African professionals who migrate to the United States and of students who remain in the country once they have their degrees. Dr. Kalambayi Kabasela, from Kinshasa, Democratic Republic of Congo, exemplifies the second trend. He has a successful practice in the nation's capital and teaches advanced general dentistry at Howard University. His experience is emblematic of the problems encountered by some African professionals and scientists who choose to stay in the West. As one of the top 20 percent of prosthodontists to use cutting-edge technology, he explains, "The state of dentistry in Congo is not advanced enough. I could not practice my specialty there.

but others have a husband and children back home. These women arrive as pioneers, a role traditionally reserved for men in most cultures. They may settle for a few months, work, and save money to enable them to start a business when they return to their homeland. African women have the second highest levels of education of any female group in the United States.

Africans continue to feel very much a part of their extended family back home. Whatever their circumstances, they send as much money as they can to their kinfolk. "The main reason I came here was to support my family," stresses a Ghanaian nurse, " I send $250 every month, which is more than I used to make. I am nothing without my family and I would never think of not providing for them, even when it gets difficult here."

Collectively, Africans remit hundreds of millions of dollars home every year. In 1999 Nigerians abroad sent $1.3 billion home, equivalent to 3.7 percent of their country's Gross Domestic Product, while the total development aid to Nigeria was only $152 million. Senegalese emigrants contributed close to 2 percent of their country's GDP. Some immigrants have established businesses in their hometowns that are run by relatives; many pay the tuition of siblings, as well as nephews and nieces.

Some immigrants, however, face restrictions in their efforts to maintain close relationships with loved ones back home. Many undocumented men and women migrated specifically in order to support their kin, yet visiting them is impossible because their illegal status would prevent them from reentering the United States, thus depriving the family of much-needed remittances.

They often feel they have no choice but to work several low-paying, exploitative jobs, to accumulate as much money as possible and return home permanently with enough capital to give their family a comfortable life. In the meantime, the very people they are attached to and came here to support may pass away. Refugees are also cut off from their families. As long as the situation they fled prevails, they have no possibility of returning home.

RELIGIOUS COMMUNITIES | As communities grow and become established they generally pool their resources to rent or buy spaces that can accommodate from a dozen to several hundred believers in order to worship in familiar surroundings. Ethiopian immigrants have established Coptic Orthodox Christian Churches. African Protestants of many denominations have also started churches. There are now hundreds of Ghanaian, Nigerian, Kenyan, and Liberian churches across the country.

However, I'm conscious of the negative effects of the brain drain and I do what I can to contribute. I have sent dental equipment and, in the future, I will also give classes at the University of Kinshasa."
Right: Many African physicians have left their countries. More than 60 percent of physicians trained in Ghana during the 1980s have emigrated. The Association of Nigerian Physicians in the Americas counts more than 2,000 members. As a result of this exodus and other factors, there are 19 physicians for 100,000 people in Nigeria, 7 in Zambia. In the United States, the ratio is 276 physicians for 100,000 people.

In New York City alone, African churches number at least 110. Some denominations were born in Africa and have established churches throughout the United States. Sometimes the national make-up of the congregation is more important than the specific denomination. For instance, the many Liberian Pentecostal Churches across the country address a diversity of Liberian issues and attract worshippers irrespective of their religious denominations.

The most recent development on the African religious landscape is the proliferation of mosques that parallels the immigration from French-speaking West Africa, where a majority of the population is Muslim. More than 20 have opened in New York City alone since the mid-1990s. There are also well-established Nigerian mosques in Chicago, Miami, Houston, Dallas, Philadelphia, and Washington, D.C.

Regardless of the congregations they serve, African religious institutions have taken on new roles in response to the needs of an immigrant population. They serve as orientation focal points for recent immigrants, conference halls, community and counseling centers, religious schools, temporary shelters, and mutual aid societies. They have become job referral centers, and imams and clergy often act as intermediaries between undocumented congregants and the authorities.

Weddings, baptisms, and holy days are occasions for gathering and sharing news, discussing social and political developments at home, and passing on information that can make life here more manageable. They also are an essential instrument of cultural continuity. It is during these events that young Africans, many of whom were born here, learn firsthand about traditions, rituals, national and ethnic culture, as well as the proper way to behave—respect for elders, sharing, and the importance of community.

BETWEEN HERE AND ABROAD | Life in African societies revolves around the community. Here, this strong commitment to community is reflected in the astonishing

A Diversity of Religions

Above, left: Africans worship in American churches, but they have also established a large number of "national" churches. There are Ghanaian, Nigerian, Kenyan, and Liberian churches in many states. Some denominations were born in Africa and have established churches throughout the U. S.

Above right: The recent increase in the number of African mosques is owing to the presence of French-speaking West Africans. In New York City alone, they have established more than 20 mosques.

Right: In areas where their communities can support them, Ethiopian immigrants have established Ethiopian or Coptic Orthodox Christian churches. They are numerous in the nation's capital but can also be found throughout California, and in New York, Georgia, Texas, and Florida.

Preserving Identity

Cultural continuity is important to African immigrants, and they make great efforts to socialize their children in their national cultures. Younger children often prefer to blend in, in order to be accepted by their American peers, but as they get older, they tend to be more self-confident and affirm their African heritage. The future of African culture in the United States is very much a subject of debate in the African community.

number of groups that have been created across the country. Every nationality has national, regional, professional, gender, and political organizations. People often belong to several, and the multiplicity of groups reflects the many layers of identity Africans bring with them and are eager to maintain. The organizations reinforce communities and create resource networks to serve them.

Some organizations are mostly devoted to the maintenance of sociocultural traditions; others are involved in development efforts in Africa. Thousands of projects throughout the continent are being funded by emigrants and managed by the locals. But African émigrés do more than share their financial resources; they also contribute their time, know-how, and ideas. The negative effects of the brain drain are thus being partially mitigated by the strong involvement—based on traditional community values—of the expatriates in the socioeconomic life of their home countries.

Today, African immigrants count on information technology to counterbalance some of the effects of the brain drain. Thanks to the Internet, their skills, expertise, and the networks they build are becoming increasingly available to colleagues and users in their countries of origin, thus transforming a problem into a potential asset. The "brain gain" that Africa can get from its expatriates is a topic widely debated and positively seen on the continent.

In the United States, Africans are linked through community newspapers, magazines, and radio and television programs. In addition, African Independent Television, a Nigerian channel, is available on cable. But the latest development in the communal life of Africans is their use of the Internet. Today, Africans from Los Angeles to Brooklyn can watch television programs and listen to radio broadcasts from their home countries on their computers. They can read their national newspapers online the same day they are published in Dakar, Nairobi, or Accra. Chatrooms link the Senegalese, Burundi, or Nigerian diasporas scattered across America, Europe, and the Middle East. Links with families are kept alive by phone, letters, fax, and e-mail. Though a wide digital gap separates the United States and Africa, major cities and many small towns on the continent have cyber cafés and communication centers that provide telephone and fax services.

THE QUESTION OF IDENTITY | Africans have several layers of identity—national origin, ethnicity, gender, class, and religion. At home, their color or "race" had no relevance. But in the United States, they find themselves defined by that specific criterion, and have to live as a racial minority in a country with a long history of exclusion and discrimination against black people. Encounters with racism are often seen as baffling and bring feelings of shock, indignation, and humiliation to people who have not grown up in societies where their intellectual, physical, social, and even human qualities were ever questioned on the basis of color.

When asked how they identify themselves, Africans, in general, say they are Africans first, and members of a national group second. To be "African" means to have a continent, to belong to a specific country, to speak one or several foreign languages, to be heir to a deep-rooted history, and to share a number of values and experiences, as well as cultural and social traits, with other Africans. To be identified as "black" only is often viewed as a negation of culture and origin that Africans regard as the most important elements of identity. They are keenly aware that they encounter racism and discrimination as black people, but they generally reject the imposition of an identity they feel does not completely reflect who they are.

Africans represent a new breed of immigrants: They are transnationals, people who choose to maintain their distinctive qualities in the host country, and retain tight links to their community of origin. As children are born or grow up in this country, issues of identity, continuity, and change become more pressing, and potential "Americanization" in the cultural sphere is a constant cause of concern. But Africans generally view their American experience as transitory, the most effective way to construct a better future at home for themselves and their relatives. Their life strategies are geared towards achieving this objective. In the meantime, they bring to the United States their robust work ethic, dynamism, and their strong attachment to family, culture and religion—just as other Africans did several centuries ago.

by Sylviane A. Diouf

From Africa to America, from the rural South to the nation at large, African Americans have changed the places they settled in, built vibrant communities, and laid the foundations for new waves of immigrants in search of better opportunities. This 1934 painting, "Aspects of Negro Life: Song of the Towers," is by Aaron Douglas.

Even though the transatlantic slave trade has created an enduring image of black men and women as transported commodities, and is usually considered the most defining element in the construction of the African Diaspora, it is indeed, as this book demonstrates, centuries of additional movements that have given shape to the nation we know today.

Always in motion, resourceful and creative, men and women of African origin have been risk-takers in an exploitative and hostile environment. Their survival skills, efficient networks, and dynamic culture have enabled them to thrive and spread, and to be at the very core of the settling and development of the Americas. Their hopeful journeys have changed not only their world and the fabric of the African Diaspora, but also the Western Hemisphere.

And they keep moving on in a movement five hundred years old that shows no sign of slowing down. By boat, on foot, by train, car, and plane, Africans and their descendants have crossed oceans and land, sailed up and down rivers, put down roots and pulled them up again. Everywhere their thirst for freedom, education, and opportunities brought them, they re-created themselves, transformed the land, the cities, the culture, and ultimately the nation. Wherever they went, they built communities and enduring institutions. And they laid the foundations for those who followed them.

The men and women of the 19th-century Northern and Western movements paved the way for those who came during the war migrations. They, in turn, not only changed the cities they settled in, but made their neighborhoods attractive destinations for people arriving from all over the black world. These immigrants brought additional resources to the African-American neighborhoods they settled in, infusing them with a new energy and creativity. And in some sort of poetic justice, although enslaved people trekked to the Deep South against their will, their college-educated descendants are now journeying back, voluntarily, to the homeplace.

But, as the chapter on colonization and emigration illustrates, thousands of

African Americans have also left their country when it became apparent that they would not find at home the freedom and equality they aspired to. Few are emigrating today, but black popular culture, from blues to soul, jazz to hip-hop, created out of the diverse influences brought about by centuries of movement, has been resonating throughout the world for decades in an unprecedented cultural out-migration.

People's diverse journeys always overlapped, and as this book shows, a southern city in, say, 1850 could be the center of several migration experiences. A particular neighborhood might be home to men and women born in Africa; American-born fugitives from rural plantations passing for free or planning their escape to Canada; Haitian immigrants having fled the Revolution; people from the southeast sold "down the river" to the Deep South; free men and women preparing their trip to Mexico, Liberia, Haiti, California, or the northern states.

Things have changed, but the migration experience has not. Nowadays, a typical northern, midwestern, or western city is a rich tapestry of people of African origin all linked, whether they know it or not, by a migration story. In the same block live the descendants of runaways and free people; the sons and daughters of southern migrants who caught a train from Alabama, Mississippi, the Carolinas, Georgia, Florida, or Louisiana during the Great Migration or the Second Great Migration; Caribbeans from English-, French-, and Spanish-speaking nations; sub-Saharan Africans; and elderly folks and young professionals planning their return or their move South.

For the past 30 years—and many to come if the trend holds—the most traveled migration paths have originated in the Northeast, the Midwest, the West, the Caribbean, Haiti, and Africa. Millions of people have been on the move, crossing borders or reversing centuries-old trends. In the 1990s, the number of sub-Saharan Africans living in the United States has doubled and that of Afro-Caribbeans increased by 60 percent. In some major cities, "Afro-immigrants" form a substantial percentage of the black population: 20 percent in several areas, 32 percent in New York City. Actually, between 1990 and 2000, a quarter of the growth of the black population, nationwide, was due to immigrants. They represented almost one million out of the 3.7 million increase in the total black population that occurred in the last ten years of the 20th century. Nationally, about 8 percent of the African-American population is foreign-born. And as these new immigrants establish lives, commerce, and institutions, more and more of their compatriots are following them.

So, for the first time in history, all the components of the African Diaspora are gathered together. The United States is the only place, the present time the only time. African Americans, Africans, Afro-Caribbeans, Central Americans and South Americans of African descent, as well as Africans and Afro-Caribbeans born in Europe live side by side, each group bringing its specificities, culture, and sense of identity. The ethnic and cultural diversity of the black population has never been greater, and richer. And it is all part of the African-American migration experience.

As globalization and other forces are changing our human geography and relations, there may be a need to redefine the African Diaspora, taking into account the new movements of peoples and cultures that no longer flow from Africa to the Western world but also go back to Africa, the Caribbean, Haiti, and Europe. Tight networks, for example, link Africans in the U.S. to Africans on the continent, Great Britain, Italy, France, and Asia. Others connect Haitians in Miami or New York to those in Montreal, Dakar, or Paris. African America now reaches all over the world and the efficient Afro-immigrant networks are a new wealth to make the most of.

Alongside these movements, what in the future could be called the new Great Migration is going on with force. When Sparell Scott wrote his poem, "When I Return to the Southland it Will Be":

> When lions eat grass like oxen
> And an angleworm swallows a whale,
> And a terrapin knits a woolen sock,
> And a hare is outrun by a snail.
> …
> I then may return to the South,
> But I'll travel then in a box

...little did he know that a few decades later, even though close to 70,000 men and women were still leaving the South each year, twice as many were heading there.

For the first time in the African-American migration experience, the movement is lead by college-educated people. In that regard, it is not unlike the immigration of Caribbeans in the early 20th century and Africans in the past 30 years, spearheaded by professionals. But contrary to them, African Americans are not leaving their countries for better opportunities; they are going back home, reclaiming the place their ancestors built, where their roots run deep, where history has been unforgiving but the future looks bright.

It is mainly those who stayed and fought that made it possible for the new migrants to come back, and the valiant struggles of those who took the risk to remain need to be celebrated in the same manner as we honor those who took the risk to leave.

Today, the face of African America looks like a New Yorker in Atlanta, a Mississippian in Chicago, a Nigerian in Houston, and a Jamaican in Miami. From coast to coast, north to south, the interaction between peoples of varied backgrounds, cultures, languages, religions, and migratory experience has produced a unique population whose expression, music, food, institutions, styles, clothes, literature, arts, and sense of identity all reflect the fertile diversity brought about by centuries of African-American migrations.

BIBLIOGRAPHY

THE TRANSATLANTIC SLAVE TRADE

Barry, Boubacar. *Senegambia and the Atlantic Slave Trade.* Cambridge: Cambridge University Press, 1998.

Berlin, Ira. *Generations Of Captivity : A History Of African-American Slaves.* Cambridge, Mass.: Belknap Press of Harvard University Press, 2003.

Curtin, Philip D., *The Atlantic Slave Trade: A Census.* Madison: University of Wisconsin Press, 1969.

_____. Ed. *Africa Remembered: Narratives by West Africans from the Era of the Slave Trade.* Madison: University of Wisconsin Press, 1967.

Diouf, Sylviane A. *Servants of Allah: African Muslims Enslaved in the Americas.* New York: New York University Press, 1998.

_____, ed., *Fighting the Slave Trade: West African Strategies.* Bloomington: Indiana University Press, 2003.

Eltis, David. *The Rise of African Slavery in the Americas.* New York: Oxford University Press, 2000.

Eltis, David and David Richardson, eds. *Routes To Slavery : Direction, Ethnicity, And Mortality In The Transatlantic Slave Trade.* Portland, OR.: Frank Cass, 1997.

Hall, Gwendolyn, *African Ethnicities in the Americas: Restoring the Links .* Chapel Hill: University of North Carolina Press, 2004.

Hall, Gwendolyn Midlo. *Africans in Colonial Louisiana: The Development of Afro-Creole Culture in the 18th Century.* Baton Rouge: Louisiana State University Press, 1992.

Heywood, Linda, ed., *Central Africans and Cultural Transformations in the American Diaspora .* New York: Cambridge University Press, 2001.

Inikori, Joseph. *The Atlantic Slave Trade: Effects on Economies, Societies and Peoples in Africa, the Americas, and Europe.* Durham: Duke University Press, 1992.

Lovejoy, Paul E., ed. *Identity in the Shadow of Slavery.* New York: Continuum, 2000

_____ and Robin Law, eds. *The Biography of Mahommah Gardo Baquaqua : His Passage from Slavery to Freedom in Africa and America.* Princeton, NJ : Markus Wiener Publishers, 2001.

———and David V. Trotman. eds. *Trans-Atlantic Dimensions of Ethnicity in the African Diaspora.* London: Continuum, 2003.

RUNAWAY JOURNEYS

Alexander, Ken. *Towards Freedom: the African-Canadian Experience.* Toronto: Umbrella Press, 1996.

Finkelman, Paul, ed. *Rebellions, Resistance, and Runaways Within the Slave South.* New York: Garland, 1989.

Franklin, John Hope, and Loren Schweninger. *Runaway Slaves: Rebels on the Plantation.* New York: Oxford University Press, 1999.

Hodges, Graham Russell, Brown, Alan Edward, eds. *"Pretends to Be Free": Runaway Slave Advertisements from Colonial and Revolutionary New York and New Jersey.* New York: Garland Pub., 1994.

Howe, Samuel Gridley. *Report to the Freedmen's Inquiry Commission, 1864: The Refugees from Slavery in Canada West.* New York: Arno Press, 1969.

Mulroy, Kevin. *Freedom on the Border: The Seminole Maroons in Florida, the Indian Territory, Coahuila, and Texas.* Lubbock: Texas Tech University Press, 1993.

Smith, Billy G., Wojtowicz, Richard. *Blacks Who Stole Themselves: Advertisements for Runaways in the Pennsylvania Gazette, 1720-1790.* Philadelphia: University of Pennsylvania Press, 1989.

Tyler, Ronnie. "Fugitive Slaves in Mexico." *Journal of Negro History,* 57 (Jan. 1972).

Twyman, Bruce Edward. *The Black Seminole Legacy and North American Politics, 1693-1845.* Washington, DC: Howard University Press, 1999.

Windley, Lathan Algerna. *A Profile of Runaway Slaves in Virginia and South Carolina from 1730-1787.* New York: Garland Publishing, Inc., 1995.

THE DOMESTIC SLAVE TRADE

Bancroft, Frederic. *Slave Trading in the Old South.* Columbia: University of South Carolina Press, 1996.

Collins, Winfield. *The Domestic Slave Trade of the Southern States.* Port Washington, NY: Kennikat Press, 1969.

Johnson, Walter, *Soul by Soul: Life Inside the Antebellum Slave Market.* Cambridge, Mass.: Harvard University Press, 1999.

Tadman, Michael. *Speculators and Slaves: Masters, Traders, and Slaves in the Old South.* Madison: University of Wisconsin, 1989.

Wesley, Charles H. "Manifests of Slave Shipments along the Waterways 1804-64." *Journal of Negro History,* 27, (April 1942).

COLONIZATION/EMIGRATION

Dixon, Chris. *African America and Haiti: Emigration and Black Nationalism in the Nineteenth Century.* Westport, Conn.: Greenwood Press, 2000.

Dorsey, Bruce Allen. "A Gendered History of African Colonization in the Antebellum United States." *Journal of Social History,* 34:1 (2000): 77-103.

Gershoni, Yekutiel. *Black Colonialism: the Americo-Liberian Scramble for the Hinterland.* Boulder, Colo.: Westview Press, 1985.

McDaniel, Antonio. *Swing Low, Sweet Chariot: The Mortality Cost of Colonizing Liberia in the Nineteenth Century.* Chicago: University of Chicago, 1995.

Mehlinger, Louis R. "The Attitude of the Free Negro Toward African Colonization, *1790-1860"* in *Not a Slave! Free People of Color in Antebellum America,* Lacy Shaw, ed. New York: American Heritage Custom Publishing Group, 1995.

Miller, Floyd John. *The Search for a Black Nationality: Black Emigration and Colonization, 1787-1863.* Urbana: University of Illinois Press, 1975.

Moses, Wilson J. *Liberian Dreams: Back-to-Africa Narratives from the 1850s.* University Park: Pennsylvania State University Press, 1998.

Redkley, Edwin S. *Black Exodus: Black Nationalist and Back-to-Africa Movements, 1890-1910.* New Haven: Yale University Press, 1969.

Shick, Tom W. *Behold the Promised Land: a History of Afro-American Settler Society in Nineteenth Century Liberia.* Baltimore: Johns Hopkins University Press, 1980.

Wiley, Bell I., ed. *Slaves No More: Letters from Liberia, 1833-1869.* Lexington: University Press of Kentucky, 1980.

THE NORTHERN MIGRATION

Berlin, Ira. *Slaves Without Masters: The Free Negro in the Antebellum South.* New York: Pantheon Books, 1974.

Bolster, W. Jeffrey. *Black Jacks: African American Seamen in the Age of Sail.* Cambridge: Harvard University Press, 1997.

Cohen, William. *At Freedom's Edge: Black Mobility and the Southern White Quest for Racial Control, 1861-1915.* Baton Rouge: Louisiana State University Press, 1991.

Curry, Leonard. *The Free Black in Urban America, 1800–1850: The shadow of the dream.* Chicago: University of Chicago Press, 1981.

Horton, James Oliver, and Lois E. Horton. *In Hope of Liberty: Culture, Community, and Protest among Northern Free Blacks, 1700– 1860.* New York: Oxford University Press, 1997.

Nash, Gary B. *Forging Freedom: The Formation of Philadelphia's Black Community, 1720-1840.* Cambridge: Harvard University Press, 1988.

Pleck, Elizabeth Hafkin. *Black Migration and Poverty, Boston 1865-1900.* New York: Academic Press, 1979.

Putney, Martha S. *Black Sailors: Afro-American Merchant Seamen and Whalemen Prior to the Civil War.* West Point: Greenwood Press, 1987.

Winch, Julie. *Philadelphia's Black Elite: Activism, Accommodation, and the Struggle for Autonomy, 1787–1848.* Philadelphia: Temple University Press, 1988.

THE WESTWARD MIGRATION

Athearn, Robert G. *In Search of Canaan: Black Migration to Kansas, 1879-80.* Lawrence: Regents Press of Kansas, 1978.

Beasley, Delilah. *The Negro Trail Blazers of California.* San Francisco: R &E Research Associates, 1968.

Billington, Monroe Lee, ed. *African Americans on the Western Frontier.* Niwot: University Press of Colorado, 1998.

Crockett, Norman. *The Black Towns.* Lawrence: Regents Press of Kansas, 1979.

Goode, Kenneth G. *California's Black Pioneers: A Brief Historical Survey.* Santa Barbara, Cal.: McNally & Loftin, 1974.

Gordon, Jacob. *Narratives of African Americans in Kansas, 1870-1992: Beyond the Exodus Movement.* Lewiston, NY: Edwin Mellen Press, 1993.

Hamilton, Kenneth. *Black Towns and Profit: Promotion and Development in the Trans-Appalachian West, 1877-1915.* Urbana: University of Illinois Press, 1991.

McLagan, Elizabeth. *A Peculiar Paradise: A History of Blacks in Oregon, 1778-1940.* Portland: Georgian Press, 1980.

Painter, Nell Irvin. *Exodusters: Black Migration to Kansas after Reconstruction.* New York: Knopf, 1977.

Ravage, John. *Black Pioneers: Images of the Black Experience on the North American Frontier.* Salt Lake City: University of Utah Press, 1997.

Taylor, Quintard. *In Search of the Racial Frontier : African Americans in the American West, 1528-1990.* New York : W.W. Norton, 1998.

BIBLIOGRAPHY

THE GREAT MIGRATION

Adero, Malaika, ed. *Up South: Stories, Studies, and Letters of This Century's Black Migrations.* New York: The New Press, 1993.

Anderson, Jervis. *This Was Harlem: 1900–1950.* New York: Farrar, Straus and Giroux, 1981.

Devlin, George. *South Carolina and Black Migration, 1865-1940: In Search of the Promised Land.* New York: Garland Pub., 1989.

Gottlieb, Peter. *Making Their Own Way: Southern Blacks' Migration to Pittsburgh, 1916–1930.* Urbana: University of Illinois Press, 1987.

Grant, Robert B. *The Black Man Comes to the City: A Documentary Account From the Great Migration to the Great Depression, 1915 to 1930.* Chicago: Nelson-Hall, 1972.

Henri, Florette. *Black Migration: Movement North 1900-1920.* Garden City, NY: Anchor Press, 1975.

Hine, Darlene Clark. "Black Migration to the Urban Midwest: The Gender Dimension, 1915-1945", in Kenneth W. Goings, ed. *The New African American Urban History.* Thousand Oaks, CA: Sage Publications, 1996.

Johnson, James Weldon. *Black Manhattan.* New York: A. Knopf, 1930.

Lemann, Nicholas. *The Promised Land: The Great Black Migration and How It Changed America.* New York: Vintage Books, 1992.

Phillips, Kimberley L. *AlabamaNorth: African-American Migrants, Community, and Working-class Activism in Cleveland, 1915 - 45.* Urbana: University of Illinois Press, 1999.

Thomas, Richard. *Life for Us Is What We Make It: Building A Black Community in Detroit 1915-45.* Bloomington: Indiana University Press, 1992.

Trotter, Joe William. *The Great Migration in Historical Perspective: New Dimensions of Race, Class, and Gender.* Bloomington: Indiana University Press, 1991.

THE SECOND GREAT MIGRATION

Bontemps, Arna. *They Seek a City.* New York: Doubleday, Doran and Company, Inc., 1945.

Chafe, William H., et al. *Remembering Jim Crow: African Americans Tell About Life in the Segregated South.* New York: The New Press, 2001.

Goodwin, E. Marvin. *Black Migration in America from 1915 to 1960: An Uneasy Exodus.* Lewiston, N.Y.: E. Mellon Press, 1990.

Honey, Maureen, ed. *Bitter Fruit: African American Women in World War II.* Columbia: University of Missouri Press, 1999.

Daniels, Douglas Henry. *Pioneer Urbanites: A Social and Cultural History of Black San Francisco.* Philadelphia: Temple University Press, 1980.

De Graaf, Lawrence, Kevin Mulroy, and Quintard Taylor, eds. *Seeking El Dorado: African Americans in California.* Seattle: University of Washington Press, 2001.

Hirsch, Arnold R. *Making the Second Ghetto: Race and Housing in Chicago, 1940-1960.* Chicago: University of Chicago Press, 1983.

Johnson, Marilynn S. *The Second Gold Rush: Oakland and the East Bay in World War II.* Berkeley: University of California Press, 1993.

Lemke-Santangelo, Gretchen. *Abiding Courage: African American Migrant Women and the East Bay Community.* Chapel Hill: University of North Carolina Press, 1996.

Moore, Shirley Ann Wilson. *To Place Our Deed: The African American Community in Richmond, California, 1910 -1963.* Berkeley: University of California Press, 2000.

CARIBBEAN IMMIGRATION

Chamberlain, May, ed. *Caribbean Migration: Globalised Identities.* New York: Routledge, 1998.

Gmelch, George. Double Passage: The Lives of Caribbean Migrants Abroad and Back Home. Ann Arbor: University of Michigan Press, 1992.

Ho, Christine G. T. *Salt-water Trinnies: Afro-Trinidadian Immigrant Networks and Non-assimilation in Los Angeles.* New York: AMS Press, 1991.

James, Winston. *Holding Aloft the Banner of Ethiopia: Caribbean Radicalism in Early Twentieth Century America.* New York: Verso, 1998.

Kasinitz, Philip. *Caribbean New York: Black Immigrants and the Politics of Race.* Ithaca: Cornell University Press, 1992.

Palmer, Ransford W. *Pilgrims from the Sun: West Indian Migration to America.* New York: Twayne Publishers, 1995.

Waters, Mary C. *Black Identities: West Indian Immigrant Dreams and American Realities.* Cambridge: Harvard University Press, 1999.

Watkins-Owens, Irma. *Blood Relations: Caribbean Immigrants and the Harlem Community, 1900-1930.* Bloomington: Indiana University Press, 1996.

HAITIAN IMMIGRATION

Eighteenth and Nineteenth Centuries:

Bell, Caryn Cossé. *Revolution, Romanticism, and the Afro-Creole Protest Tradition in Louisiana, 1718–1868.* Baton Rouge: Louisiana State University, 1997.

Everett, Donald. "Émigrés and Militiamen: Free Persons of Color in New Orleans 1803-1815." *Journal of Negro History,* 38 (Oct. 1953).

Fiehrer, Thomas. "The African Presence in Colonial Louisiana: An Essay on the Continuity of Caribbean Culture." *Louisiana's Black Heritage,* ed. Robert R. McDonald et al. New Orleans, Louisiana State Museum, 1979.

Gaspar, David Barry, ed. *A Turbulent Time: The French Revolution and the Greater Caribbean.* Bloomington: Indiana University Press, 1997.

Hunt, Alfred. *Haiti's Influence on Antebellum America: Slumbering Volcano in the Caribbean.* Baton Rouge: Louisiana State University, 1988.

Twentieth Century:

Catanese, Anthony. *Haitians: Migration and Diaspora.* Boulder, CO: Westview, 1999.

Laguerre, Michel. S. *American Odyssey: Haitians in New York City.* Ithaca, N.Y.: Cornell University Press, 1984.

_____ *Diasporic Citizenship: Haitian Americans in Transnational America.* New York: St Martin's Press, 1998.

Lawless, Robert. *Haiti's Bad Press.* New York: Schenkmann Press, 1992.

Portes, Alejandro and Alex Stepick. "Haitian Refugees in South Florida, 1983–1986." (Occasional Papers Series Dialogue no. 77), Latin American and Caribbean Center, Florida International University, 1987.

Stepick, Alex. *Pride Against Prejudice: Haitians in the United States.* Boston: Allyn & Bacon, 1998.

Woldemikael, Tekle Mariam. *Becoming Black American: Haitians and American Institutions in Evanston, Illinois.* New York: AMS Press, 1989.

Zéphir, Flore. *Haitian Immigrants in Black America: A Sociological and Sociolinguistic Portrait.* Westport, CT: Bergin & Garvey, 1996.

RETURN SOUTH MIGRATION

Adelman, Robert. "Homeward Bound: The Return Migration of Southern-born black Women 1940 to 1990." *Sociological Spectrum,* 20, 4, (fall 2000), 433-464.

Gates, Henry Louis, Jr. *America Behind the Color Line: Dialogues with African Americans.* New York: Warner Books, 2004.

Johnson, James H. Jr. and David M. Grant. "Post-1980 Black Population Redistribution Trends in the United States." *Southeastern Geographer,* 37 (1), (1997).

Johnson, James. "Recent African American Migration Trends in the U.S." *Urban League Review,* 14, 1, (1990).

McHugh, Kevin. "Black Migration Reversal in the U.S." *Geographical Review,* 77, 2, (1987).

O'Hare, William P. "Blacks on the Move: A Decade of Demographic Change." *Washington D.C. Joint Center for Political Studies.*

Stack, Carol B. *Call to Home: African Americans Reclaim the Rural South.* New York: Basic Books, 1996.

AFRICAN IMMIGRATION

Apraku, Kofi Konadu. *African Emigrés in the United States: A Missing Link in Africa's Social and Economic Development.* New York: Praeger, 1991.

Arthur, John A. *Invisible Sojourners: African Immigrant Diaspora in the United State*s.Westport, Conn.: Praeger, 2000.

Attah-Poku, Agyemang. *The Socio-Cultural Adjustment Question: The Role of Ghanaian Immigrant Ethnic Associations in America.* Brookfield, VT: Avebury, 1996.

Babou, Cheikh Anta. "Brotherhood Solidarity, Education and Migration: The Role of the *Dahiras* Among the Murid Muslim Community of New York." *African Affairs,* 101, no. 403 (April 2002), 151-70.

Diouf, Sylviane A. "The West African Paradox." Zahid H. Bukhari, Sulayman S. Niang, Mumtaz Ahmad, and John L. Esposito, eds., *Muslims' Place in the American Public Square.* Walnut Creek: AltaMira Press, 2004.

Djmaba, Yanyi K. "African Immigrants in the United States: A Socio-Demographic Profile in Comparison to Native Blacks." *Journal of Asian and African Studies,* 34, no. 2 (May 1999): 210-15.

Halter, Marilyn. *Between Race and Ethnicity: Cape Verdean American Immigrants, 1860-1965.* Urbana: University of Illinois Press, 1993.

Holtzman, Jon. *Nuer Journeys, Nuer Lives: Sudanese Refugees in Minnesota.* Needham Heights, MA: Allyn & Bacon, 2000.

Wamba, Philippe. *Kinship: A Family's Journey in Africa and America.* New York: Plume, 2000.

INDEX

A

Abache **28**
Abbot, Lyman 48
Abbott, Robert Sengstacke 122
Abdul-Jabbar, Kareem 163
Abolition movement 42, 60, 61, 73, 100
Adams, J. H. 122
Africa: brain drain 204–205, 206–207; emigrants 204, 207, 210; immigration 66, 69, 74, 76–77, **77**
African Civilization Society 73, 74
African immigrants **198–211**; population 200–201, 214
Africatown, Ala. 29
Agassiz, Louis 26
Agriculture **2–3**, 136–137, **137, 138**
Aguilera, Valmond G. **189**
Ahonkai family **198**
Alabama: slave trade 29, 32, 37, 46, 47, 60; wages 123
Alexander, "Pop" **43**
Alexandria, Va.: slave trade 48, **56, 57**
Ali, Noble Drew 128
All-black towns 29, **100–106, 111**
Allen, Richard 70, 74
American Colonization Society 65, 66, 67, 69, 74
American Revolution 32, 66, 73
Angola: slave trade 20, 22, 26, 28
Aristide, Jean-Bertrand 177
Arkansas: emigration 100, 136; fugitive slaves 38; immigration 66
Arts 107, 133, 147, 172, 181–182, 206
Atlanta, Ga.: domestic laborers 148; immigrants 169, **184, 189,** 201
Atlanta University: commencement **192–193**
Atwell, Joseph Sandiford 158
Audacious, Nebr. 104
Automotive industry 123
Azikiwe, Nnamdi 199

B

Back-to-Africa movement 74, 76
Badgett, Henry 61
Bahamas: emigration 162, 166, 168
Ball, Charles 39, 48
Baltimore, Md.: immigrants 161, 169, 171, 172; slave trade 48
Bambara people **14,** 26
Barbados: emigration 157, 158, 161, 166, 169; exploitation of blacks 159; slavery 23, 157, 159
Belafonte, Harry 163
Bell Aircraft: discrimination 142, 149
Benin 16, **17**; slave trade 16, 26, 29
Benin, Bight of: emigration 172; slave trade 20, 28
Benitez, Rosa **195**
Bethel African Methodist Episcopal Church, Chester, Pa. **91**
Bethlehem Baptist Association of Chicago 123
Biafra, Bight of: slave trade 20, 26, 28
Bibb, Henry 71, 73
Black colleges and universities **192–193**, 199
Black Nationalism 73, 76, 132

Black Panthers Party 153
Black Star Steamship Line 76, **77**
Blackmon, Barbara **186**
Blyden, Edward Wilmot 74, 77, 158
Boardinghouses 83, 86, 89, **93**
Boeing Company: discrimination 149
Boley, Okla. 104; town council **104–105**
Boley, William 104
Bonaparte, Napoleon 171–172
Boston, Mass.: black population 80, 95, 179; employment 79, 83, 91, 92; immigrants 90–91, 158, 161, 166, 169, 179, 180, **180**; protests 87; racism 83; schools 86; slaves 39, 41, 83
Boyer, Jean-Pierre 70
Brackettville, Tex.: former slaves **39**
Braithwaite, William Stanley 158
Brazil: slave trade 22; slaves 16, 23, 28
Breedlove, Sarah 106
Brent, Linda 33
Bridgetown, Barbados 161
British West Indies: emigration 157; sugar industry 158–159
Brooklyn, New York, N.Y.: churches 128–129; employment **144**; immigrants 162, **164–165, 169**
Brown, Claude 141
Brown, Henry 33, **33,** 42
Brown, John 54, 100
Brown, Peter 98
Brown, William Wells 42
Brownlee, Nebr.: migrants **6–7**
Buffalo, N.Y.: southern blacks 80
Buffalo soldiers **101, 106**
Burke, Rosabella and William 67
Burns, Anthony 42
Burris, Samuel D. 37
Burton, I. B. 104
Burton, T. W. 47
Bus boycotts 140
Butler, Benjamin 42

C

California: Black Panthers 153; black population 98, 135; churches 209; emigration 201; immigration 98, **101,** 135, 136, 147, 149, 200, 201; World War II 141–142
Canada: emigration 70; fugitive slaves 42; immigration 71, 73, 100
Cape Verde: emigration 199, **201**
Caribbean immigrants **1, 156–169,** 214; see also Haiti: emigrants
Carnival **156,** 169, **181**
Carter, Mae Bertha 139
Case, Michael C. 101, 103
Catholicism 172, 181
Celestin, Joe **178**
Charles, Ray 147
Charleston, S.C.: emigration 74; employment 81; free blacks 79, 80, 89; immigration 171; slave trade **24,** 48, 55, 59; slave uprisings 158
Cheney, Lee **43**
Cherry, F. S. 128

Chicago, Ill.: Black Panthers 153; black population 80, 123; churches 128; employment 120, **125,** 126; housing 127; immigrants 119, 139–140, 142, 147, 149, 180; mosques 208; nightlife **148**; politics 132; riots 129, 131, 149
Chicago Defender 122, 140
Chicago Urban League 119, **124–125,** 126; handbill **126**
Chisholm, Shirley 163
Church of God, Philadelphia, Pa. 128
Churches: African immigrants 207–208, **208**; communications role 92; community importance 90, 128–129, 133, 208; Coptic Orthodox Christian 207, **209**; migration clubs 120, 129
Cincinnati, Ohio 133; black population 80; communication network 90, 94; employment 83, 92; free blacks 87, 92; fugitive slaves 39, 41; racism 83; schools 86
Civil rights 86–87, 111, 140, 152, 167, 173
Civil War 39, **40,** 42–43, 61, 173, **173**
Clay, Jefferson L., II **194**
Cleveland, Ohio: black population 95, 127; emigrants **194**; fugitive slaves 39
Clotilda (slave ship) 29
Cochrane, Alexander 32
Coffin, Charles Carleton 61
Coffles **47,** 47–48
Collins, Winfield H. 55
Colorado: immigration 106
Congo, Democratic Republic of 206–207
Connecticut: emigration 70; immigration 166
Coptic Orthodox Christian Churches 207, **209**
Cordley, Richard 43
Cornish, Samuel E. 158
Cotton industry 115, **117,** 136–137, **138,** 139
Craft, Ellen and William 39, 41
Cuffee, Paul 66, **66**
Cugoano, Ottobah 22, 23

D

Dallas, Tex.: mosques 208
Davenport, Charles 116
Davis, Gertie and Nelson **43**
Davis, Hector 61
Day, Ava Speese 104
Dearfield, Colo. 106
DeKalb County, Ga.: celebrities **196**; vocational training **195**
Delany, Hubert T. **131**
Delany, Martin R. 73–74, 77
Delaware: fugitive slaves 39; population trends 136; slave trade 45, 46, 61
Delille, Henriette 172
Democratic Party 65, 131, 132; primary voting **187**
Denver, Colo. 106, **108–109,** 111
DePriest, Oscar 132
Detroit, Mich.: black population 80, 95, 123; churches 128; emigration **194**; factories **125**; Housewives' League **147**; immigration 149
Didley, Bo 147
Divine, Father 128–129

Dominican Republic: immigration 159, 161, 171, 173
Douglass, Frederick **33,** 42, 71, 73, 103
Drake, St. Clair 163
Drew, Timothy 128
Du Bois, W. E. B. 95, 133, 158, 163
Dumas Hotel, Cincinnati, Ohio 90
Duvalier, François 176–177, 179
Duvalier, Jean-Claude 177, 179

E

East St. Louis, Ill.: race riots 129
Education: commencement **192–193**; immigrants 182–183, 204, **204,** 205, 207; racism 7, 83, 86; women 207
Elliott, Robert Brown 158
Emancipation Proclamation 173
Emeagwali, Philippe 204
Employment: agriculture 132; assistance **124–125**; entrepreneurs 106, **108,** 131, 132, 162–163, **164–165, 178,** 206; immigrants 180, 205; industrial **84–85,** 110, 120, 123, **125, 144–145**; networking 91; North (region) 81, 83, 117, 123, 125; professional positions **130,** 162–163, 206–207, 215; racism 81, 83, 95, 129, 142, 151; railroads 120; sailors 92, **93**; South (region) 81; teachers 132; wages 98, 123, 126; women 79, 83, 86, **88, 93,** 110, 126, **134**; World War II 110, 141, 142, **144–145,** 148
Entrepreneurs 106, **108,** 131, 132; immigrants 162–163, **164–165, 178,** 206; women 206
Equiano 23; autobiography **22**
Ethiopian immigrants 200, 201, 204, 207, **209**
Exodusters 101, 103

F

Families: importance 54, 61, 182–183, **198,** 206–207; slavery **44, 50–51,** 53–54, 56, **81**
Farrakhan, Louis 163
Fauset, Arthur Huff 129
Fedric, Francis 53
First African Baptist Church, Richmond, Va. 92
Fisher, Rudolph **131**
Florida: agriculture 166; black population 136, 167, 179; churches 209; emigrants **2–3**; fugitive slaves 37, 38; immigrants 162, 168–169, 171, 176–180; slave trade 28
Ford, Barney 106
Ford, Henry 123
Forest, Joe 38
Forrest, Nathan Bedford **55**
Forten, James 70, 74
Frazier, E. Franklin **131**
Free blacks: kidnap of **53,** 54, 86–87; migration North 87, **87,** 92; migration routes map 62–63; in the South 79–80, 89; travel restrictions 86
Fugees (band) 182
Fugitive Slave Act 42, 54, 71, 87

G

Gara, Larry 42
Garnet, Henry Highland 73, 87

Boldface indicates illustrations.

Garvey, Marcus **75,** 76, 77, 132, 168
Geffrard, Nicolas Fabre 70
Georgia: churches 209; emigration 136, 147; fugitive slaves 39, 41; immigration **189;** slave trade 28, 46, 47–48, 54, 61; slaves 23, 26, 32, **36**
Ghana: emigration 200, 205, 207; first president 199; immigration 69; physicians 205, 207; *see also* Gold Coast
Ghettos 127, 152
Gibbs, Mifflin W. 98
Gold Coast: slave trade 16, 20, 23, 26
Gold rush 98, **99**
Grace, Charles M. 128, 129
Grayson, Mary and Renty **39**
Great Depression: agriculture 136–137, **137;** Caribbean migration 166
Great Dismal Swamp, N.C.-Va.: maroons 37–38
Great Migration 9, 10, **114–133**
Green, Walter **43**
Greenwood, Okla. 131, 132–133
Guinier, Lani 163
Guy, Rosa 163

H

Haiti: emigrants 169, **170–183;** immigrants 69–71; political situation 171–172, 176–177
Hall, Prince 158
Hampton, Va.: family **81**
Hanson, Josiah 42
Harber, Sybil **78**
Harding, Vincent 163
Harlem, New York, N.Y. **114, 121;** churches 128; Convention of Negroes **74;** entrepreneurs 206; immigrants 147, 162, 169, 206; maroon community 37; riots 149, **151;** UNIA parade **132**
Harlem Renaissance 131, 133, 152
Hart-Celler Act 167
Haywood, Felix 38
Health care 127, 132, **161,** 178; career preparation **195**
Hickman, Williana 101
Higgs, R. H. 168
Hill, Fanny Christina 110
Hodges, William 80–81, 89
Hodges, Willis 81, 83
Holly, James 70, 71, **71**
Homestead, Fla.: agriculture **138**
Homesteaders 100, 103, 104
Housewives' League of Detroit **147**
Housing: discrimination 127, 148, 149, 151; overcrowding **149;** protests **150;** public housing projects **188**
Houston, Tex.: mosques 208
Howard University, Washington, D.C.: students **94**
Hughes, Langston 7, **131,** 133
Hughley, Stephanie S. **184**

I

Illegal immigrants 205, 207
Illinois: abolition 39; fugitive slaves 41; racial restrictions 86; wages 123
Immigration: laws and legislation 163, 166–167, 176, 177

Immigration and Naturalization Service: Haitian policies 177, 178–179; protests **183**
Indian Territory 38, 98, 100, 103
Indiana: abolition 39; fugitive slaves 41; racial restrictions 86
International Migration Society 69
Islam 17, 19, 26; mosques 208, **208;** Nation of Islam 128

J

Jackson, Minerva 106
Jackson, Oliver Toussaint 104, 106
Jackson, Polly **35**
Jacobs, Harriet 33
Jamaica: agriculture **160;** colonial rule 159, 161; emigration 66, 161, 166, 169; immigration 73; slave trade 157, 159
Jamestown, Va.: first Africans **24–25**
Jarrett, Vernon 142, 147
Jean, Wyclef 181–182
Jim Crow laws 116, 141, 161, 168; protests **187**
Johnson, Carmen **189**
Johnson, Charles S. **131**
Johnson, James Weldon 120, 158
Johnson, Lyndon 167
Johnson, John Rosamond 158
Jones, Maud 139
Jordan, June 163
Julian, Hubert 168

K

Kabasela, Kalambayi **206,** 206–207
Kaiser, Henry J.: shipyards 142, 149
Kansas: abolition 100; black settlements 43; emigration 73, 103; fugitive slaves 38–39; immigration 98, 100–101, 103
Kansas City, Mo.: civil rights campaigns **187**
Keel, Norris **165**
Kennedy, John F. 167, 176–177, 193
Kentucky: emigration 100, 101, 103; fugitive slaves 39, 41–42; slave trade 46, 53, 61
King, Martin Luther, Jr.: birthday celebrations **180**
King, Roswell 32
Kinkaid Homestead Act of 1904 104
Kongo (kingdom) 17; slave trade 16
Ku Klux Klan 54, 65, **140,** 168

L

Labor unions 110; racism 126, 149
Lane, James H. 39
Lange, Mother Mary 172
Langston, John Mercer 103
Langston City, Okla. 103–104
Lawrence, Jacob 120
Lawrence, Kans.: fugitive slaves 38–39, 43
Lee, Mary Custis 67
Lee, Robert E. 67
Levitt, Joshua 48, 53
Lewis, Cudjoe **28**
Liberia: immigration 16, **65–69,** 73, 74, 76, 77; Seal **68**
Liberian Pentecostal Churches 208
Lincoln, Abraham 71
Lincoln University, Pennsylvania 199
Littig, Tex. **105**

Little Haiti, Miami, Fla. 180, 181
Logan, Charles 59
Lorde, Audre 163
Los Angeles, Calif.: black population 107; immigration 97, 147; industry 147; Watts Uprising 111
Louisiana: black population 147; emigration 100, 103, 106, 136; fugitive slaves 38; immigration 171, 172; slave trade 19, 26, 28, 53, 60, 92
Lumpkin, Robert 61
Lynchings 116, **118,** 119, **119,** 140

M

Madison, James 28
Mali: emigrants **14;** slaves from 26
Manigault, Louis: runaways **36**
Maps: contemporary migrations 154–155; free peoples migrations 62–63; slave migrations 12–13; war migrations 112–113; West Africa, 1600s 18
Maroon communities 37–38, 43, 66
Marshall, Paule 163
Martin, Sella 47–48
Maryland: free blacks 79; fugitive slaves 39; immigrants 200; population trends 136; slave trade 46, 48, 60, 61; slaves 19, 23, 26, 45
Mason, Bridget 107
Massachusetts: black population 167, 179; employment 79; immigrants 162, 167, 179, 199; slave trade 23, 45–46
Mathis, Willie 90
Matzeliger, Jan Earnst 158
McCabe, Edwin P. and Sarah 103
McCarran-Walter Act 166–167
McCoy, James 139–140
McDonald, Alexander 55
McGill, Mrs. Urias R. **64**
Memphis, Tenn.: racism 140; slave trade 54
Meredith, James **193**
Meredith, Joseph 193
Mexico: emigration 97; fugitive slaves 38; immigration 97–98; slaves 16
Miami, Fla.: black population 179; immigrants 168–169, **170, 176,** 179, 180, **183;** mosques 208
Michigan: abolition 39; racial restrictions 86
Middle Passage **20, 21,** 22–23
Migration: assistance 125, 126, 129, 133; maps 12–13, 62–63, 112–113, 154–155; motivation 179, 200, 205; transportation 47–48, 53, 98, **101,** 119–120, 161
Miller, Kelly 133
Miller, Lewis 47
Minneapolis, Minn.: immigrants 201
Mississippi: agriculture **138,** 139; black population 147; emigration 100, 101, 103, 139–140, 147; fugitive slaves 37; slave trade 47, 60; slaves 94; State Senators **186**
Missouri: emigration 100, 101; fugitive slaves 38–39; slave trade 46, 59, 61
Mitchell, Arthur W. 132
Mob violence 129, 131; *see also* Lynchings; Race riots
Mobile, Ala.: slaves 29
Montana: buffalo soldiers **101**

Montgomery, Ala.: bus boycott 140; Ku Klux Klan **140**
Moore, Lake 104
Morehouse College, Atlanta, Ga.: commencement **192–193**
Moses, Austin 46
Moses, Robert 163
Mosques 208, **208**
Mount Olivet Baptist Church, New York, N.Y.: emigrants awaiting ship **67**
Muhammad, Elijah 128
Muhammad, Wallace Fard 128
Murray, Emily **195**
Music 147, 169, 172, 181–182

N

Napoleon I, Emperor (France) 171–172
Natchez, Miss. 48, **190,** 190–191
Nation of Islam 128
National Association for the Advancement of Colored People (NAACP) 126–127, 163
National League on Urban Conditions among Negroes 125, 126
National Youth Administration: training programs **144**
Nebraska: immigration **6–7,** 104
New Bedford, Mass.: immigrants 91, **201**
New Deal 137, 139, 152
New Jersey: abolition 39; immigrants **2–3, 176;** slave trade 45–46
New Mexico: immigration 97
New Mount Pilgrim Mission Baptist Church, Chicago, Ill. 139–140
New Orleans, La.: civil rights 173; employment 81; free blacks 80; immigrants 161, 171, 172–173; slave trade 48, 53, 61, **61;** slaves 92; wars 32, 61
New York: abolition 39; Black Panthers 153; black population 167, 179; churches 209; emigrants **190, 194;** fair-housing ordinance 151; fugitive slaves 39; immigrants 141, 162, 166, 167, **176,** 179, 200, 201; mosques 208; slave trade 23, 28, 45–46; slaves 157; UNIA convention 76
New York, N.Y.: black population 80, 95, 115, 123, 200, 214; churches 208; employment 83, 91; entrepreneurs 131, **164–165;** immigrants 81, **120–121,** 149, 161, **164–165,** 168–169, 171, 180, 200, 201, **202–203,** 214; parades **202–203;** protests 87; racism 83
Newark, N.J.: churches 128; fugitive slaves 41
Newport News, Va.: employment **84–85**
Newspapers 122, 158; role in migration 122, 163
Newton, Huey 153; trial **153**
Nicodemus, Kans. 100–101, **102**
Nigeria: doctor-patient ratio 207; emigrants **198, 200–204,** 207, 208, 211; first president 199; slaves from 26, 29
Nkrumah, Kwame 199
Norfolk, Va.: Haitian immigrants 171
North Carolina: emigration 136; free blacks 79; fugitive slaves 37–38; migrant workers **2–3, 137;** slave trade 46, 47–48, 61; slaves 33, 90; wages 98
North Miami, Fla.: mayor **178**

North (region), U.S.: discrimination against southern blacks 87, 89; employment 83, 85, 117, 123, 125; immigrants 80, **81,** 89, 119, 133; racism 65

Nova Scotia, Canada: Black Loyalists 66; Freedom Certificate **73**; fugitive slaves 41

O

Oakes, Ziba 55, 59

Oakland, Calif. 107, 142; Black Panthers 153

Ohio: abolition 39; former slaves **35**; fugitive slaves 41, 42; immigration 89; racial restrictions 86

Oklahoma: black population 147; emigration 69, 73, 136; homesteaders 104, **105**; immigration 103–104

Olivera, Isabel de 97

Omohundro, R. F. and Silas 61

Ontario, Canada: fugitive slaves 42

Oregon: racial restrictions 86

Overland Trail, Wyo. **101**

Owens, Charles 107

Owens, Robert C. 107

P

Page, Margaret **191**

Pan-African movement 77

Panama Canal 161, 163

Parker, Sarah **43**

Peace Mission Movement 128–129

Pennsylvania: abolition 39; fugitive slaves **33,** 39; slave trade 23, 45–46

Pennsylvania Railroad 120

Pentecostal churches 128, 129

Petersburg, Va.: slave trade 48

Philadelphia, Pa.: black population 80, 95, 123; churches 128; emigration 98; employment 83, 91; fugitive slaves 39, 41; immigration 161, 171, **198,** 205, 206; meetings 87, 97; mosques 208; women entrepreneurs 206

Pinckney, Charles C. 46

Poitier, Sidney 168

Political power 131–132, 152–153, **178,** 186, **186, 187**

Poole, Elijah 128

Port Hudson, La.: black troops **173**

Portland, Oreg.: employment 110; population 110

Powell, Colin 163, 168

Project Southern Cross 191

Protestantism 181, 207

Providence, R.I.: job network 91

Puerto Rico: immigration 161; slaves 16, 28

R

Race riots 129, 131, 149, **151,** 193

Racism: in education 7, 83, 86; in employment 81, 83, 85, 126, 142, 151; in housing 127; against immigrants 168, 211; North (region), U.S. 65, 86–87; role of newspapers 122; scientific 26; and slavery 29; view of youth 182–183; West (region), U.S. 7, 149

Railroads: employment 120

Randolph, A. Philip 151

Randolph, J. T. 56

Randolph, Peter 90

Red Summer 129

Redpath, James 70

Reed, James 163

Religion 172, 181, 207–208; see also Churches; Islam; Mosques

Republican Party 131, 132

Rhode Island: immigrants 200; slave trade 28

Richburg, Dave **194**

Richburg, Diana **194**

Richmond, Calif.: shipyards 142

Richmond, Va.: churches 92; slave trade 46, 48, 61; women working **88**

Riggs, J. S. 55

Roberts, Joseph Jenkins 69

Rollins, Sonny 163

Roosevelt, Franklin Delano 151

Rowland, Dick 131

Rural-urban migration 136, 152

Russwurm, John B. 158

Ryan, Thomas 55

Rydall, E. H. 107

S

Sacramento, Calif.: immigration 98

Salinas, A. J. 55

Sam, Alfred 69

San Francisco, Calif.: black population 107; employment 110; Huey Newton's trial **153**; immigration 98

Sand Hills, Nebr. 104

Santa Fe, N.Mex.: immigration 97

Santo Domingo 171; immigration 70

Savannah, Ga.: immigrants 171; slave trade 61

Schools see Education

Scott, Sparell: poem 215

Sea Islands, Ga.: slaves 32

Seaborn, George 55

Seale, Bobby 153

Seattle, Wash. 110–111

Segregation 86, 140, 148; signs **141**

Seminole Indians: fugitive slaves 37, 38

Senegal: emigrants 200, 201, 207

Senegambia: slave trade 16, **19,** 20, 26; spread of Islam 17

Sengstacke, Flora **122**

Shadd, Mary Ann 73

Sharecroppers 66, 80, 95, 137, **138,** 139

Shepard, Harriet 33

Sierra Leone: immigration 16, 66, 67; slaves from 24, 26

Singleton, Benjamin 100

Slave trade: advertisements **24,** 45–46, **52,** 54, **55, 58,** 59; children **21, 52, 55**; domestic **44–63**; economics 20, 22, 55, 60; family separations **44, 50–51,** 53–54, 56; impact 61, 94–95; justification 60–61; kidnap and sale of free blacks **53,** 54, 86–87; laws and legislation 26, 28; markets 47, **55, 58, 61**; Middle Passage **20, 21,** 22–23; traders 54, 55, 56, 59; transatlantic **14–29**; transportation 47–48, 53

Slaves: communications 90; demographics 53; ethnicities 26; fugitives **30–43**; jobs 23, 26; migration routes map 12–13; population 15, 23, 45, 60; reparations 153; repatriation 29; revolts 16, 19, **20,** 23, 171; violence against **17,** 22, 29, 31–32, **57**; women 32–33

Smith, Eric **194**

Smith, Mamie 133

Smith, Tek **195**

Smith, Venture 22

Sneed, Henry 73

Somalia: emigrants 200–201

Soulouque, Faustin 70

South Carolina: emigration 136; free blacks 79, 80; fugitive slaves 37, 38, 39; politicians 158; slave trade 28, 46, 47, 48, 55, 59, 157; slaves 23, 26, **27,** 46, 159; voting **187;** War of 1812 32

South (region), U.S.: agriculture 136, 139–140; black population 147, 185; emigration 119, 133, 135, 141, 215; immigration **94, 184–197,** 215; racism 95

Spear, Cesar 83

Spear, Chloe 83, 86

Spelman College, Atlanta, Ga.: commencement **192–193**

St. Amand, Fred and Sandra **178**

St. Augustine, Tex. **111**

St. Paul, Minn.: Somali immigrants 201

Stewart, Alvan 60

Stewart, Dora **43**

Stirling, James 56

Stokes, E. H. 61

Stuyvesant Town, New York, N.Y.: housing protest **150**

Sudan: emigrants 201, 205

T

Taylor, Koko 139

Temple Baptist Church, Dorchester, Mass.: Haitian-Americans **180**

Tennessee: emigration 100, 101, 103, 104, 107; slave trade 46; wages 98

Texas: black population 100; churches 209; emigration 73, 103, 107, 136, 201; fugitive slaves 38; immigration 97–98, 200, 201; slave trade 28; wages 98

Thompson, John **33**

Topeka, Kans. 101, 103

Toussaint L'Ouverture, François Dominique 70, 171

Trail of Tears 98

Triangular Trade 22

Trinidad: emigration **165,** 168, 169; immigration 71

Trotter, William Monroe 163

Tubman, Harriet 41, **43**

Tulsa, Okla.: race riots 131, **133**

Turner, Henry McNeal 74

Tuskegee Institute, Ala.: donors 107

Tyson, Cicely 163

U

Underground Railroad 32, 39, 41–42, 100

Undocumented aliens 205, 207

Union Hotel, Chattanooga, Tenn. **90**

United States: doctor-patient ratio 207; emigration 65–67, 69, 73–74; foreign-born black population 158, 162, 166; immigrants 158, 161–163, 169, 176, 200–201, 214; immigration restrictions 163, 166–167; slave trade 16

Universal Negro Improvement Association (UNIA) **74,** 76, 132, **132,** 168

University of Mississippi 193

U.S. Coast Guard: and Haitian refugees 174, 178

U.S. Constitution: slavery 26, 28, 100; voting rights 65, 116, 140

U.S. House of Representatives: first elected black congressman 132; protests **176**

U.S. Supreme Court 95, 136, 186

V

Vesey, Denmark 158

Vigilante (slave ship) **21**

Virginia: emigration 69, 80–81, 89, 100, 106, 201; employment 83; freed slaves 79; fugitive slaves 33, 37–38, 39, **41,** 42; immigrants **24–25,** 201; slave trade 46, 53, 54, **56, 57,** 60, 61; slaves 19, 23, 26, 32, 45, 90, 157; wages 98

Voting: primaries **187**; registration 153; rights 116, 131, 140, 151, **151,** 167

Vodou (religion) 172, 181

W

Walker, Charles 106

Walker, Madam C. J. 106, **108**

Walker, Margaret 163

Wallace, Michelle 163

War of 1812 32, 71

Ward, Samuel Ringgold 42, 87

Ware, John 73

Ware, Mildred: with children **72**

Washington, Booker T. 95, 104, 107, 133, 163

Washington, D.C.: churches 209; employment **82;** free blacks 79–80; housing **149;** immigrants 169, 200, 201; mosques 208; population trends 136; protests **176;** slave trade 48; slaves **81**

Waters, Muddy 147

Watts Uprising, Los Angeles, Calif. 111

Weatherly, Thomas C. 47, 55, 59

Wells, Ruth 151

West (region), U.S.: black population 97, 110, 149; employment 110; immigration **96–111,** 135–136; racism 7, 111

Wiley, John 140

Williams, Bert 158

Williams, Henry 92

Williams, Peter 74

Williams, Thelma Wallace **190,** 190–191

Women: domestic work 83, 148; education 207; employment 79, 83, 86, **88, 93,** 110, 126, **134;** entrepreneurs 206; income sources 92; independence 86, 206–207; industrial workers **127, 134, 146,** 148

Women's League, Newport, R.I.: executive board **88**

World War I: migration north 115–117

World War II: Caribbean migration 166; employment 110, 141, 142, **144–145,** 148; westward migration 110

Wyoming: wagon train **101**

Z

Zambia: doctor-patient ratio 207

Zimbabwe: emigrants 205

ACKNOWLEDGMENTS

In Motion: The African-American Migration Experience, the Schomburg Center's website from which this book is derived, has been based on research by distinguished scholars whose contributions the Center gratefully recognizes:

Paul E. Lovejoy – *The Transatlantic Slave Trade*
Loren Schweninger – *Runaway Journeys*
Michael Tadman – *The Domestic Slave Trade*
Nemata Blyden – *Colonization and Emigration*
James Oliver Horton – *The Northern Migration*
Quintard Taylor – *The Westward Migration*
Carole Marks – *The Great Migration*
Thomas C. Holt – *The Second Great Migration*
Winston James – *Caribbean Immigration*
Caryn Cossé Bell and Alex Stepick – *Haitian Immigration*
Mary Alice Hudgens – *Return to the South*
Sylviane A. Diouf – *African Immigration*

Special thanks go to Lou Potter for turning scholarly essays into popular narratives.

We are indebted to all the institutions and photographers who allowed us to include their images in the book and the web site.

We are grateful to the Migration Project staff: Yukiko Yamagata and John Parsons; and to Mary Yearwood, Curator of the Photographs and Prints Division, Schomburg Center for Research in Black Culture; and Karen Van Westering, Publications Director, The New York Public Library.

Finally, many thanks to the talented people at the National Geographic Society, especially Lisa Lytton for her editorial talent. Thanks to Nina Hoffman, publisher of the National Geographic Book Division; Kevin Mulroy, editor-in-chief; Jane Menyawi, photo editor; Rebecca Lescaze, text editor; and designer Bill Marr.

In Motion: The African-American Migration Experience was made possible by the support of the Congressional Black Caucus through a grant administered by the Institute of Museum and Library Services.

STAFF

PUBLISHED BY THE NATIONAL GEOGRAPHIC SOCIETY

John M. Fahey, Jr., *President and Chief Executive Officer*

Gilbert M. Grosvenor, *Chairman of the Board*

Nina D. Hoffman, *Executive Vice President*

PREPARED BY THE BOOK DIVISION

Kevin Mulroy, *Vice President and Editor-in-Chief*

Charles Kogod, *Illustrations Director*

Marianne R. Koszorus, *Design Director*

STAFF FOR THIS BOOK

Lisa Lytton, *Project Editor*

Rebecca Lescaze, *Text Editor*

Bill Marr, *Art Director*

Jane Menyawi, *Illustrations Editor*

Gary Colbert, *Production Director*

Richard S. Wain, *Production Project Manager*

Meredith C. Wilcox, *Illustrations Assistant*

MANUFACTURING AND QUALITY CONTROL

Christopher A. Liedel, *Chief Financial Officer*

Phillip L. Schlosser, *Managing Director*

John T. Dunn, *Technical Director*

Vincent P. Ryan, *Manager*

Clifton M. Brown, *Manager*

ILLUSTRATION CREDITS